IDENTITY AND INTEGRATION

DAMES

Dansk Center for Migration
og Etniske Studier

**EUROPEAN RESEARCH CENTRE
ON MIGRATION & ETHNIC RELATIONS**

Identity and Integration
Migrants in Western Europe

Edited by

ROSEMARIE SACKMANN
University of Bremen, Germany

BERNHARD PETERS
University of Bremen, Germany

THOMAS FAIST
University of Applied Sciences, Bremen, Germany

ASHGATE

Published by
Ashgate Publishing Limited
Gower House
Croft Road
Aldershot
Hants GU11 3HR
England

Ashgate Publishing Company
Suite 420
101 Cherry Street
Burlington, VT 05401-4405
USA

Ashgate website: http://www.ashgate.com

British Library Cataloguing in Publication Data
Identity and integration : migrants in Western Europe. -
  (Research in migration and ethnic relations series)
  1.Immigrants - Cultural assimilation - Europe, Western
  2.Group identity - Europe, Western 3.Transnationalism
  4.Social integration - Europe, Western 5.Europe, Western -
  Emigration and immigration
  I.Sackmann, Rosemarie II.Peters, Bernhard III.Faist,
  Thomas, 1959-
  305.9'0691

Library of Congress Cataloging-in-Publication Data
Identity and integration : migrants in Western Europe / edited by Rosemarie Sackmann,
  Bernhard Peters, and Thomas Faist.
      p. cm. -- (Research in migration and ethnic relations series)
  Includes bibliographical references and index.
  ISBN 0-7546-3211-3
    1. Immigrants--Cultural assimilation--Europe, Western. 2. Group identity--Europe,
  Western. 3. Social integration--Europe, Western. I. Sackmann, Rosemarie. II. Peters,
  Bernhard, 1949- III. Faist, Thomas, 1959- IV. Series.

  JV7590.I34 2003
  304.8'4--dc21

                                                                          2003048165

ISBN 0 7546 3211 3

Printed and bound in Great Britain by MPG Books Ltd. Bodmin, Cornwall

Contents

List of Contributors

Ursula Apitzsch is Professor of Sociology and Political Science and Dean of the Faculty of Social Sciences at the Johann Wolfgang Goethe University (Frankfurt am Main). She published widely in the fields of migration, culture, ethnicity and biographical analysis. She coordinates an EC sponsored European project ('EthnoGeneration') on women as entrepreneurs and the chances of the second generation in migrant business. In 1999 she edited a book on migration and tradition building (Migration und Traditionsbildung, Westdeutscher Verlag, Wiesbaden).

Rainer Bauböck (D. Phil, Senior Lecturer), sociologist and political scientist, member of the Research Unit for Institutional Change and European Integration of the Austrian Academy of Sciences. He teaches at the Universities of Vienna and Innsbruck. He has been visiting fellow and guest professor at the universities of Warwick (UK), Princeton (USA), Malmö (Schweden), Bristol (UK). He has published widely on migration, multiculturalism, nationalism, citizenship, and political theory.

Godfried Engbersen is Professor of Sociology at the Erasmus University of Rotterdam, the Netherlands. He studied sociology at the University of Leiden and worked at the Universities of Leiden, Utrecht and Amsterdam. He is the author of numerous books, including (with Romke van der Veen) *Moderne armoede* (Modern Poverty, 1987); *Cultures of Unemployment* (Westview Press, 1993) (with Jack Burgers) *De Ongekende Stad I en II* (The Unkown City I and II, 1999). Since 1997 he has been the editor of the *Annual Dutch Report on Poverty and Social Exclusion* (Amsterdam University Press).

Thomas Faist is Professor of Political Science and Director of International Studies in Political Management (ISPM) at the University of Applied Sciences Bremen. He received his PhD from The Graduate Faculty, New School for Social Research in New York. His research interests focus on transnational and social policy. His latest books include *The Volume and Dynamics of International Migration and Transnational Spaces* (Oxford University Press, 2000) and *Transstate Spaces* (Ashgate, forthcoming). Currently, he is engaged in a comparative research project on the politics of dual citizenship in Europe.

Yasemin Karakaşoğlu (D. Phil.) is Assistant Professor at the University of Essen (Germany). She studied Turkology, Political Sciences and Modern German Literature in Hamburg and Ankara. She received her PhD from the University of Essen. Her main fields of interest are Islam in Germany, second generation Turkish migrants and migrant children in the German education system.

Riva Kastoryano (Dr.) is a senior research fellow at the CNRS (National Centre for Scientific Research) and teaches at the Institute for Political Studies in Paris. Her work focuses on relationships between identity and states, on minority and community formation in western democratic societies. Her publications include *Negotiating Identities. States and Immigrants in France and Germany* (Princeton University Press, forthcoming). She is the editor of *Quelle identité pour l'Europe? Le multiculturalisme à l'épreuve* (Paris, Presses de Sciences-Po, 1998).

Tariq Modood is Professor of Sociology and Public Policy and Director of the Centre for the Study of Ethnicity and Citizenship at the University of Bristol, UK. His publications include (co-author) *Ethnic Minorities in Britain: Diversity and Disadvantages* (PSI, 1997), (joint ed.) *Debating Cultural Hybridity* (Zed Books, 1997) and (joint ed.) *The Politics of Multiculturalism in the New Europe* (Zed Books, 1997). His most recent publication is 'The Place of Muslims in British Secular Multiculturalism' in N. Alsayyad and M. Castells (eds), *Muslim Europe or Euro-Islam: Politics, Culture and Citizenship in the Age of Globalisation*, New York (Lexington Books, 2002).

Bernhard Peters is Professor of Political Theory at the University of Bremen and Co-director of the Institute for Intercultural and International Studies (InIIS). He received his Ph. D. (1991) and his Habilitation in sociology (1993) at the Johann Wolfgang Goethe University in Frankfurt. He has published books and articles on topics in the field of social theory. His current research interests concern aspects of cultural differentiation in contemporary societies, public culture and public discourse, and relations between normative and empirical theory.

Kathrin Prümm (D. Phil., Social Science, Osnabrück) is currently teaching Political Theory, Political Systems and International Migration at the University of Applied Sciences at Bremen. Her research activities focus mainly on conditions of life, cultural differences and citizenship of immigrants and minorities in Germany. In her dissertation she concentrated on the process of naturalisation of Turkish migrants in Germany.

Rosemarie Sackmann (Dr. rer. soc.) is Assistant Professor at the University of Bremen and member of the Institute for Intercultural and International Studies (InIIS). Previously she was engaged in research on gender, culture and regional differences. Her current research interests concern migration, societal integration and multiculturalism in Europe.

Sven Sauter (D. Phil.) studied cultural anthropology, psychoanalysis and sociology. He is currently visiting professor in the Faculty of Education at the Johann Wolfgang Goethe University (Frankfurt am Main).

Tanjev Schultz (MA) is research fellow and PhD candidate at the Institute for Intercultural and International Studies at the University of Bremen, Germany. He studied political science, journalism, philosophy and psychology at the Free University of Berlin and the Indiana University Bloomington (USA). Research interests: public sphere, political communication, migration and multiculturalism.

Margret Spohn (Dr.) studied sociology and intercultural education. She has undertaken research in intercultural relations. Currently she is working in the administrative unit for intercultural co-operation of the City of Munich.

Thijl Sunier is senior lecturer in Cultural Anthropology at the University of Amsterdam. He completed his PhD thesis, entitled *Islam in Beweging. Turkse jongeren en islamitische organisaties* (Islam in Motion. Turkish young people and Islamic organizations) in 1996. He has conducted comparative research among Turkish Youth in the Netherlands, France, Germany and Great Britain. He is also senior researcher engaged on nation building and multiculturalism in France, the Netherlands and Turkey. His publications include articles and books on migrants and Muslims in Europe, Islam and Politics in Turkey and Central Asia.

Chapter 1

Introduction: Collective Identities and Social Integration

Rosemarie Sackmann

Symbolic boundaries, cultural differences and ethnic conflicts have gained significance and new meanings in a global situation characterized by a dissolution of traditional political and societal structures. While communications, political and economic interactions increasingly cross the borders of states, nations and ethnic communities, symbolic borders and separate group identities are nevertheless asserted. International migration combines these two tendencies in an exemplary way. In this context, the perceived efforts of migrants to maintain their cultural and ethnic identities are often blamed as a cause of conflict within nation states. What some see as a development that enriches a society's cultural reservoir, others take as a threat to their own culture and conception of themselves.

In the wake of September 11th and the successes of political parties who build their election platforms on the issue of immigration, today the whole subject of migration is assuming an ever greater significance within the public debate. Increasingly, doubts are being expressed concerning the scope for integrating culturally different groups and the practicability of multi-cultural concepts of society. During the last decades especially Muslim migrants have been discussed as a potential threat to social integration (cf. Nonneman, 1996).

While keywords such as cultural difference and collective identity, or assimilation and integration are constantly used by the general public, these concepts have become controversial in the scientific community (cf. Ranger, Samad and Stuart, 1996). Concepts of ethnicity and identity have been criticized as essentialist, as a reification of constantly changing and contested social perceptions or as filling statistical classifications with fictitious subjective meanings. The concepts of assimilation and integration have been suspected of a homogenizing bend. However, the usefulness of concepts like integration or collective identity depends not on the word itself, but on appropriate meanings and analytical differentiations. And the controversies about the role of objective classifications or descriptions and subjective meanings and constructs can be reconciled to some degree by proper distinctions and the analysis of connections and interrelationships.

For analytical purpose we might use 'positioning' and 'self-localization' as complementary concepts. Positioning refers to structural conditions and structured practices through which members of a society get a position within the social structure. Of course, positions within a structure are not fixed and neither are social structures. Research on self-localization on the other hand tries to reconstruct the point of view of the individuals, of the social actors. Self-localizations include a wide range of identifications, patterns of orientation and self-conceptualizations, feelings of belonging and perceptions of symbolic boundaries. Research in the perspective of self-localizations is also interested in connections between processes of self-localization and positioning.

We can now combine these perspectives with the familiar distinction between migrants as *categories*, as *social groups* and as bearers of *collective identities*. Such a distinction permits a differentiated view of integration processes with regard to different parameters and to possible interactions between them. (The first part of this volume provides some theoretical perspectives on these concepts and relationships.)

Immigrants as *population categories* are determined in the first instance by the socio-statistical characteristics of immigration and descent. These characteristics give rise to different types of ascription by members of the host society. For instance, migrants are imagined to be groups with special preferential social relationships, with a collective identity, with a different culture. Immigrants are perceived as groups of people who are culturally different. Arising from this broadly interpreted difference, a number of further ascriptions are deduced, concerning the capacity for assimilation and integration of different categories of immigrants, for instance.

Sometimes, migrants take up these ascriptions. The act of *categorical* self-location refers to the fact of immigration, or descent from migrants, and to the fact of differentiation between immigrants and the native population in the country of immigration. The adoption of categorical ascriptions can be the expression of discrimination or stigmatization experiences. Immigrants perceive themselves as members of some social category with unequal status. This might become one particular element of collective identity (see below).

The self-conception of the respective country of immigration provides a framework for the perception of its migrants. The acceptance of immigrants as citizens who are equal in status depends to some degree on their legal status as citizens or non-citizens, of course. But full recognition is only possible via social processes which result in a new determination of societal self-conceptions in the country of migration (cf. Bauböck in this volume). The frequently heated debate on immigration issues in Western Europe has also made it clear that in the wake of immigration, self-conceptions are under pressure for change. Reactions to this pressure can be seen e.g. in the way public institutions are adapting their schemas of categorization and perception (cf. Engbersen in this volume).

Societal schemas of ordering and systems of categories present a point of departure for scientific analysis. And as long as systematic positioning effects are connected with immigrant status, scientific analysis will not be able to manage without the category 'immigrant'. Nevertheless, the warnings against reification and essentialization which have been iterated in the past ten years or so should not be ignored. It is possible to guard against such risks. Reflected socio-scientific analysis makes it possible to examine ascriptions with respect to their reality content (cf. the contributions by Karakasoglu and Spohn in this volume). The investigation of processes of change in immigrant categories supersedes essentializations (cf. the contribution by Prümm, Sackmann and Schultz in this volume). The perception of immigrants as social actors cancels out reifications (cf. the contributions by Apitzsch and Sauter in this volume).

If we now look at forms of *self-localization* by immigrants, we should distinguish between *group-formation* and the formation of *collective identities*. A perspective on immigrants as *social groups* refers to the social organization of the immigrant community, i.e. to special preferential social relationships (choice of friends or partners; social nets of co-operation) and to forms of social organization such as associations to represent interests, organizations for self-help, cultural associations, sport and leisure clubs. The membership in organizations and the composition of circles of friends and acquaintances can exert an influence on the social identities of individuals. Migrant organizations can be places of communication about collective identities whereby identity models are reproduced or changed (see the contribution of Sunier in this volume). However, collective identities of some kind may well exist without much group organization or actual community formation (compare Peters, this volume).

We perceive *collective identity* as a component of the culture of a group (compare Peters in this volume; 1993; 1998). The culture of an immigrant community comprises systems of symbols and symbolic contents which play a role in the lives of members of the group, which are shared by the group members, i.e. by all members or at least a real majority, and which are used for orientation and in communication and interaction. Prominent among these symbols and frames of interpretation there are those which refer to the character or to the destiny of the group. The sum of these cultural elements forms the collective identity of the group. Collective identities can be of different density or extensiveness. Their articulation can be diffuse and vague, or differentiated and multifaceted. Note should also be taken of certain structural relationships between different collective identities. Certain memberships and identities mutually exclude one another. An interesting question would be to look into conflicts of loyalty which might ensue from having membership in different groups and the sharing of different collective identities. The interesting case today is the relation between national identification with host societies and identification with an immigrant community. For immigrant communities of non-Christian religion, this question is connected with the problem of the relation between their own religious identification and membership in a national community which exhibits many cultural elements characterized by the Christian religion. This may entail the collective identity of most immigrant communities being of a 'hybrid' type. It does not simply consist of identification with the national identity of the country of immigration. Rather, certain elements of identification with the country of origin join together in an immigrant identity which also bears elements of identification with the country of immigration (compare the contribution of Modood in this volume).

It is not to be expected that immigrants constitute a homogenous group, sharing one and the same collective identity. Rather, it is to be expected that existing social lines of differentiation also bear an influence on the relationship of individuals to constructions of collective identity. Differences between generations, between social classes and gender differences can be systematically taken into consideration in the analysis. Nor is the concept fixated on ethnic identity. It is quite possible that empirical application of the concept may ascertain an orientation of the collective identity of immigrant groups toward the class position, or perhaps a clear reference to gender roles.[1] The analytical concept put forward here is characterized by openness vis-à-vis different theories and by a high degree of analytical differentiation.

The contributions to the first part of this volume are mainly engaged in conceptual and theoretical clarifications.[2] Parts two and three of the book

---

[1] Different influences may be at work here. On the one hand, traditional cleavage structures of the host countries may influence the self-description of immigrants. On the other hand, immigrants may experience significant influencing factors inherited from their country origin, such as class alignment, for instance.

[2] First drafts of the contributions have been presented to a workshop at Bremen in February 2001. Our thanks are due to the Heinrich-Böll-Foundation and the University of Bremen. Without their financial support this meeting would not have been possible.

analyze examples for various forms of self-localization. In part 2, the contributions analyze patterns of orientation among Turkish migrants in Germany and The Netherlands.[3] Part 3 takes up a 'transnational' perspective. Included are a transnational/post-modern perspective, the trans-national social spaces approach, and one contribution that combines the transnational perspective with other theories of integration. Since the transnational approach is still in a stage of development, searching for its specific content and shape and clarifying its relation to other approaches, the diversity in the third part of this volume is a reflection of the state of the art.

Part I: Collective Identity and Social Integration

The first part begins with an analytical reconstruction of the concept of collective identity. The proposition put forward by *Bernhard Peters* in his contribution is that of a discursive concept of collective identity: Questions like 'who are we, what sort of group do we constitute?' can only be sensibly voiced and resolved within the context of real or imaginary communication. On the basis of this definition, Peters formulates a critical appraisal of other concepts of collective identity.

In his contribution, *Rainer Bauböck* specifies normative criteria for the evaluation of collective identity in its institutionalized form. This has to do with public culture and insofar it has primarily to do with the collective identity of immigration societies. The proposition advanced by Bauböck is that all modern societies are internally multicultural. Within this context it is up to the state to bring about the creation of a public culture to represent the political community in its entirety. This becomes the basis for communication, it offers a cultural repertoire (memories, identity; explicit norms and values regulating political conflict; implicit norms and styles of behaviour broadly shared across communities within society). Bauböck distinguishes between four aspects of the public culture: linguistic, historical, political and civil culture. His text deals with the first two.

Whereas Bauböck is engaged in questions of political theory, the contribution by *Godfried Engbersen* is sociological in its orientation. Engbersen puts forward a general model of societal integration. Modern societies are integrated in three dimensions: in the functional dimension (which affects questions of co-ordination), the moral dimension (questions of justice and solidarity) and the expressive dimension (questions of

---

[3] Turks are the largest category among Muslim migrants in Western Europe and about one third of the Muslim population are migrants from Turkey (cf. Vertovec and Peach, 1997).

identity). At the same time, though, one has to distinguish between the different spheres of integration (e.g., law, labour market, education system, religion). Making reference to the integration of migrants over the course of the past forty years in the Netherlands, Engbersen illustrates that different spheres were alternately at the centre of debate and politics. Engbersen's observations are directed towards the necessity for differentiated and reflexive policies. It is the task of the state to find a new balance between the functional, the moral and expressive dimensions of integration.

The last two contributions in this first part turn the focus onto the migrants. *Tariq Modood* deals with questions concerning the collective identity of migrants in the UK. He finds it of particular interest that for the South-Asian migrants, notwithstanding the British reference system on the basis of race or class, it is religious identity which primarily determines localization. Modood endeavours to arrive at an evaluation of this collective identity. Among other things, he investigates the question whether this entails a form of collective identity which is characterized by a particular insularity against the host society.

Ursula Apitzsch is especially interested in domestic culture. This does not mean, though, that she perceives her object of research in the private sphere. On the contrary, Apitzsch critizes prevailing concepts about publicly recognized forms of life conduct. Whereas freedom of religion is institutionalized in the public sphere of host societies, the subsequent recognition of cultural difference is not sufficient to cover the cultural-religious practices of Islamic migrants, a difference which is articulated in everyday forms of life conduct (rules concerning clothing, for instance). Rules which have been shaped on the model of Christianity leave no room for these forms of expression. Apitzsch advances the proposition that this will lead to a situation in host societies in which they have to redefine their self-conception.

Part II: The Self-Localization of Migrants

Like Ursula Apitzsch, *Yasemin Karakasoglu* also emphasizes that integration policy in Germany has so far failed to create an adequate practice for the accommodation of religious difference. Politicians and large sections of the public still perceive the visible forms of Muslim life style, like the headscarf for instance, as the expression of an undemocratic, theocratic and dogmatic world view. Karakasoglu shows that this perception is misplaced. Veiled and unveiled Islamic students of education differentiate between their orientations as Muslims and their orientations as teachers. They have a well developed sense of educational and professional principles, which are not mixed up with their religious belonging. Karakasoglu believes that the new academic elite, especially women, who are culturally and structurally integrated and who insist on their right to religious freedom, will change the meaning of integration for Muslims in the future.

Thijl Sunier's analysis points to an alternative way of influencing the process of integration. He examines the Turkish Muslim organizations in The Netherlands with a special focus on the way their orientations are changing with the changer of generation. For the first generation, the organizations represented a means for creating the infrastructure for exercising their communal religion. Only a few of these organizations were attributable to the initiative of migrants, rather they were organizations for migrants and created by actors of Dutch society. Eventually, Turkish Muslim organisations also became active in Holland. The organizations were in competition with one another. In a parallel development, the presence of the second generation in the organizations was making itself felt. These two changes were instrumental for the increasing focus on the issue of identity and allegiance. Sunier shows that the ethnic collective within Turkish Islamic organisations has been redefined by second generation migrants. The redefinition includes a greater importance of localization processes within the Dutch society.

The second generation differs greatly from the first – this is a general finding in migration research. Often the first generation receives less attention than following generations. Notwithstanding, *Margret Spohn* focuses her research on the first generation males. She shows that different concepts of family relations among migrants have existed prior to their migration to Germany. It is important to note that, while the process of migration may foster the change of models, changes may occur within an repertoire of models that have already existed in the Turkish context. Thus, while adaptations to specific experiences in migration processes influence reconstructions of cultural patterns and orientation models, this does not necessarily mean that migrants have to adopt new models from the context of their country of settlement.

The contribution by *Kathrin Prümm, Rosemarie Sackmann* and *Tanjev Schultz* adds research findings on self-localizations of Turkish migrants in Germany to the picture. The term 'self-localizations' refers to two kinds of localization processes, one with regard to groups and one with regard to places of belonging. The differentiation makes it possible to analyse relations between the two localizations. The research findings indicate that the self-naming as 'Turk' does not imply a feeling of belonging to Turkey.

And for most respondents the group of 'Turks' they refer to, are Turks in Germany rather than Turks in Turkey. This definition of the group of belonging is found among first generation migrants as well as among their children, but the concepts of collective identity vary between the first and the second generation.

Part III: Where is 'Home'? The Perspective of Transnational Theories

The contribution by *Sven Sauter* deals with issues of belongingness and self-localization from a post-national/post-modernity perspective. Based on the example of young members of a folklore group, Sauter shows how references to the homeland and the country of settlement are combined by the second generation. The youths do not want to make the choice, they want to maintain both references which proffer them the space for self-localization. 'Home' does not connect them with any one location, but rather with a space filled with different local and transnational references. Social ties which stretch beyond national boundaries. Cultural and social adaptation, though, is consummated by local rather than national allegiances: 'The sociospaces of the members of the folklore group are related and located in the urban space of their suburb. (...) A well-balanced form of cultural approbation mixes the ethnic resources of their life history, the suburb they actually live in, with own (youth-) subculture orientations and the traditional autochthone feeling of belonging to a smaller part of the city' (chapter 11).

In her contribution which deals with the Turkish transnational community in Europe, *Riva Kastoryano* also reveals that there is an overlapping of different spaces. Whereas the community formation of Turkish migrants is to a great extent shaped by the prevailing institutional frames within the country of immigration, at the European level there emerges a space for action within which the migrants' organizations assume the status of negotiating partners for their respective countries of settlement and countries of origin, seemingly from outside. These migrants' organizations view Europe as a democratic space positioned above the national state and the European space furnishes them with an actor status not (not in all cases) enjoyed within the national frame. The identity references in these determinations of groups are not based on territory (neither with regard to the country of settlement, nor to the country of origin), but rather on ethnical, religious and regional boundaries. The interplay between these factors leads to 'deterritorialized nationalisms'.

Thomas Faist explores the issue whether theories of trans-national social spaces actually replace the old models of integration processes, or whether they complement such concepts. Basing his investigation on the migration of Poles to Germany, Faist draws comparisons between the assimilation model, the model of cultural pluralism and the transstate-spaces approach. The migrations of Poles to Germany provide a good example for such a comparison, since they entail migration relations which, although long established, are changing in form. The proposition advanced by Faist is that a multi-perspective analysis of immigrant integration is necessary. The empirical analysis finds that all three models of integration capture essential parts of the Polish immigrant experience in Germany. Faist argues that the different theories capture different types of migrations. Which model is appropriate depends on the migration causes (for example: forced or voluntary), the relation to the homeland (if the migrants have specific reasons to be interested in homeland affairs) and the situation in the country of immigration (for example: situations of discrimination). Generally, one approach may not fit to entire categories of migrants but rather to subgroups within a category. The multi-perspective analysis clarifies the conditions under which the different models can be applied.

Finally, the postscript highlights some common features of the contribution by placing the findings in the wider landscape of research on migration and integration.

References

Nonneman, G. (1996), 'Muslim Communities in the New Europe: Themes and Puzzles', in: G. Nonneman, T. Niblock and B. Szajkowski (eds), *Muslim Communities in the New Europe*, Ithaka Press, Reading, pp. 3-23.

Peters, B. (1993), *Die Integration moderner Gesellschaften*, Suhrkamp, Frankfurt am Main.

Peters, B. (1998), *Identity Questions*, Arbeitspapier 10/98, InIIS, Universität Bremen.

Ranger, T., Y. Samad and O. Stuart (eds), (1996), *Culture, Identity and Politics*, Avebury, Aldershot.

Vertovec, S. and C. Peach (eds), (1997), *Islam in Europe. The Politics of Religion and Community*, Macmillan, London.

PART I
COLLECTIVE IDENTITY AND SOCIAL INTEGRATION

Chapter 2

Collective Identity, Cultural Difference and the Developmental Trajectories of Immigrant Groups

Bernhard Peters

Introduction

'Collective identity' has become a very popular term in recent years, partly in debates and research about 'national identities', but also with respect to minority groups (like ethnic groups or immigrants) (Brubaker and Cooper, 2000). Within the new discourse of multiculturalism, however, 'collective identity' has been used with marked ambivalence. So have the terms 'assimilation' and 'integration'. But while group identities might be seen as part of the pattern of multiculturalism, these latter terms have fallen in stronger disrepute because of their even stronger connotations of cultural homogeneity and reduction of 'difference' (Brubaker, 2001). In the older research on immigration, a process of identification with the new host society (or nation) had sometimes been seen as one dimension of cultural assimilation, most prominently in Gordon's conceptual scheme (Gordon, 1964). Objections to this view have come from two directions. The reality and normative desirability of 'assimilation' have been questioned, and the implied target of assimilation has been put into doubt. If there are no homogenous and coherent national identities, what is there to identify with? Similarly, and more generally, with 'integration'. If current societies are not really 'integrated' any more (in some specific understanding of this term, which might include some notion of moral or more general cultural consensus), the target for the 'integration' of immigrants equally blurs.

There are several ways, however, to understand these theoretical developments and disagreements. They could be due to new results of empirical research. They could be influenced by changing normative standards and commitments. Or they might reflect conceptual changes and differences on a more abstract level. It is this last question which will mainly be pursued in this chapter. There are conceptual confusions and infelicities about the term collective identity. Some parts of the controversies surrounding this term could be removed by a more precise formulation, and the term might retain its usefulness. First, then, a discussion of some problematic uses of 'collective identity', and as a consequence some proposals for conceptual clarification.

1 Collective Identity: Some Misunderstandings

Many criticisms of the term 'collective identity' refer to its connotations of wholeness, unity, homogeneity, and continuity or permanence. Many understandings of collective identity draw some kind of parallel with certain conceptions of individual identity, and fill the term collective identity with normative or evaluative content. Identity is then used as a 'success' term. In current discourses about multiculturalism and cultural differences, it is often implied that collective identity is somehow based on cultural difference. We could call this the 'differentialist' use of 'identity'. Furthermore, there is the popular opposition between two 'theories' of collective (especially national or ethnic) identity, which concerns its 'primordial' or 'constructed' characteristics. These are unfortunate conceptual uses and subsequent controversies.

Collective and Individual Identities

While we might suppose that some kind of consistent and coherent individual identity is necessary for a 'normally' functioning personality, it is not obvious that the analogue statement is true for the collective case – i.e. that a consistent, coherent *and* consensual identity is necessary for the stability or proper functioning of all kinds of social units (which does not say if it is more important for certain kinds of collectivities than for others).

   The term 'social identity' is sometimes used to denote that element of individual identity which consists in identifications with relevant groups (Tajfel, 1981; Tajfel, 1982). Following common sociological assumptions (as articulated above all in the theoretical tradition of social interactionism), individual identity is partly developed by this kind of group identification or by the acquisition of membership roles in such groups. The question 'who am I' or 'what kind of person am I' is partly answered by reporting relevant membership affiliations: I am a German, a European, a Catholic, a member of the professoriate and so on.[1] Collective identity as understood

---

[1] This *may* imply 'identification' with those groups in the sense of support for strong collective identities (identification with the 'fate' of the group, as it were, support of

here is different from social identity in this sense.

Questions about collective identity are distinguishable from questions about individual identity. Questions like 'who are we', 'what kind of group are we', 'what does it mean to be German', 'what binds us together', 'how do we interpret our common past', 'what are we striving for' are different from the question 'who am I', and even from the question 'where do I belong'. Such questions can only be asked in a meaningful way in the context of some real or imagined conversation within a group.

Thus, collective identity is a social phenomenon, not an attribute of individuals. While it is true that collective identities need carriers, i.e. persons who hold the collectivity and communication beliefs about it, or who participate in symbolic activities which relate to the collectivity, it is nevertheless not very useful to think of collective identity just as the sum or aggregation of individual beliefs, attitudes and activities. Collective identities have properties of their own. For instance, elements of collective identity which are embodied in social practices, as well as in external carriers of symbolic meaning must be studied as such, not just as aggregated properties of individuals. Collective identities are created and recreated in social processes of communication, cultural transmission and contestation, and their existence and character cannot be separated from these processes.

Sometimes the notion of collective identity is treated as an *analogue* to individual identity. The group or collectivity is then treated as some kind of collective personality. This is also misleading. On the social level there is above all the basic problem of agreement and disagreement, which is different from the problem of the consistency of individual beliefs and attitudes. The notion of individual identity is itself understood in different and contested ways. But in most uses we can find the supposition that personal identity is something positive, a necessary element of personality development and a successful life. Personal identity has something to do with a successful integration of different parts of a personality and of individual biography into some kind of coherent unity. The concept of collective identity should be more neutral. It should leave open if all kinds of social units should be expected to have a collective identity which unites them on the basis of some consistent and shared self-image, a shared and coherent understanding of the common past and future, shared ideals about the character of the collectivity and so on. I take it that this question, which

---

collective goals and so on). It may also just imply acceptance of certain roles and standards of behavior which are expected from the individual members of such groups. One can learn and accept e.g. gender roles or occupational roles without explicit identification with corresponding groups.

has both normative and empirical aspects, *should* be kept open, subject to further inquiry.

What are the *relations* between individual and collective identity? As the above mentioned notion of 'social identity' implies, individual identity is in part formed or constituted by participation in collective identities, by collective identifications. Loyalty to a group, being accepted as member of a group (by other members or by non-members), seeing oneself involved in the life of a group, in some collective project, being proud of one's group, being interested in the well-being of the group or in collective achievements, feeling responsible for activities attributed to the group may all be important parts of individual self-understanding, a basis for self-esteem, an important element of the goals or ideals one pursues, a source of meaning for one's life.

On a general level, not much more can be said. How important collective identifications are for various individuals, and what the relative importance of different collective identifications may be, are open empirical questions. For some people, collective identifications might be important, for others much less so. And forms of collective identity might have different relevance to different people. There may also be important situational and historical factors which influence the relevance or salience of collective identifications - e.g. situations of conflict or group mobilization. There is e.g. not much empirical evidence to support the notion that participation in a *national* collective identity is (or has been, for specific historical periods) the *most important* collective identification in most people's lives. Surely there are other candidates, e.g. family, other small groups, churches, occupational groups. Not much is empirically known about these things.

The relevance of collective identities to individual identities should be distinguished from the importance of more general cultural influences on individual lives. Certainly the national culture, and in some cases some other group culture is a very important influence in people's lives. It provides them with a cultural repertoire which helps them to develop goals and standards, to master tasks and problems, to give meanings to their lives. All this, however, does not necessarily imply the adoption of identifications with the national collective. One can become acculturated within a national culture while being largely indifferent to the national collectivity. Collective identity is after all only a particular *part* of collective culture, as will be elaborated later.

Collective Identity, Culture and Difference

Should the term 'collective identity' imply some kind of cultural homogeneity and coherence? Does it have to fall foul of empirical statements that modern cultures are in fact heterogeneous and incoherent? Does it have to fall foul of normative judgements that homogeneity is to lament, cultural pluralism to applaud?

Now these empirical and normative questions should not be prejudged by the use of the term 'collective identity' itself. Collective identity might just be understood as the sum of collective representations, of symbols and meaning which refer to the collectivity itself, as a special part of the collective culture.[2]

There are many elements of a group culture or national culture which are not necessarily part of collective identity: stocks of knowledge, many values and norms with no specific relation to the life of a particular community, patterns of individual identity, elements of expressive or aesthetic culture: music, literature and so on, which do not carry meanings that relate specifically to the community. Some of these elements may be shared with other communities, some may be special. The composition of the whole cultural repertoire and its patterns of distribution among the membership make up the cultural profile, the peculiar cultural character of a group. But that does not necessarily make them part of the collective identity of the group. They become elements of collective identity only insofar as they are regarded as such by the members, and insofar as they are seen as expressing a specific cultural character of the group or as constituting a specific cultural heritage or tradition. The boundaries between the general culture and those 'reflexive' elements which make up collective identity are not very sharp, of course, since representations of cultural features are an important part of collective self-images. And the

---

[2] In an interesting discussion of the concept 'national identity', Bikhu Parekh sets an encompassing understanding of collective identity against more limited understanding. The latter may refer to self-understanding or to shared values and commitments; the wider notion 'includes the central organising principles of the polity, its structural tendencies, characteristic ways of thinking and living, the ideals that inspire its people, the values they profess and to which its leaders tend to appeal, ... their propensities to act in specific ways, their deepest fears, ambitions, anxieties ...' , (Parekh 1995, p. 257). Defined in this way, 'collective identity' loses its distinctiveness - it becomes the total of all important properties (institutional and cultural) of a polity. It achieves the same general meaning as 'culture' in Taylor's famous encompassing definition. Or at least it gains the meaning of 'way of life' or 'ethos'. A more restricted and specific understanding might be more useful, however. Therefore I plead for a more restricted, and also for a less unitary understanding. Parekh's notion of collective identity is explicitly modeled after a strong notion of individual identity. This may be misleading, too, as later explained in the text.

maintenance of a distinct group culture can become an important collective goal and as such a part of collective identity. But collective reflections of the group culture only provide a selective, partial, possibly not entirely accurate representation of that culture. There are probably many cultural elements which remain implicit, unreflected.

The strength of collective identity is also not dependent on the degree of cultural difference or dissimilarity between the group and its social environment. *Individuality* is not *dissimilarity*. Collective identity and cultural difference are not the same kind of phenomenon. Since collective identities are necessarily unique, because they refer to a particular collective, its features (cultural and otherwise), its situation, history and so on, they always provide *some* element of cultural dissimilarity. But if we understand something like different world views, value systems, beliefs and so on by cultural difference or dissimilarity, then we find that marked differences in these attributes are not a necessary condition for a distinct collective identity. Members of different collectivities can become quite similar in overall cultural profile, in most beliefs, values, individual goals and life-plans and so on, without losing a distinct collective identity. Two groups with extremely similar cultural characteristics can nevertheless maintain quite strong collective identities. Italian renaissance city states or contemporary English soccer clubs might be examples. Group solidarity is not dependent on cultural difference. A collective memory, narratives about the history of the group makes for collective identity, but is unrelated to current cultural differences in other areas.[3]

So cultural assimilation of immigrant groups or minorities, or cultural convergence between state-bounded societies or even larger units does not necessarily result in a weakening of collective identities. There may be other relations, however. Strong group identities may lead to a high valuation, to a large subjective relevance of small cultural difference. We may assume, on the other hand, that the confrontation with cultural otherness, with very dissimilar cultural environments will strengthen collective identities.

---

[3] This implies that 'cultural conflict' and 'identity conflict' may not be the same. In the first case, conflict may result from incompatible cultural orientations (e.g. norms or values which are not mutually acceptable). In the second case, group solidarities based e.g. on common histories or collective memories may shape conflict constellations, or experiences of disrespect for one's community may sharpen conflict. Huntington's diagnosis of a 'conflict of civilizations' is ambiguous in this respect. Insofar as he refers to conflicts of historically grounded collective identities, counter-arguments which refer to cultural similarities between civilizations or dissimilarities within them will not prevail.

Collective Identity, Boundaries, the Other

These remarks may sound like a notion of group identity which simply stresses the maintenance of social boundaries, in the spirit of F. Barth (Barth, 1969). Barth and other authors see features of group culture simply as markers of the delineation of group boundaries. Otherwise cultural content does not seem to matter much and cultural features are seen as quite malleable.

The proposition that collective identity is not necessarily dependent on important cultural differences does not imply such a thesis. Both the elements of collective identity (self-perceptions, group histories, collective aspirations and so on) and the group culture as a whole may be quite rich and complex, may have their own weight, a relevant influence on group life, may provide both limits and opportunities to cultural change. All this has to be determined empirically, of course. And the maintenance of group boundaries is certainly not the only function or effect of collective identities.

Similarly, there are understandings of collective identity which focus on difference, distinction, or otherness. Collective identity, in this view, is primarily produced by the construction of boundaries, by the maintenance of distinctions between in-group and out-group, by the exclusion of the other, or by focusing on the differences between members and non-members. Groups create their self-image by drawing contrasts to their social environment, to images of the other.

Now it is certainly true that contrasts and comparisons are common elements of collective identities. But it is not *obviously* true that they always play the central role for the constitution of these identities. This should not be decided by definition.[4] There seem to be cases where collective identity is very much centred on problems of the group itself, e.g. on its history and collective future, where concern for difference and otherness is very muted.

These are questions about the *contents* of collective identities. These must be distinguished from questions about the origins of collective identities or about the processes of creation and recreation. Here, external definitions often play a role. Groups have experiences and perceptions of the ways they are perceived, described and otherwise treated by the outside world, and this influences their self-perceptions. Sometimes groups may partly adopt external definitions, sometimes they may reject external perceptions and develop counter-images. Also, experiences of hostility,

---

[4] For criticisms on such a 'differentialist' notions of identity see Shils, E. (1995, p. 107), (Parekh 1995, p. 256).

mistreatment and disrespect may form elements of collective identity.

How Collective are Collective Identities?

If we use a weak and inclusive notion of collective identity, as developed here, and drop the unitary associations of this term, it becomes obvious that we have to ask the same questions about collective identity which have been asked about the role and character of group culture or especially national culture in general. There are familiar objections to the idea of a common culture and collective identity in modern societies. To sum them up, in a somewhat oversimplified or exaggerated way:

There is no national culture and identity that is a coherent system of beliefs or meanings. Contemporary culture and collective identity is eclectic, syncretist, internally fragmented, a jumble of heterogeneous elements, not an organic whole at all.

Neither is there cultural consensus. There are no cognitive and normative belief systems and no collective self-perceptions which are widely accepted as valid and binding. There is widespread controversy, dissensus, pluralism, difference, diffidence, at most some fragile acceptance, imposed by the more powerful groups.

There is therefore also no core or essence of a national culture and identity which would be relatively durable, which would change only very slowly, following largely its own logic. Cultural elements are constantly and opportunistically produced or constructed, especially by certain powerful elites, and adapted to changing political and economic circumstances.

More generally, there is no cultural determinism. Culture does not regulate or direct social action, like a computer program steering some complicated piece of machinery. Instead, social actors use cultural elements as a 'tool kit' for the fabrication of interpretations and accounts, suited to their interests and plans.

Certainly, these statements have some force. But do they give a complete and accurate picture? If we get around in different countries, if we read the newspapers, watch TV, if we go to public meetings, talk to people, if we live in a country for a while, try to understand its politics, the ways of life we encounter – do not we feel very distinctly that there *are* very real and consequential cultural differences? And that there are collective self-images, historical narratives, collective ideals and other elements of collective identity which seem to have a recognizable influence? And if we look at some of the relevant comparative literature on political culture, value change, social movements, nationalism and so on, we find at least some confirmation (not conclusive, but suggestive) of the supposed influence of national cultures and identities. And even if there is reason for doubt if there are unitary national identities - what is it, then, that so many people are talking about under this heading? Or what does it mean that there are public debates about national identity?

And of course there is a lot of cultural invention going on, but does it start from nowhere? And do we really approach culture as a tool kit, which we can grab at will and handle freely? At least we had to learn to handle these tools and this has left some imprint on us. And where did those tools come from, how were they produced and distributed or made available to us? Are there not accumulated cultural repertoires which we have to make our own before we can start to remould them?

Now it is not too difficult to describe in a general manner some kind of middle position between the polemical extremes. We do not have to follow the obviously false alternative between the assumption of national cultural homogeneity and cultural determinism on the one hand and the assumption of randomness or total manipulability of cultural variation on the other.

It is more plausible to describe a national public culture and collective identity as a field of contention. There is a lot of variation of cultural elements, a lot of difference, a lot of disagreement. But the whole ensemble is not just chaotic, without some kind of order or pattern. Cultural elements are more a repertoire than a definite blueprint for action, but it is still a repertoire with a distinct composition. And a repertoire only exists insofar as it is already to some degree mastered by the actors - who are what they are because of their mastery of or familiarity with that specific repertoire. Contention is widespread, but not random. There are fault lines, cleavages, camps, central issues and topics, certain inventories of ideas and arguments to support different positions. Despite all disagreement, there are probably some common assumptions, some common language, some shared images and ideas.

All this has to be properly specified or qualified, of course. There might be further differentiations of collective identities, in addition to the alignment of adversary camps or the contests between different interpretations or discourses. Not only might there be different versions of collective identity which are supported by different parts of a national population. There might also be different degrees of interest. Aspects of collective identity might be more important for some people than for others. Public debates about questions of collective identity may be followed primarily by certain segments of the public, and active participation in public will be even more selective. In a certain part of the literature on national identity, statements about features of these identities seem to be derived from statements by intellectuals, journalists or politicians. It is not obvious how much influence those debates and statements have on the general population.

'Primordialism' vs. 'Constructivism': What are the Questions?

From the literature on nationalism, ethnicity and collective identity, we are familiar with the opposition of 'primordialist' and 'constructivist' accounts of these phenomena. Most of the time, primordialism is flogged somewhat ritualistically. Collective identities are not given by nature or biology, and they are not unchanging essences. Instead they are changing, adaptable and 'socially constructed'.

This opposition is somewhat misleading, however. It is based on a conflation of two questions. First, what are the causes or origins of collective identities, how are they produced or created, transmitted, changed, and how variable are they as a result? Second, what is the content of collective identity, what kinds of meaning do we find there, what kinds of understandings about the nature of the collectivity and the relations between its members?

'Primordialism' is most often criticized as an answer to the first question. It is, however, better understood as answering the second question, and at least some important proponents of 'primordialism' mean it that way (Geertz, 1994; Eisenstadt and Giesen, 1995).

Relating to the second question, 'primordialism' means that there are certain elements of collective identity which are *understood* or *experienced* as unconditionally binding, pre-given and not subject to voluntary choices, of primary importance and particular force, connected with strong sentiments. These understandings may relate to solidarities between group members, identification with a group and its welfare, concern about the continuance of cultural traditions, life-forms or collective projects (which may in turn be connected with attachments to territories or landscapes).

Such an identification of 'primordial' understandings and sentiments in some collective identity could be criticized in several ways. It could very simply be criticized as inaccurate because these interpretations and sentiments are just not there, or not strong, or confined to certain parts of the population. Some elements of these understandings could be criticized as factually inaccurate; this pertains above all to historical interpretations and collective memories or stories, which are often invoked to support attachments to the group or a territory. This or other evidence may be used to support a diagnosis that certain 'primordial' collective self-understandings are the result of manipulation or self-deception.[5] All these claims would have to be supported by proper evidence, of course. None of these possible criticisms rules out the possibility that there might be quite genuine, authentic beliefs and sentiments of a 'primordial' character.

The last mentioned criticism touches on the first question again. What are the origins or causes of collective identities, and how stable or malleable are these identities? One causal account may be that collective identities are invented in some more or less deliberate or intentional way by interested parties, possibly to mask ulterior motives, to give some appearance of legitimacy to specific interests, or to manipulate people in the interest of the inventors (Nagel 1994; Hechter 1987). Besides intentional manipulation, elements of self-deception or rationalization might also be involved. This opportunistic or instrumental or self-serving use of collective identities is apparently sometimes meant when people talk of 'social construction' (Eller and Coughlan 1993). This understanding is then set against the notion that collective identities emerge in some way naturally and universally, possibly as a result of biological mechanisms, or as a result of some unanalyzed universal social or cultural mechanism.

There looms a false alternative, however. Apart from intentional invention and instrumental use for particularistic interests, there might be many other forms of social 'construction' or production or creation of collective identities, other forms of generating meanings. There might be processes of cultural creation and transmission which are not simply driven by specific interests, which are indeed prior to or more basic than the formulation of an 'interest'.

And as to permanence or change of collective identities, there are several questions, from the factual question of degrees of change in collective self-understanding, as noted by outside observers, to the more complicated question about the causes of permanence or change, and to questions about the role, which ideas about historical continuity play within collective identities. Biological inheritance might not be the only basis for the durability of certain social and cultural features, and the rejection of biological explanations or of some notions of an unchanging human nature does not settle the question of permanence and variability.

---

[5] Beliefs about primordial relationships could of course also be criticized in a straightforward normative way, as some kind of inappropriate collective egoism or ethnocentrism, or as traditionalism that cannot stand up to rational criticism. But it is not obvious that e.g. certain special obligations and solidarities could not be justified normatively.

2 Collective Identity: An Alternative Formulation

First of all, 'collective identity' should be understood as an area of culture, as a special class of cultural elements. In any given social unit we find stocks of symbols and meanings which make up the cultural repertoire of that unit. Among these symbols and meanings there are some which pertain in a special way to an understanding of the social unit itself - to its current state, its character, its problems, its achievements, its history, its future. The totality of these cultural elements makes up a collective identity.

How do we Identify These Symbols and Meanings?

We find them in acts or processes of communication and expression (both linguistic and non-linguistic). We find them in the minds or memories of people - as symbolic competencies, beliefs, images and so on. We find them in all kinds of artefacts which become carriers or stores of symbolic meaning. We discover these meanings by asking people about their beliefs, by interpreting artefacts, by studying communications and expressive practices.

Discursive and presentative meanings. We can distinguish between discursive and presentative symbols and meanings.[6] Discursive meanings can be articulated in written or spoken language. Discursive meanings can also be contested. They come with claims to validity (Habermas) which can be argued - questioned or criticized, justified or defended. Discursive meanings are what is usually meant by terms like 'ideas' or 'beliefs'. Presentative meanings are represented by non-linguistic symbols or symbolic practices (signs, pictures, music, rituals etc.) or by non-literal, figurative or poetic uses of language ('fiction', poetry, metaphor etc.). Representative meanings can be interpreted in ordinary language, of course, and works or practices with representative meanings can be evaluated and criticized in various ways. But this does not really make presentative meanings into discursive meanings. We can argue about the meaning of a painting, or a piece of music, or a ritual, but we cannot make it an idea or belief - even if we can sometimes *connect* it to certain ideas or beliefs.

Collective identities are not only made up by ideas, beliefs, narrations or interpretations which are discursive in the mentioned sense. There are also presentative meanings in rituals and non-discursive symbols. There are collective representations in art forms, in popular entertainment, in literature, in stories and fairy tales, in signs, photographs, advertising

---

[6] I borrow these terms from S. Langer (1957).

graphics, in architecture, memorials, public rituals, in consumer goods, fashion, and for sports. The roles and relations of discursive and presentative meanings within collective identities are an intriguing problem. It could be argued that (especially in modern culture) discursive meanings are in some ways more important, especially with respect to changes of identity and contests about identity. In any case I will (without arguing this point) direct my primary attention to discursive meanings.

Meanings, practical dispositions and sentiments. There are complex relations, not easily analysed, between symbols or meanings, on the one hand, and actors' practical dispositions and affects, on the other. By 'practical dispositions' I mean phenomena like desires, preferences, a readiness to act according to certain normative expectations, to follow certain rules and so on. The corresponding actions may derive from explicit choices and decisions, or they may be more or less habitual and unreflective. Symbolic meanings (evaluations of objects or states of affairs or activities, normative expectations and so on) are implicated in these dispositions, and many components of collective identity, which are of evaluative or normative character, imply a disposition to certain behaviours. Similarly, affects or sentiments which are often formed by symbolic interpretations can be expressed in symbolic forms and can be evoked by symbols.

I mention these relations because common understandings of collective identity often refer to certain practical dispositions or sentiments as parts of those identities. Think of concepts like pride, trust, or solidarity, which combine evaluative judgements or normative expectations and obligations with certain feelings. And there are concepts like 'love of the country', with diffuse and manifold aspects of meaning, sentiment and inclinations to act. We can follow this usage and include such sentiments and dispositions in the meaning of 'collective identity'. But we have to keep in mind that the relations between articulate normative or evaluative beliefs and actual practice can be complicated - such beliefs do not invariably lead to corresponding actions.

Salience and reflexivity. There is great variability in the salience of various elements of collective identity, and of collective identity as a whole. In many contexts, these elements remain in the background, as unstated assumptions and beliefs, as taken for granted. Collective beliefs or other elements become more or less explicit, objects of attention or possibly objects of reflection, if they are taught in a deliberate way, or if they are questioned or disputed or celebrated.

Collective identities as a whole also differ in the degree to which their creation or reproduction is accompanied by explicit articulation and critical examination. There can be more traditional identities, which are transmitted or adopted without much questioning, and there can be more 'reflective' collective identities which are subject to collective examination, deliberation, and possibly reformulation. It is commonly assumed that modern culture has generally become more reflective in this sense. If this applies to collective identities, or to what extent, remains to be seen.

Strong or weak identities. 'Thick' or 'thin' collective identities. Collective identity, as the notion is explicated here, is a descriptive term which does not imply much about the specific content or strength or degree of acceptance of collective representations. Collective identity exists wherever there are collectivities, where some of these cultural elements are present. Not all of the elements that were mentioned above need to be present or to be articulated.

These elements may be weakly developed and somewhat marginal for the members of the social unit, or they may be more central and more important to the members. And collective identities may have a narrow or 'thin' character (as in those cases where a group or organization shares a small range of common interests or goals - which may nevertheless be quite important for the members - and where there is little historical depth and not much of a self-image beyond the narrow purpose and corresponding instrumental features of the unit). Or they may be rich, complex, 'thick', of considerable historical depth, with detailed conceptions of group character, strong elements of collective solidarity and so on.

In this rather weak and inclusive sense, almost every social unit with at least minimally developed boundaries and a minimum of internal communication will have a collective identity in this sense: face-to-face groups as well as larger ones, groups with mostly informal structures and formal organizations.[7] Families, friendship circles, organizations and associations of all kinds, professional or occupational groupings, religions, state-bounded societies (which will be discussed presently), may be

---

[7] 'Collective representations' might be a better, somewhat more neutral term than 'collective identity'. (This is Durkheim's term, of course. Durkheim, however, used the term in a somewhat different way.) Or 'collective self-understandings'. These terms have their own problems, however. Terms like 'representation' or 'self-understanding' do not bring out the normative, evaluative, practical components of the symbolic elements which are parts of collective identities. There is also a problematic feature that they share with collective identity: misleading associations of a group personality or group mind.

civilizations or continents or other transnational units.[8]

More complex identities will be found in larger, more encompassing groups or communities,[9] also in groups with a longer life-span, where elements of collective identity, not least a collective memory have time to develop and accumulate. Transgenerational groups, which include whole families or members of all ages and life-stages, where membership is primarily inherited and new members are introduced in the life of the community primarily by primary socialization, are both encompassing and long-lived. The most important cases are: Religious communities; Symbolic communities which define themselves by a common history, common traditions, common cultural practices or features ('ethnic' groups); but also classes, under certain circumstances; and of course state-bounded societies - i.e. the classical case of national identity.

Relations Between Overlapping or Nesting Identities

Collective identities might be nesting (e.g. national and sub-national, regional identities) or overlapping. The latter is true e.g. for collectivities which are at least partly transnational in scope, but have national 'wings' or departments or sub-units. Examples would be international religious communities or professional organizations of scientists.

Substantively, the relationships between collective identities with overlapping memberships *may* be competing: the strength of the identities in question might be inversely related, one kind of identity would gain strength by weakening the other allegiance. So one might assume some kind of competition between national and regional identities, for example, or between collective identities of immigrant groups and the national identity of the host society. This kind of relationship is not a necessary one, however. Relationships between collective identities might as well be indifferent (non-rivalling) or even mutually supportive. Insofar as group

---

[8] Gender and sexual orientation are often quoted as examples of collective identity. But especially in the case of gender it is not clear whether the term, as defined here, applies, or to what degree. This depends upon the degree to which male and female (or other) identities are really understood as *group* identities or more as *differing types of personal identity*. Of course this varies among individuals. Some women do understand themselves as members of a (historical, transgenerational) group. Others probably do not. There could well be different gender roles, even different cultural characteristics of (many) men and women, with there being a male or female collective identity.

[9] Encompassing groups are those who combine a broad range of activities and concerns and are relevant to large parts of the lives of their members (rather than to specialized interests and activities) (Selznick, 1992, pp. 358-360). Membership in a state-bounded society or possibly in an ethnic group is more encompassing in this sense than membership in a business organization.

membership and orientation towards a collective identity demands individual attention, commitment, or even some kind of active support or participation, there is always some kind of competition. The amounts of energy and attention that individuals can mobilize are certainly variable, but nevertheless limited, and choices about allocation are always necessary. Most of the time these may be made habitually, however, without much reflection. Relationships between group memberships and collective identities can nevertheless be mutually supportive in some respects, especially in the case of nested identities. Family traditions, local and regional attachments, membership in a national church, and/or membership in voluntary associations may support people's national identifications.

Incompatible or conflicting relations between collective identities may emerge in several ways. In most cases, there are conflicts between social units, where collective identities are implicated. In certain cases, collective identities may produce conflict, because they imply conflicting orientations and demands. Or conflicts may affect certain elements of collective identity (e.g. collective pride or self-respect), and this may aggravate conflict. There may be all kinds of conflicts between collectivities with mutually exclusive memberships. How collective identities might be implicated in such conflicts, if there are elements of collective identity which give group conflicts a special character and possibly make them harder to resolve, is an important question (which I cannot discuss in this paper, however). In the case of nested or overlapping memberships and collective identities, there may simply be conflicting demands which are put on the individual by the respective groups and their collective self-understandings, without open conflict between the groups as a whole. This is more or less the familiar case of role conflict. Demands of family membership may conflict with patriotic duties. In conflicts between groups, where overlapping memberships play a role, conflicts of loyalty emerge. In conflicts between states, for example, class solidarity may conflict with national loyalty.

Authors have made various statements about competing or conflicting collective identities. Often assertions are made that collective identity has some primacy about other collective identities, either in a descriptive or a normative sense. Subnational or transnational collective identities (based on ethnicity, class, religion) have been seen as dangerous for national unity. On the other hand, national identity has often been described as the winner in most of these conflicts. National identities have trumped both international class solidarity and more particularistic group attachments.

It is, however, not so easy to evaluate general statements of this kind. The impact of collective identities on people's orientations and actions is very much influenced by specific contexts, situations and characteristics of group conflict. It is true, of course, that stability of a political order requires that allegiance to the state *on certain matters* is dominant over competing group loyalties. But modern political orders respect individual attachments to families, religious communities and other collectivities, and this is a precondition for their stability. There is some kind of balance, not simply predominance. Most of the time it is also not evident to which degree acquiescence in demands of the state is based on national identifications or on other factors, like power, coercion, various institutional mechanisms for the diffusion of conflict and so on.

Identities: 'Good' and 'Bad'

Collective identity is, like individual identity, sometimes used as a 'success term' with implicit normative connotations. A 'lack' or 'deficit' of collective identity is then seen as a problem. There are also some related terms, which point to certain forms of collective identity which are clearly considered as bad. These are terms like ethnocentrism, chauvinism or racism.

As I have explained above, I would propose an understanding of collective identity that is more neutral. That makes it necessary to identify empirically the consequences or implications of some form of collective identity, and to specify explicitly the normative criteria one might wish to apply in the evaluation of collective identities.

I will not be able to discuss such normative criteria in a systematic way here. We might consider very briefly, however, some possible criteria for evaluation, which are implicitly or explicitly used in descriptions of collective identities.

Insofar as collective identities contain norms, values or (as in the case of national identities) principles of political order, these may be evaluated according to the criteria of some moral or normative political conception. In this sense we could speak e.g. of 'liberal' and 'non-liberal', or 'democratic' or 'non-democratic' collective, or national identities. However, the case of *group-specific* moralities or solidarities poses some special normative problems. How do they relate to more general, or universal norms or obligations? What kinds of *special* obligations, loyalties, solidarities among the members of some collectivity could be justified? And how should conflicts between competing loyalties be resolved? These problems have generally been discussed with respect to *national* loyalties or allegiances and their relation to universal moral principles (sometimes framed as questions about the relation between 'nationalism' or 'patriotism' and 'cosmopolitanism'). Many authors have argued that certain special obligations or allegiances could well be justified on universalistic grounds, but there is considerable controversy about these matters (Spinner, 1994; Tamir, 1994; Cohen, 1996; Miller, 1996; McMahan and McKim, 1997).

There are other kinds of evaluations, relating to more formal or pragmatic features of collective identity. The following five pairs of concepts denote some of these kinds of evaluation. These concepts have both descriptive and evaluative content. They denote certain features of collective identities and at the same time imply a certain evaluation of these features.

Deep or shallow. Deep identities are distinguished by intense commitments or solidarities and by a long time horizon (rich collective memories and felt collective aspirations for the future). Shallow identities are based on a narrow range of common interests or concerns, low solidarity and short time horizons.[10] In a communitarian perspective at least, deep collective identities might be clearly preferable. The reasons for this would have to be spelled out in more detail, of course. And probably everybody would agree that there can be pretty ugly deep identities in this sense. So this criterion would have to be combined with some of the following.

Coherent and fragmented. These terms may mean two different things. 'Fragmentation' of collective identity may mean that the relevant collectivity is ridden by internal conflicts and divisions and that there are different and incompatible versions of collective identity held by different sub-groups. Or it may mean that the elements of collective identity themselves, although widely accepted, are a jumble of incoherent pieces, so that collective identity cannot fulfil its function to give orientation and meaning to the lives of the members. It is of course a matter of judgement how much consensus in the first sense is desirable, depending on the circumstances, and how much coherence in the second sense is possible.

Genuine or manipulated. This one is harder to explain, because 'genuine' or 'authentic' might mean different things. Manipulated collective identities are the result of some kind of deception by interested parties (elites, powerful groups, and so on) who somehow, by persuasion or propaganda or compulsory education or control of public communication or other such means get other people to accept certain forms of collective identity. If

---

[10] The distinction between 'life-style enclaves' and 'communities of memory' in *Habits of the Heart* (Bellah, R. N., R. Madsen, et al., 1985) is an example for this kind of evaluation.

these are not freely accepted, if acceptance is not based on some kind of undistorted cultural exchange, it might be regarded as a criterion of inauthenticity. There might also be forms of self-deception in the adoption of collective identities, the acceptance of self-serving beliefs, resulting from motives which one hides from oneself. But this is slippery conceptual ground.

Inclusive or exclusive. This could mean greater or lesser readiness to accept newcomers into the group. An inclusive collective identity could also be understood as a tolerant one, with norms of acceptance and respect for a variety of life-forms or other orientations and behaviours. An exclusive identity may mean a tendency to stigmatize or exclude members or subgroups which do not conform to the standards of the group. There might of course be very good reason to disapprove of certain behaviours, and no collectivity will or should tolerate everything. So this criterion has to be qualified somehow. Also the readiness to accept newcomers into the group may be normatively contested in various cases.

Open or closed. This refers primarily to the cognitive dimensions. A closed group identity would be one which does not admit internal or external criticism and is not ready to correct erroneous perceptions or judgements, be it of the group itself or of the outside world. An open collective identity would further reflect on its own premises, critical evaluation of its contents, and readiness to correct mistakes.

Co-operative or aggressive. This one is more or less self-explanatory. Aggressive collective identities will put perceived group interests first under all circumstances, will pursue them in an aggressive way, and will possibly tend to see the group threatened by a hostile environment. Co-operative identities will be more trusting, ready to compromise or seek fair solutions which take into account legitimate interests of others, and will use restraint in the choice of means for the pursuit of their interests.

The last two criteria have been developed in the literature on ethnocentrism and group prejudice. All these criteria are pretty vague, as formulated here. They would need to be specified, and the corresponding normative judgements to be spelled out and justified much more clearly. It would also be necessary to specify them for different types of groups. Obviously, different criteria should be applied to families, churches or states. This enumeration of concepts which often play a role in the description of collective identities should only hint to a need to make the criteria for evaluation more explicit.

3 Identity, Assimilation and Integration: Some Closing Remarks

With respect to the analysis of the developmental trajectories of immigrants (or, to be more precise, of the members of immigration flows from individual countries and their descendants), this conceptual elaboration might open up certain possibilities for empirical research. It would lead to probe deeper into the multiple dimensions of collective identity than much of current research. This research is mostly oriented to notions of collective identity which are borrowed from social psychology (where collective identity is understood of that aspect of self-categorization which is oriented towards the group-membership of the individual) and often focuses on one particular aspect (feelings of loyalty, pride, and above all attitudes towards other groups). A more differentiated approach might be useful, and some examples are given in other chapters of this volume.

Such an approach alerts us to the possible development not only of various differing kinds of collective identity among immigrants, but also of different relationships between group identities of immigrants and other dimensions of what has traditionally been called assimilation and integration. Above all, group identity might develop differently (if not entirely independently) both from the *social organization* of immigrant groups and of their *cultural and other differences* from other parts of the host society. Table 2.1 gives a simplified representation of various ways in which immigrant categories could develop over time within the host society.

Table 2.1 Development trajectories of immigrant categories

	Collective identity	Community organization	Cultural distinctiveness	Dissimilar socio-economic profile
1	+	+	+	+
2	+	+	+	-
3	+	+	-	-
4	+	-	-	-
5	-	-	-	+

'Community organization' here refers to all kinds of organisations, associations or even more permanent circles and networks. 'Dissimilar socio-economic profile' refers primarily to the distribution of educational attainment, income and wealth, and occupancy. 'Dissimilar' means, that the distribution of these features is markedly different for the immigrant category compared to the rest of the population. This includes the (remote) possibility that the immigrant category might show a 'better' distribution with respect to one or more of these dimensions. 'Cultural difference' does not just mean a different distribution of cultural attributes like religious beliefs of affiliations or of more or less family centred cultural practices (food, codes of polite conduct, dress norms and so on), but deeper differences in beliefs, value patterns and associated practices which do not just affect some parts of family life, but more general behavioural orientations.

Now there are more possible and plausible combinations of these attributes than Table 1 shows. The combinations which are represented in the table are just meant to alert us to the possibility that socio-economic 'equalization' *might* go hand in hand with the retainment of group life, social organization and cultural distinctiveness among immigrants (line 2) - that is part of what is normally meant by normative conceptions of 'multiculturalism'. However, there are other possibilities. Cultural distinctiveness (in any deeper sense) might go first (value differences and differences in cognitive beliefs might become insignificant, religious convictions and practices might adopt to a pluralist model and so on). Community organization might follow, except for some loose kinds of cultural organizations (which do not require a lot of engagement) and some kinds of interest representation. Collective identity together with some kinds of identity-articulating practices and rituals (both private and collective, like parades, holidays and so on) might still survive. This is the pattern that has been described as 'symbolic ethnicity' (Gans, 1979; Waters and Lieberson, 1988; Waters, 1990; Gans, 1994).

The primary example for a development towards 'symbolic ethnicity' are European immigrants in the US in the 19th and 20th centuries - the most extensively documented and researched case of immigrant adaptation over three or more generations in a Western society.

Today it is often assumed that current immigration which streams into Western countries will produce markedly different patterns. Why would one predict such a different development? Here is a list of possible assumptions: Host societies may differ from earlier cases: less accommodating or tolerant (more rejectionist), or more tolerant or supportive of cultural pluralism (less assimilationist) (and the US may themselves have become different from earlier periods). Host societies may be less culturally homogenous, or more culturally differentiated themselves, and forces of cultural assimilation may be weakened thereby. Economic and social conditions may be less favourable, restricting mobility, locking immigrants into certain social positions. Characteristics of immigrants and immigration streams may differ (no distinct immigration 'waves' and 'lulls', producing a clear succession of generations, but continuous streams; differences in skills or human capital; differences in social and cultural characteristics). Immigrants may have become more assertive, may have more resources and opportunities for collective mobilization and organization, and they may use this to resist assimilation in certain (especially cultural) areas. Ease of travel and communication as well as (in some cases) geographical proximity may further continuing relations with the country of origin ('transnational social spaces').

Do these conditions apply, and to what degree? And above all: Will they lead to different development trajectories for immigrants - away from a path of slow upward mobility (over two or three generations), general cultural assimilation with respect to cognitive orientations and basic value patterns, and of retention of some kinds of symbolic identity with some associated private or community rituals? Should we expect instead (in the long run) stronger segmentation, stronger retention of distinct end encompassing group cultures, stable and enduring community institutions and organizations, stronger political salience of immigrant identity, incompatibility between immigrant and national identity, maybe blocked mobility and enduring conflict? Will national identities and national cultures with certain recognizable shared patterns be dissolved as a consequence, to be replaced by patchworks of identity and culture or by general flux and hybridity?

Because of the as yet limited time span of the new immigration into Western countries it is hardly possible to empirically confirm or disconfirm these expectations conclusively. But at least we might check the existing evidence for the assumption that current developmental trajectories of immigrants into Western countries are really very much different from earlier cases (European immigration into the US). This cannot be done here. But as I read the literature, there is much evidence that assimilation processes seem still to be well at work. Why should we really assume that current developments will be profoundly different? Given our earlier experience with the immigration into Western countries in the 20th century, the burden of proof should really be on the other side.

References

Barth, F., Ed. (1969), *Ethnic Groups and Boundaries: The Social Organization of Cultural Difference*. Bergen-Oslo / London, Universitets Forlaget / Allen & Unwin.

Bellah, R. N., R. Madsen, et al. (1985), *Habits of the Heart*, Berkeley, CA, University of California Press.

Brubaker, R. (2001), 'The Return of Assimilation? Changing Perspectives on Immigration and Its Sequels in France, Germany, and the United States', *Ethnic and Racial Studies* 24(4), pp.531-48.

Brubaker, R. and F. Cooper (2000), *Beyond 'Identity'*, Theory and Society 29,1, pp.1-47.

Cohen, J., Ed. (1996), *For Love of Country. Debating the Limits of Patriotism*. M. Nussbaum and Respondents. Boston, MA, Bacon Press.

Eisenstadt, S. N. and B. Giesen (1995), 'The Construction of Collective Identity', *Archives Européennes de Sociologie* 36, pp.72-102.

Eller, J. D. and Coughlan, R. M. (1993), 'The Poverty of Primordialism: the Demystification of Ethnic Attachments', *Ethnic and Racial Studies 16*, pp.183-202.

Gans, H. (1979), 'Symbolic Ethnicity: The Future of Ethnic Groups and Cultures in America', *Ethnic and Racial Studies 2*, pp.1-20.

Gans, H. J. (1994), 'Symbolic Ethnicity and Symbolic Religiosity: Towards a Comparison of Ethnic and Religious Acculturation', *Ethnic and Racial Studies*, pp.577-92.

Geertz, C. (1994), 'Angestammte Loyalitäten, bestehende Einheiten', *Merkur* 452(Mai 1994).

Gordon, M. M. (1964), *Assimilation in American Life: The Role of Race, Religion and National Origins*, New York, Oxford University Press.

Hechter, Michael (1987), 'Nationalism as Group Solidarity', *Ethnic and Racial Studies*, pp.415-26.

Langer, S. K. (1957), *Philosophy in New Key: A Study in the Symbolism of Reason, Rite and Art*, Cambridge, MA, Harvard University Press.

McMahan, J. and R. McKim, Eds. (1997), *The Morality of Nationalism*, Oxford, Oxford University Press.

Miller, D. (1996), 'On Nationality', *Nations and Nationalism* 2(3), pp.409-21.

Nagel, J. (1994), 'Constructing Ethnicity: Creating and Recreating Ethnic Identity and Culture', *Social Problems* 41, pp.152-76.

Parekh, B. (1995), 'The Concept of National Identity', *New Community* 21(2), pp.255-68.

Selznick, P. (1992), *The Moral Commonwealth: Social Theory and the Promise of Community*, Berkeley, University of California Press.

Shils, E. (1995), 'Nation, Nationality, Nationalism and Civil Society', *Nations and Nationalism*(1), pp.93-118.

Spinner, J. (1994), *The Boundaries of Citizenship*, Baltimore, MD, The Johns Hopkins University Press.

Tajfel, H. (1981), *Human Groups and Social Categories*, Cambridge, Cambridge University Press.

Tajfel, H. (ed.) (1982), *Social Identity and Intergroup Relations*, Cambridge, UK, Cambridge University Press.

Tamir, Y. (1994), *Liberal Nationalism*, Princeton, NJ, Princeton University Press.

Waters, M. and S. Lieberson, (eds.) (1988), *From Many Strands: Ethnic Racial Groups in Contemporary America*, For the National Committee for Research on the 1980 Census, New York, Russell Sage Foundation.

Waters, M. C. (1990), *Ethnic Options: Choosing Identities in America*, Berkeley, University of California Press.

Chapter 3

Public Culture in Societies of Immigration

Rainer Bauböck

Defining Public Culture[1]

In October 2000 a German politician, Friedrich Merz, the leader of the parliamentary faction of the Christian-Democratic party CDU, launched a debate on the need for immigrants to integrate into the *Leitkultur*, a term which has been translated variously as 'guiding' or 'defining' culture. In the controversy that followed, the president of the Jewish community in Germany asked whether the outbreaks of racist violence in the Eastern provinces should be seen as part of this defining culture that immigrants would have to accept. In its party manifesto on immigration policy of 6 November 2000 the CDU replaced the original formula 'a German defining culture' with an apparently less nationalistic one: 'a defining culture in Germany' (CDU, 2000).[2]

The idea I want to develop in this paper is that public culture in societies of immigration must be self-transformative. In a way this is the very opposite of a defining culture that sets the terms of integration, although both share the assumption that democratic societies exposed to immigration need a common cultural framework that is supported by their political institutions. It may therefore be useful to start with a brief look at how the CDU defines the 'defining culture'. The manifesto lists three elements: constitutional principles and values, the German language and the Christian-occidental community of values. The first two items will also figure in my own list. In these regards the dispute is not about whether to include, but how to interpret these elements. It is the last item that reveals

---

[1] A first version of this text was given as a lecture at the conference: Globalisation in the Local Community, 27-29 November 2000 at Malmö University, Sweden. Special thanks to Bernhard Perchinig and Thomas Faist for helpful comments.

[2] For an analysis of underlying nationalist assumptions of the CDU approach see Klusmeyer (2001).

the intention of the political campaign. Immigrants can endorse con-stitutional principles and they can make efforts to learn the language of the receiving country. However, a Christian-occidental culture can be neither chosen nor learned. Combining the markers of religion (Christian) and geographic origin (occidental) creates a boundary between the natives and certain groups of immigrants that is meant to exclude the latter. Ethnic Germans from Eastern Europe or migrants from other EU member states already belong to this Christian-occidental community, the two million immigrants from Turkey do not. The authors of the CDU manifesto seem to be fully aware of this. They even felt the need for some fine-tuning, in order not to exclude the wrong groups: thus, ironically, Judaism is listed among the sources of *Christian*-occidental culture.[3]

Before I turn to my own list of elements of public culture, I will try to explain my use of this concept and why I think it is relevant for integration in societies of immigration. George Bernhard Shaw famously quipped about England and America being two nations separated by the same language. Since English has become the global language of academic discourse the scope of misunderstanding in transatlantic debates due to different uses of the same term has become much broader. The way American and European legal and political theorists use the term 'public' is a good example. In Europe, the dominant interpretation links 'public' to publicity, i.e. to communication that is open in the sense of being addressed to an unspecified or unlimited audience. In economic theory the main characteristic of public goods, such as clean air or city parks, is that nobody can be excluded from enjoying them. Jürgen Habermas' (1962) theory of the public sphere (*Öffentlichkeit*) builds on this interpretation. In this framework, public culture means the symbols, norms and values, world-views and styles of communication shared by persons and groups who interact in the public sphere. In the US, however, the term 'public' more often refers to the political sphere only. It signifies the *res publica*, the public interest or the common good of the political community. Thus, for John Rawls the public culture of a democratic society 'comprises the political institutions of a constitutional regime and the public traditions of their interpretation, as well as historic texts and documents that are common knowledge'. He demarcates this public political culture from the

---

[3] The full quote is: 'Integration requires therefore, besides learning the German language, to take a clear decision in favour of our political and constitutional order and to insert oneself into our social and cultural ways of life. This means to accept the value order of our Christian-occidental culture in Germany, which has been shaped by Christianity, Judaism, the philosophy of antiquity, humanism, Roman law and enlightenment' (CDU, 2000, my translation, RB).

'background culture' of civil society (Rawls, 1993, pp. 13-14). The point of this distinction in Rawls' theory is that comprehensive religious and moral doctrines belong to the background culture, but not to the public culture. The latter contains only those norms and values that all citizens can share as equal and free members of the political community irrespective of their religious and moral views. On Rawlsian grounds the CDU's 'defining culture' should be classified as non-public precisely because it is not a suitable basis for the political commitment a democratic society can expect from all its various groups, be they natives or immigrants.

David Miller, who defends the need for shared national identities in democratic societies, defines public culture quite differently and in a way that comes close to the CDU's *Leitkultur*:

> A public culture may be seen as a set of understandings about how a group of people is to conduct its life together. This will include political principles such as a belief in democracy or the rule of law, but it reaches more widely than this. It extends to social norms such honesty in filling in your tax return or queueing as a way of deciding who gets on to the bus first. It may also embrace certain cultural ideals, for instance religious beliefs or a commitment to preserve the purity of the national language. Its range will vary from case to case, but it will leave room for different private cultures within the nation. Thus, the food one chooses to eat, how one dresses, the music one listens to, are not normally part of the public culture that defines nationality (Miller, 1995, p. 26).

Miller admits that the boundary between public and private culture will often be controversial. His definition is obviously much broader than Rawls', and more communitarian than a Habermasian conception of the public sphere as a non-exclusive discursive space. What I find worrying about Miller's account is the potential conflation of empirical description with normative legitimation. By starting from shared understandings in society, Miller immunizes the content of a national culture against the critique that some of these traditions and beliefs may conflict with liberal and democratic norms. A public culture is not merely an inventory of widely shared beliefs and practices in a society, but it is also interpreted prescriptively as that part of a society's culture that immigrant must assimilate into. The CDU's notion of 'defining culture' takes a further step and makes this hidden normative assumption explicit.

If we define a public culture instead more narrowly as those elements of a society's culture that have been shaped and are sustained by its political institutions, then the contents and boundaries of a public culture become a field for political action. Such a political conception is relevant both for explaining how the imagined communities of nationhood have been forged and for envisaging how they should change in response to immigration.

This conception of public culture does not coincide with either the Habermasian public sphere or the Rawlsian interpretation. The former is too wide for my purpose while the latter is too narrow. Different from Rawls (and similar as Miller) I want to start from a descriptive notion of public culture that looks first at those areas where all democratic states try to assert control over cultural developments in society. In a second step we can then address the question what *ought* to be the content of this culture in a democratic and liberal society of immigration. On the one hand, such a two-step procedure will help to avoid the communitarian fallacy of regarding shared understandings as an ultimate validation of moral principles and political institutions. On the other hand, it will ensure that our normative considerations will remain much closer to real-world contexts. We will be less tempted to abstract from structural features of contemporary societies that should be included in a more extensive notion of what at Rawls has called the objective circumstances of justice (Rawls, 1971, pp. 126-7).[4] We are also less likely to overlook, as many liberal theorists do, those cultural activities of state institutions that do not establish formally neutral legal rules but promote a particular cultural identity within a society that is itself culturally heterogeneous. Our attention will thus be drawn to normatively problematic aspects of state-backed cultural hegemony that are ignored in Rawls' theory and are defended as legitimate in Miller's approach.

In order to distinguish a public culture from the Habermasian notion of public sphere, it is important to emphasize that state institutions are not the

---

[4] For Rawls, the circumstances of justice refer to the general human conditions that make cooperation both possible and necessary (Rawls, 1971, p. 126). Objective circumstances include features of human society such as a dependency of each individual on others and 'moderate scarcity of resources', so that there is neither abundance that makes cooperation superfluous nor extreme scarcity under which humans have to fight for survival against each other. My suggestion here is that we may have to include structural features of *modern* societies among the objective circumstances of justice when discussing what justice requires in the realm of public culture. State involvement in reproducing a public culture for the wider society is a general feature of modernity that ought to be accepted as a starting point before we can ask how norms of liberty and equality of citizens should determine liberal policies in this area. Normative theories that ignore the structural features of modernity lead to utopian models of a just society. This may be a worthwhile intellectual endeavour, but the conclusions of such approaches are generally irrelevant for assessing and changing institutions in contemporary states. For example, many libertarian theories of justice start with denying any legitimate role of the state in matters beyond collective security. This implies that liberal states should simply refrain from interfering in any way with the cultural affiliations and practices of their citizens (see for example Kukathas, 1998). However, in the absence of state-sponsored languages and education we would not have large scale modern societies in the first place and could not discuss in a meaningful way how immigrants and other minorities are affected by cultural policies.

sole force shaping the culture of a civil society. They compete in this respect with the institutions of economic markets and kinship systems. On the one hand, the contemporary market economy creates volatile and highly diversified patterns of life style and consumer culture. On the other hand, primary socialization in the family reproduces the more stable cultural milieus of class, regional, ethnic and religious communities.[5] While consumer culture is no longer confined within national border and becomes increasingly global, the intergenerational reproduction of distinct cultural communities and milieus makes all modern societies internally multicultural. In this context of heterogeneity the specific role of the modern state is to create a public culture that is roughly coextensive with the political community (Gellner, 1983). Such a public culture fulfils four fundamental tasks: it provides, first, a standardized idiom of communication; second, a repertoire of collective memories and identity; third, a set of explicit and implicit norms and values regulating political conflict and decisions; and, finally, a set of implicit norms and styles of behaviour that are broadly shared across different communities within society. In a shorthand way we can identify these four aspects as linguistic, historical, political and civil culture.

Miller and many other authors identify the phenomena I have just described as elements of *national* culture. I hesitate to use this term because it signals a degree of homogeneity and comprehensiveness that often cannot be achieved and in most cases is undesirable to aim for. First, a national culture in the singular is obviously inappropriate for multi*national* states that are composed of several autonomous political communities.[6] Yet it is also questionable in multi*ethnic* societies where heterogeneity resulting from immigration cannot be easily reconciled with a nationalist view of collective identity. Secondly, a national culture is generally regarded as providing an overarching identity that includes but also dominates other particular identities. It is, in Will Kymlicka's words, a societal culture 'which provides its members with meaningful ways of life across the full

---

[5] I regard civil society as an intermediary sphere of voluntary associations that emerges from a rough equilibrium in an institutional triangle formed by markets, state and kinship (Bauböck 1996).

[6] Miller is aware of this difficulty. He attempts to resolve it by postulating that multi-national states can be stable democracies only if they are 'nested nations' with an overarching national identity shared by majorities and minorities (Miller, 2000, pp.125-41). However, in multinational democracies such as Britain, Belgium, Canada or Spain it is only the historically dominant group that regards the overarching identity as their *national* identity, whereas minorities tend to see them as a more contingent political affiliation. Instead of sharing a common understanding of their nationality, these societies tend to be deeply divided over rival interpretations of that identity.

range of human activities, including social, educational, religious, recreational, and economic life, encompassing both public and private spheres. These cultures tend to be territorially concentrated, and based on a shared language' (Kymlicka, 1995, p. 67).[7] As I have already pointed out, I would rather regard the public culture of contemporary democracies as incomplete and constantly competing with other centrifugal forces in civil society that pull towards more global or more local cultural styles.

What is the significance of a public culture so defined for societies of immigration? The integration of immigrants depends crucially on four conditions: economic opportunities, legal equality, cultural toleration and recognition, and an inclusive and pluralistic public culture. Economic opportunities for immigrants must allow for upward social mobility within and between generations. Legal equality can be achieved through combining extensive rights for settled non-citizens with guaranteed access to formal citizenship through naturalization or at birth. Toleration and recognition refer to the distinct ethnic, linguistic and religious communities formed by immigrants; they ought to enjoy equal liberties to use their languages and practice their religion, some public recognition and some special exemptions from general rules.[8] In contrast with such legal accommodation of cultural minorities the fourth condition of integration refers to the public culture of the wider society. My conjecture is that even taken together the first three conditions are not sufficient for integration. The public culture must reflect the fact of immigration and transform itself in response to it.

My focus on this fourth requirement should, however, not in any way signal a lesser importance of the other three conditions. I have a particular reason for choosing this focus. I am a citizen of Austria where the first and second conditions of integration are seriously underdeveloped. There is still strong legal discrimination against non-EU migrants in this country (Davy, 2001; Waldrauch, 2001) and surveys show that their social mobility is significantly lower than, for example, in neighbouring Germany (Fassmann et al., 1999). I wrote the first draft of this paper in November 2000 while holding a guest professorship in Sweden. My impression from the literature is that, compared to other European countries, the Swedish record is rather good on the legal equality and cultural recognition dimensions, and probably not much worse than that of many other countries when it comes to economic opportunity. However, I have a suspicion, nourished only by anecdotal evidence, that this good record has not overcome a strong sense of exclusion among immigrant communities in this country. Like other

---

[7] For a critique of Kymlicka's concept of societal culture see Carens (2000, pp. 64-77).

[8] For a useful classification of cultural minority rights see Levy (2000, chapter 5).

small European nations Sweden seems to find it easier to tolerate the presence of immigrants as long as they remain culturally distinct foreigners. It is much more difficult to learn to regard unassimilated others as true Swedes, that is, as ordinary members of the globalizing society which Sweden has become. If this observation is correct, this may signal a deficiency in the public culture. One pragmatic reason why this should raise concern is that it creates a potential for nationalist populist parties and racist movements to stir up anti-immigrant sentiments in the population, a potential that has recently become manifest in neighbouring Denmark and Norway. The dilemma is that this potential cannot be substantially reduced through integration policies on any of the other three dimensions. On the contrary, opportunities, equal rights and cultural recognition for immigrants may be exploited rhetorically to fuel resentment among the native population against minority privileges. This can only be prevented through a changing perception of the collective 'We'. And the primary responsibility for transforming the public culture to make it more inclusive lies with a country's political institutions.

I will now turn to analysing the various elements of public culture. In this short chapter I will only be able to discuss the first two of the four items I have listed: language and history. I will discuss them separately, asking each time what might be the task of political institutions in democratic societies experiencing continuous and large-scale immigration. I have to leave it to the readers' imagination how the answers that I will suggest might apply to a transformation of the political and civil culture.

Language

First and most obviously, democratic community requires the capacity of all citizens to communicate. State bureaucracies need standardized languages for internal coordination and for the services they provide to the general public. Citizens need skills in these languages in order to effectively communicate with state institutions and in order to participate effectively in political debates. These arguments can be added to Ernest Gellner's (1983) well-known theory that linguistic homogenization within a state territory is required by the industrial division of labour, a theory which may be somewhat less relevant for a postindustrial economy. These political and economic reasons lead to a simple conclusion: While the modern liberal state is by and large neutral in religious matters, it is structurally incapable of being similarly neutral with regard to linguistic difference. This fact of linguistic establishment must be taken into account in normative considerations about language policy in multicultural societies.

On the one hand, a state-backed dominance of specific languages within a national territory is not necessarily oppressive in the same way that state support for certain religious doctrines would be. People who speak a common language remain free to state any moral conviction they have and to disagree profoundly in their views. In fact, they can only disagree profoundly if they can communicate their disagreements in a common language. Because a certain amount of linguistic homogeneity within society is a functional precondition for democracy, state institutions have not merely a negative duty to allow the free use of minority languages in civil society, but also a positive duty to enable all citizens to participate in a common public culture, for example by establishing public schools where these languages can be learned.

On the other hand, this argument does not require the establishment of a single national language. In liberal states official multilingualism can be sustained in two ways that are normally combined: as regional monolingualism and as statewide multilingualism. In multilingual federations like Belgium, Switzerland or Canada provincial governments have established their own languages that dominate the regional public culture. In order to integrate such monolingual provinces into a democratic federation, the federal institutions must to a certain extent be multilingual so that they can communicate with citizens in several officially recognized languages. Federal integration will also be promoted through multilingual education that encourages citizens to learn at least one language spoken in other parts of the federation. This shows another relevant difference between language and religion. In contrast with monotheistic religions, language communities are not mutually exclusive. Learning second and third languages requires efforts, but besides its positive impact on political integration it also yields benefits for individuals by offering them additional opportunities and enhancing their mobility.

Such policies of official multilingualism are not about minority rights. They are ways of shaping a common multilingual public culture that reflects the composite character of a federal polity. I do not think that similar policies would be required or even appropriate in response to the fact of immigration. Territorial linguistic establishment is connected to claims of political autonomy and self-government. Immigrant communities normally do not raise demands for this type of recognition and they would be ill advised to do so. These communities are generally concentrated in major cities, but dispersed throughout the country so that they do not form a regional majority within a stretch of territory where they could become autonomous. And even where sufficient numbers concentrate in a sufficiently large territory, it is not self-evident that this would back claims to autonomy and linguistic establishment. Immigration would turn into invasion if outsiders, after being admitted, could simply claim for themselves any part of the territory where they form a numerical majority. Multinationalism and immigration give rise to different recognition claims (Kymlicka, 1995, chapter 2; 1998, chapter 2). Confusing them plays into the hands of political forces that are interested in portraying immigration as invasion.

How should societies of immigration then respond to linguistic diversity resulting from recent immigration? I suggest that public policy ought to be guided by a mix of four principles: linguistic liberty, assimilation, accommodation and recognition.

Liberty Liberal democracies must guarantee not only the right of immigrants to use their own languages in the private contexts of family, neighbourhood or ethnic association, but also in the public sphere of civil society where other people will be exposed to these immigrant languages. A liberal state has no business regulating the language of shop signs, advertising, private print or audiovisual media. Private schools may be regulated in various ways because government has a duty to guarantee the right of every child to school education, but there should be no discrimination if immigrants want to set up a private school where their languages will be the medium of instruction. Even if the state does not actively intervene to promote minority languages, the free exercise of linguistic liberties will profoundly transform the public face of civil society. Regions with high concentrations of immigrants such as South California or urban districts like Berlin-Kreuzberg have become visibly and audibly multilingual through processes that involve hardly any state-sponsored multiculturalism.

Assimilation The second task is to promote the acquisition of dominant languages, not only through public education for the children of immigrants, but also for newcomers. I have provocatively called this a principle of assimilation because it in fact endorses a public policy that speeds up a process of language shift that normally occurs between the second and third generation. The main justification for this is that immigrants need skills in the dominant language for their economic as well as their political integration. Providing these skills is a genuinely public task because in most cases the need to earn a living prevents labour migrants from investing time and money into language acquisition.

Linguistic assimilation programmes are still compatible with linguistic liberty as long as immigrants remain free to retain and promote their original languages. Assigning responsibility for language programmes to public institutions is also important to prevent a policy that blames the immigrants for their failure to integrate. A number of European states today require language skills as a key condition for naturalization without supporting or creating easily accessible language courses.

In 1998 the Netherlands have introduced a programme of mandatory Dutch language courses for new arrivals. At the time of writing, in April 2002, draft legislation is pending in Germany and Austria that would extend similar requirements to immigrants already in the country for five years or less. In the Austrian legislation this retroactive 'integration contract' is meant to be enforced with an ultimate sanction of deportation, but there is no corresponding duty of the government to provide accessible and fully financed language courses for those immigrants who are obliged to take them. Linguistic assimilation policies are, however, legitimate only when they assume a convergence of public interests and private interests of the immigrants themselves. Mandatory language courses for adults must then be justifiable as a form of benign paternalism, for example as securing immigrants' long-term interests in upwards social mobility by enabling them to set aside their short-term interests in earning income in low-skilled jobs. The Austrian programme illustrates a form of coercive assimilation that cannot be justified in these terms. Instead of convergent interests there is an underlying assumption of conflicting public and private interests. This is articulated in the ruling Freedom Party's campaigns against *Überfremdung* (swamping by aliens), which call for the assimilation of immigrants because their languages pose a danger to the public culture of the receiving society.

Accommodation Although in the long run communicative capacities among all members of a society of immigration can be most efficiently achieved through assimilation into one or a few official languages, in the short run accommodation of linguistic difference is often more appropriate. Learning a new language takes a long time and full fluency is usually only achieved by a next generation already born in the country. Therefore communication between immigrants and private and public institutions of the receiving society can be severely hampered if services are provided exclusively in the established languages. This is particularly important in institutional environments that are experienced as stressful, such as hospitals, police interrogations or courtrooms. In such institutions, immigrants may have a moral right to not only to use their native languages but also to be understood when they speak them (Patten, 2001). More generally, public policy in countries of immigration should accommodate immigrant languages by providing a broad range of translation and interpreter services, bilingual forms and ballots, information sheets and public broadcasting in immigrant languages.

Recognition The second and third tasks, as I have described them, focus only on the communicative value of languages. However, languages also have what we can call identity value. The first language we learn as small children is very different from second and third languages we acquire later on as foreign idioms. It is significant for who we are as persons and – according to some linguistic theories – it may even shape our perception of the world. 'Mother tongues' are also markers of collective identity not just for groups that claim territorial autonomy, but also for ethnic minorities who live dispersed among a majority population.

This identity value of immigrant languages justifies some recognition rights, for example offering optional courses in immigrant languages in public schools for children of the second or third generation.[9] Such programmes are generally not needed for bridging communication gaps in the wider society, but they enable children to communicate better with their parents and grandparents, to maintain links with relatives in the country of origin and to insert themselves into the ethnic communities in the surrounding society. From the perspective of public policy this is a way of recognizing immigrants as linguistic minorities. The essential difference with linguistic establishment is that the programme is designed to serve the needs of the minority and does not oblige the linguistic majority to participate. Children from the native majority should be free to attend immigrant language courses and there ought to be some intercultural teaching in the mandatory curriculum where they learn basic facts about the primary languages of their classmates of immigrant origins. However, in contrast with national minorities such as the Catalans or Quebecois, immigrants have no claim to establish their languages as the general medium of instruction in public schools. And the principle of linguistic freedom demands that even for the minority participation in mother-tongue education should be optional rather than mandatory.

All the public policies I have listed are rather common in democratic societies of immigration. On the one hand, changing the public culture so that linguistic difference is taken into account does not require radical steps that would lead to splitting society into a myriad of autonomous groups. On

---

[9] Programmes in immigrant languages in public radio or TV combine a communicative and an identity value.

the other hand, taking the four principles I have suggested seriously will have the effect of transforming monolingual public cultures into more and more multilingual ones. Even the countervailing principle of assimilation will not prevent this change as long as new immigrants keep arriving and reinvigorate minority language communities.

History

History is the second element of public culture that I want to consider. This will probably raise suspicions among readers who are historians. In the 19th century history became important not only as an academic discipline but also as the handmaiden of nationalism. National historiography is not necessarily ideological in the sense of distorting the facts. Writing history from the perspective of a nation in its present composition and territorial boundaries already excludes many other possible historical narratives about the same events and reinforces the false belief that nations are subjects of history rather than its contingent products. Today serious historians are reluctant to write national histories. Much contemporary historiography is global, regional or local in scope rather than national. It should still be possible to write the history of states, the evolution of their system of government, the expansion or shrinking of their territory without portraying it at the same time as the history of a nation, in the sense of a people sharing an ancient origin, a common culture and a strong sense of identity.

Democracy needs, however, also a sense of historical continuity that refers to the political community rather than merely to the territory or the institutions of government. A democratic polity is always an intergenerational community (Bauböck, 1998). Membership is acquired at birth either through descent from citizen parents or through being born within the territory. A polity is thus not a voluntary association of persons who have chosen to belong to this state rather than to another one. It is also not a spatial aggregation of individuals who merely happen to reside in the same territory at the same time. Democratic decision-making needs a stable framework that is meant to last over generations. This framework includes stable territorial borders and a stable constitution. Democracy can only survive if minorities whose interests are overruled in a present decision have fair opportunities to revise these decisions and win the next time. This reason for democratic loyalty would be subverted if each new generation or maybe even each new election changed the borders and the basic rules for lawmaking. Minorities would defect by seceding and majorities would manipulate the constitution to turn temporary minorities into permanent ones. If citizens of a democracy do not imagine that they share a common future submitting to political authority would become irrational or based on naked coercion. It is, however, impossible to imagine a common future without also imagining a shared past.

To test this hypothesis we may consider three different situations. Think first of a democratic regime that has been stable and whose basic institutions have enjoyed broad popular support over several generations. This very fact generates a sense of inherited achievements that will always need to be improved or adapted to new circumstances but should not be completely undone. Second, imagine a democratic regime that has been born out of a revolution or the military defeat of an authoritarian *ancien régime*. This foundational event creates a shared history. It will be constantly referred to when exploring the options for the future. The writings and speeches of 'founding fathers' (or mothers) will figure prominently in the collective historical memory. Where the previous regime was particularly atrocious 'never again' will become a national motto. This slogan is not only a call for preventing a return of the old regime, but even more an urge to remember its evils and a pedagogic device for teaching the basic values of the democratic constitution to new generations. Third, consider the most unlikely case: a foundation *ex nihilo*, a settler regime established in an uninhabited territory or, closer to historical reality, a settler regime that has decimated and pushed into the hinterlands the aboriginal population. Even in this context, a democratic regime will generate historical narratives that tell the stories and invoke the heritage of Pilgrim Fathers in New England or British convicts being deported to Australia. And, one should add, if it is a really democratic regime, it will not only remember the oppression from which the first settlers fled, but also the oppression they exercised over the indigenous peoples whose lands they occupied and cultivated.

Finally, I want to suggest that the imagination of a shared history is not merely an element of a background culture in civil society, but also of the public culture, as I have tried to define it. Historical memories will have a special place in the families who trace back their origins to revolutionary heroes, writers of the constitution or victims of the previous regime. Certain associations in civil society and political parties will defend a particular interpretation of the nation's history. But such private narratives and associational activities are not sufficient to create a collectively shared memory. Only state institutions can ensure that a historical narrative becomes hegemonic in society. They do so through references to an official history in national symbols, such as flags, anthems or national holidays, in political speeches and in school curricula. Hegemony does not mean that everybody shares a deep conviction about, or emotional affiliation to, these historical narratives. Citizens need not take them all that seriously as long as they take them for granted.

My claim that democratic regimes have to imagine a shared history raises a formidable challenge for societies of immigration. It seems to exclude immigrants from the public culture almost by definition. How could newcomers, who arrive with a memory of the history of their own countries of origin, see themselves, and be seen by native citizens, to share the past of the receiving country? Different from settlers and colonists they do not initiate a new history in the places where they enter. And the more diverse the origins of immigration are, the less likely is it that their historical baggage will somehow become part of the mainstream public culture. This seems to leave them no other options than either permanent segregation within the polity or full assimilation. And, in contrast with the possibility of multilingualism, assimilation of immigrants into a national history seems to imply also dissimilation from their origins.

If they or the receiving society choose the option of segregation, immigrants and their descendants will remain foreigners even after becoming citizens. They will cultivate their own historical memories and tell their children stories about what happened back home a long time ago. And the native population will continue to regard them as people from a different country even when they have been born in the same hospitals as their own children. Divided histories will divide the citizens of native and migrant origin. This is just as bad for democratic integration as when the native population itself is divided by the memories of irreconciled factions of a past civil war.

If the second option is chosen, immigrants will have to forget where they came from. In the US Hispanic children will learn in school that their ancestors sailed across the Atlantic on a boat called Mayflower, in France Algerian children will learn that their forefathers stormed the Bastille, in Germany Turkish children will learn to be ashamed of the Holocaust rather than of the genocide of Armenians. Although an assimilationist conception of public culture need not deny the fact of immigration as such, it denies that the historical content of the public culture is affected by this fact. This kind of integration through assimilation may have worked in some countries for some time. However, it is unlikely to work under conditions of full liberties of speech and association, which allow immigrants to make their own voices heard. And it is also undesirable because excluding the memories of immigrants distorts history and impoverishes the public culture. In the US the big immigration from around 1900 was rather successfully assimilated during the period between the 1920s and the

1950s. But we should not forget that there were two preconditions that today cannot or should not be brought about: an immigration stop in the aftermath of World War I and an aggressive Americanization policy that in fact denied immigrants basic cultural freedom.

So how can a society of immigration escape this unpalatable choice? I think that there is a third option. First, the rules of membership themselves must be changed in response to immigration (Bauböck, 1994). In countries of immigration, acquisition of citizenship at birth must not be exclusively based on descent, or else several generations of immigrant descent may remain formally excluded from the polity. Alongside introducing some form of *ius soli* the second significant element of reform is to turn naturalization from a discretionary decision of authorities into an entitlement of applicants without demanding that they have to renounce their previous citizenship. This change of rules does not undermine the intergenerational continuity of the polity. It would not promote an image of the polity as a voluntary association because the children of immigrants would acquire citizenship automatically at birth. And as long as first generation immigrants would still have to apply for naturalization rather than being automatically turned into citizen without their consent, the polity would still remain a community membership in which implies certain commitments and is therefore distinct from a mere aggregation of residents.[10] The important effect of such a reform of citizenship law is that the mechanisms that ensure historical continuity of the population base of a democratic community no longer define immigrants as outsiders. By giving them a right of access to citizenship, they are already included in the imagined community even before they choose to join it formally.

Reforming citizenship in this way will have important long-term effects on popular conceptions of collective identity. Maybe a generation from now, there will be a lot of research on how the German citizenship reform of 1999 has transformed ethnic conceptions of nationhood. However, this is merely a precondition for a change of historical consciousness and, given the largely formal character of citizenship in many western democracies, the desired effects cannot be taken for granted. The historical dimension of public culture should also be reshaped directly and in the short run.

---

[10] Rubio-Marín (2000) has suggested that in order to guarantee the inclusiveness of citizenship in societies of immigration immigrants could be naturalized automatically as long as they are permitted to retain their previous nationality. I think that this proposal underestimates the symbolic significance of citizenship, which is expressed in the need for individual consent of adults in the acquisition or loss of this status and in the commitments that immigrants are deemed to make when they apply for naturalization.

The alternative to segregation and assimilation would then consist in the task of weaving the histories of immigrant communities into the larger tapestry of a shared public history in such a way that they remain visible as strands of different colour. How can this be achieved without multiplying the colours to the point where they merely yield an overall impression of a bland grey and without selecting some colours arbitrarily, which would mean that excluded groups cannot recognize the tapestry as also telling their own stories?

Identity politics may be opposed by arguing that a proliferation of recognition claims will diminish the value of recognition towards zero. This is an objection not to be lightly dismissed. Its basic steps are the following ones:

1. Once a state gives special recognition to a particular group it creates an incentive for other groups to discover their particular oppression and collective identity and to construct their claims in the language of victimhood.
2. Because of the basic democratic commitment to equal respect and concern for all citizens all such claims must be treated equally, so if one group is recognized, all must get similar recognition. After recognizing national minorities one must recognize immigrant ethnic groups, then persons of mixed origins and dissenters may also claim to be victimized groups because they do not fit into recognized group patterns and, finally, the native majority will complain that they are the victims of reverse discrimination. This process of proliferation is greatly accelerated by the fact that recognition groups are not mutually exclusive because they intersect. Gender, class, sexual orientation, age, physical or mental handicap, etc. can all serve as grounds for recognition claims.
3. Special recognition is a 'socially scarce' or 'positional good' (Hirsch, 1977). Once everybody gets it, it is no longer special and thereby loses its value. So after giving special recognition to all who might claim it, we end up in a situation where all are again equal and nobody is specially recognized. The detour we have taken may, however, be quite costly in terms of social cohesion.

At an abstract level this argument is hard to beat. But it loses much of its bite once we start to look at claims for the public recognition of histories in a historical perspective. It will then turn out that recognition claims are different in kind and migrants generally do not aspire to the same kind as indigenous minorities. Including immigrant groups in the public history of the receiving society need not also involve compiling the official histories of all countries of origin. A public history is a narrative about how a *particular* society has changed over time. Writing the history of immigration is the key to incorporating the history of immigrant groups. How then could such a history be sufficiently selective but still representative?

My first suggestion is that new light could be thrown on historical encounters between sending and receiving countries. Let me mention and once again illustrate this with an example from Austria. Serbs and Turks, the two largest national origin groups of immigrants, arrived in the late 1960s as guestworkers. Yet they also figure prominently in quite different roles in the Austrian collective memory. Serbia was the historical enemy of the late Habsburg monarchy and the killing of the designated successor to the Austro-Hungarian throne by a Serb nationalist in Sarajevo served as the pretext for Emperor Franz Josef to start the First World War. When I went to school, the Turkish siege of Vienna in 1683 was reported as a major turning point in European history and a defining moment for Austria's national identity. Although it was Jan Sobieski, a Polish king, who saved us from Kara Mustafa's troops, it was in our territory that the survival of Christian-occidental culture was decided.

Today in public discourses the historical connection between our past and current immigration is mainly exploited by right wing populist rhetoric. However, the enemies of past wars do share a common history that can be reinterpreted as a reason for unity in the present. The best example is the original plan of the founders of the European Economic Communities to create an economic as well as a political union that would weld together nations that had been at war with each other for so many centuries. There is no need for historical revisionism to achieve this end. All that it is required is an ethical interpretation of historical enmity as constituting itself a reason for reconciliation and future cooperation. The presence of an immigrant population whose historical narratives tell the other side of the story should be an incentive to explore how the shared history could be written in such a way that it creates prospects for a shared future.

My second point is that migration often flows in riverbeds carved out by already established historical links. It is simply not true that most migrants are rational economic opportunity seekers that choose their destination by calculating wage differentials, unemployment rates or currency exchange rates. Or, to put it more precisely, only short-term migrants calculate in this way. Long-term immigrants are rational enough to include in their calculations costs of settlement, benefits of cultural skills that may help them in particular places but may be worthless in others, and foreign policy relations that will make it more difficult for the receiving country to deport them back home. This is one reason why migrants from former colonies so often choose the former colonial power as a destination. In contrast with a past connection through war, colonial ties are causally relevant for creating postcolonial migration flows. There are many other ways how states are involved in creating the particular type of migration that they receive. Recruiting guestworkers is only the most obvious one. As Saskia Sassen (1988) has pointed out, direct capital investment may also lead to migration flows in the opposite direction. All these well-known findings of migration research are so many arguments for regarding immigration as a legacy of the receiving society's own past, or as a result of its attempts to shape its own future, rather than as a historical accident to which it was involuntarily exposed.

Thirdly, even where no historical connections of the first or second type can be uncovered, large-scale immigration itself opens a new page in history. An exchange of populations is the most important mechanism for connecting previously unconnected histories. This has probably been true ever since the early days of humanity. Once migrants settle and start to intermarry with the local population, their own biographies and memories create new angles for interpreting and linking the histories of the countries from which they have come and of those where they take up residence. This dynamic is very strong in modern mobile market economies and liberal democracies that defend the freedom of marital as well as cultural choices. In such a context the segregationist or assimilationist options do not emerge naturally but have to be imposed. Such political imposition does not require racial segregation laws or the suppression of minority languages. It is quite enough to create a national public culture in which these two options seem the only feasible ones.

I would like to add a caveat to this point. Nothing I have said about the need to integrate the histories of immigrants into a public culture is meant to deny the liberty and opportunity for migrants to build a minority identity that focuses specifically on their origins and to retain thus a sense of their own history as a separate one. Not all migrants are involved in homeland politics or conceive of themselves as members of diaspora communities, but quite a number of them do (Cohen, 1997). The reasons for such orientation towards national projects outside the society of residence are many and most of them should be fully respected. They include, for example, the histories of political refugees who have suffered persecution and whose main goal is to overthrow a repressive regime in their home country; of stateless nations like Kurds or Palestinians for whom mobilizing their diaspora is a way to stake their claims in the international arena; of religious communities whose doctrines refer to a holy land and for whom living in a country where their religion is in the minority implies special burdens and duties. What I have said about language is also true for history: the need for constructing a shared public culture is not incompatible with the freedom for immigrants to organize themselves as distinct minorities.

Conclusions

I have initially stated the main idea of this paper as that of a self-transformative public culture. Let me conclude by explaining how the various suggestions I have made could be summarized under such a heading. Consider first, my proposals for reforming citizenship laws. They entail that the polity is constantly transformed in its population base in such a way that neither territory nor descent finally determine who belongs to it. State authorities, who represent the present citizens, also no longer exercise control over new admissions through discretionary naturalization. The political community opens up its membership for those who live permanently in the territory while retaining the connection with those who have emigrated. Yet it still asserts the consensual character of belonging by leaving it to the individuals concerned to apply for admission or to sever the ties through expatriation. Self-transformation therefore does not mean abandoning the allocation of membership to the contingent forces that determine migration flows. The self-transformative character of the rules of membership that I have endorsed goes together with a self-assertion as a democratic community that embraces the dual principles of inclusion and consent.

Similar considerations apply to the linguistic and historical dimensions of public culture. Public history becomes self-transformative if it is no longer written as that of a particular nation. National identity is constructed by excluding or assimilating groups whose collective memories relate them to other places and polities. The alternative perspective is that ongoing immigration uncovers, or newly establishes, historical links that require a constant rewriting of the past.

In contrast with integrating the history of immigrants into shared public narratives, linguistic accommodation appears to be additive rather than transformative. Certainly, immigration changes also the vocabulary of the dominant languages. *Döner* has become a German word and *tandoori* chicken and *balti* meat are national dishes in England. However, it would be naïve to regard the adoption of ethnic food or music by the native population as a sign of cultural openness. The true test is still the strength of public support for the use of immigrant languages in institutions like schools, hospitals or courts. Linguistic public culture is then not self-transformative in the sense of constantly remixing native and imported languages. Neither is it a mission of public policy to protect immigrant languages against extinction. The task is rather to facilitate communication in a multilingual polity while respecting chosen linguistic identities.

Ongoing large-scale immigration will inevitably transform the receiving society's public culture in the wider sense of the background culture of civil society. The task of initiating a deliberate self-transformation through political reform in the areas that I have outlined is a more daunting one. One of the major problems in liberal democracy is the tension between its two defining elements. Political liberalism defends the rights of individuals and minorities against the danger of majority tyranny, but democratic institutions and decisions can only be sustained if they enjoy broad popular support. Constitutionalism and the rule of law have thus been described as self-imposed constraints on democracy through which majorities tie their own hands for the sake of equal liberties of all. Because democratic majorities consist of changing groups of individuals who benefit from these liberties it is rational for them to endorse such constraints. The specific problem of securing rights for cultural minorities is that majorities have no self-interested reason in tying their hands in this way because they know that they will never themselves be in the position of the minority. For this reason, describing the rights of immigrants as a constraint on the interests of democratic majorities may be correct for the purposes of moral theory but offers little guidance for how to win majority support for this task.

The idea that the changing public culture of a society of immigration is the result of self-transformation offers a more attractive interpretation. It rejects the construction of native majorities and immigrant minorities as permanently separate groups and promotes instead the image of a heterogeneous public (Young, 1990) with a shared interest in representing as well as in integrating its diverse groups.

References

Bauböck, R. (1994), *Transnational Migration. Membership and Rights in International Migration*, Edward Elgar, Aldershot.

Bauböck, R. (1996), 'Social and Cultural Integration in Civil Society', in R. Bauböck, A. Heller, A. Zolberg (eds.) *The Challenge of Diversity. Integration and Pluralism in Societies of Immigration*, Avebury, Aldershot, 1996, pp. 67-132.

Bauböck, R. (1998), 'Sharing history and future? Time horizons of democratic membership in an age of migration', *Constellations*, Vol. 4, No. 3, January 1998, pp. 320-45.

Carens, Joseph, H. (2000), *Culture, Citizenship, and Community. A Contextual Exploration of Justice as Evenhandedness*, Oxford University Press, Oxford.

CDU (2000), Arbeitsgrundlage für die Zuwanderungs-Kommission der CDU Deutschlands, retrieved on 15 April, 2002, from www.cdu.de/ueberuns/buvo/pmueller/arbeitsgrundlage.htm

Cohen, R. (1997), *Global Diasporas: An Introduction*, University of Washington Press, Washington.

Davy, U. (2001), *Die Integration von Einwanderern. Vol. 1: Rechtliche Regelungen im europäischen Vergleich*. Campus, Frankfurt am Main.

Fassmann, H., Münz, R. and Seifert, W. (1999), 'Ausländische Arbeitskräfte in Deutschland und Österreich: Zuwanderung, berufliche Plazierung und Effekte der Aufenthaltsdauer', in H. Fassmann, H. Matuschek, E. Menasse (eds.) *Abgrenzen - Ausgrenzen - Aufnehmen. Empirische Befunde zu Fremdenfeindlichkeit und Integration*, Drava, Klagenfurt, pp. 95-114.

Gellner, E.t (1983), *Nations and Nationalism*, Blackwell, Oxford.

Habermas, J. (1962), *Strukturwandel der Öffentlichkeit : Untersuchungen zu einer Kategorie der bürgerlichen Gesellschaft*, Luchterhand, Neuwied, Berlin.

Hirsch, F. (1976), *Social Limits to Growth*, Harvard University Press, Cambridge, Massachusetts.

Klusmeyer, D. (2001) 'A "guiding culture" for immigrants? Integration and diversity in German', *Journal of Ethnic and Migration Studies*, Vol. 27, No. 3, pp. 519-32.

Kukathas, C. (1998), 'Liberalism and Multiculturalism – The Politics of Indifference', *Political Theory*, Vol. 26, No. 5, pp. 686-99.

Kymlicka, W. (1995), *Multicultural Citizenship. A Liberal Theory of Minority Rights*, Oxford University Press, Oxford.

Kymlicka, W. (1998), *Finding Our Way. Rethinking Ethnocultural Relations in Canada*, Oxford University Press, Toronto.

Levy, J. (2000), *The Multiculturalism of Fear*, Oxford University Press, Oxford.

Miller, D. (2000), *Citizenship and National Identity*, Polity Press, Cambridge.

Miller, D. (1995), *On Nationality*, Oxford University Press, Oxford.

Patten, A. (2001), 'Political Theory and Language Policy', *Political Theory*, Vol. 29, No. 5, pp. 691-715.

Rawls, J. (1971), *A Theory of Justice*, Harvard University Press, Cambridge, Massachusetts.

Rawls, J. (1993), *Political Liberalism*, Columbia University Press, New York.

Rubio-Marín, R. (2000), *Immigration as a Democratic Challenge. Citizenship and Inclusion in Germany and the United States*. Cambridge, Cambridge University Press.

Sassen, S. (1988),. *The mobility of labor and capital. A study in international investment and labor flow*, Cambridge University Press, Cambridge.

Waldrauch, H. (2001), *Die Integration von Einwanderern. Vol. 2: Ein Index rechtlicher Diskriminierung*. Campus, Frankfurt am Main.

Young, I. M. (1990), *Justice and the Politics of Group Difference*. Princeton University Press, Princeton, New Jersey.

Chapter 4

Spheres of Integration: Towards a Differentiated and Reflexive Ethnic Minority Policy

Godfried Engbersen

1 Introduction

Two years ago, in the early part of 2000 Dutch journalist Paul Scheffer published a much talked-about essay entitled 'The Multicultural Drama' in *NRC-Handelsblad*, a Dutch quality paper. In this essay Scheffer advanced the thesis that the integration of immigrants and ethnic minorities in the Netherlands is a human drama. He pointed to the high unemployment figures among established and new immigrants, the emergence of black schools with high dropout rates, and the concentration of poverty in strongly segregated districts in the large cities. In his opinion the poor integration of ethnic minorities is the result of a detached and permissive Dutch policy in respect of minorities that does not confront ethnic minorities sufficiently with the Dutch language, culture and history.

Before discussing this line of reasoning, I would like to draw attention to the new imagery that is being used. Whereas Dutch policy in respect of minorities used to be characterized by water metaphors ('the ferry can't take any more passengers', 'streams of migrants', 'stemming the tide of migrants', 'building dikes to preserve Dutch culture against a tide of foreign influences'), the metaphor of *drama* is now becoming popular (cf. also Engbersen and Engbersen 1991). Scheffer's analysis seems to relate to two branches of drama. First of all, *tragedy*, in which the unavoidable destiny of underprivileged immigrants is the central theme. The other branch of drama that plays a role in his analysis is that of *absurdist drama*. Dutch institutions (read: educational, social security, and asylum institutions) would treat migrants in an indifferent and quasi-tolerant way. Furthermore, many of the migrants would have lost their mooring, as old cultural anchors are not replaced by new Dutch ones. The result would be an anonymous and indifferent multicultural society in which marginal immigrants do not observe rules and regulations any longer, and which prefers negotiation to punishment.

Scheffer's article led to a heated debate. For months the correspondence page of *NRC-Handelsblad* featured contributions from Dutch intellectuals and citizens who either agreed or disagreed with Scheffer. Scheffer had certainly hit a nerve, particularly because he placed a strong emphasis on the importance of Dutch culture and language. Two years later the Dutch were confronted with the late populist politician Pim Fortuyn, who came to prominence when his party made a strong showing in the local elections of Rotterdam. Fortuyn, who was brutally murdered on the eve of the national elections, called for the Netherlands' borders to be closed ('This is a full country', he said. 'I think 16 million Dutchmen are about enough') and pleaded for the assimilation of ethnic minorities. According to Fortuyn, Islam was a 'backward religion'.

On empirical grounds, much can be said against Scheffer's pessimistic analysis and Fortuyn's statements. A growing proportion of the new generation of minorities have found their way in the Dutch educational system and a growing number of minorities have built up an existence in self-employment. In the last decade we have also witnessed a strongly decreasing unemployment rate among ethnic minorities (SCP, 2001a and 2001b). In this contribution, however, I would like to limit myself to the assumption that thorough acquaintance with the Dutch language and culture is the most important prerequisite for integration. In this respect the left-wing intellectual Scheffer and the populist Fortuyn are not as original as some might be inclined to think. After all, since the mid-nineties of the previous century, the Dutch government has been focussing its policy more and more at the so-called '*inburgering*' of vulnerable groups of ethnic minorities through compulsory instruction in the Dutch language and culture (WRR, 2001).[1]

In this chapter, I would like to discuss the Dutch minorities and integration policy, and the various ways in which the notion of 'integration' has been interpreted. I will then formulate a critique and present an alternative integration model containing various dimensions and spheres of integration. First of all, however, I would like to discuss the controversial notion of 'integration'.

---

[1] Note by the editors: '*Inburgering*' stands for the process by which immigrants become adopted to and established in the country of immigration.

2 Dimensions of Integration

The Dutch literature on social integration often features dichotomies. The intellectual origin of these dichotomies can be traced back to the study by Gordon (1964) on processes of assimilation in American society. For example, some authors distinguish between *structural integration* and *socio-cultural integration*. The former is described as 'full participation in social institutions' and the latter as 'the social contacts that members and organizations of minorities maintain with society as a whole, and the cultural adaptations to that society' (Vermeulen and Penninx, 1994: 3, cf. also Dagevos, 2001). On the other hand, Veenman (1995) distinguishes between two aspects of integration. Firstly, *formal participation* in sectors such as education and the labour market and *informal participation* with ethnic minorities in the sphere of leisure activities. Secondly, *the attitudes* of ethnic minorities towards the significance of participation in the receiving society. Veenman adds that 'informal participation' together with 'orientation towards the receiving society' are indicators of the 'ethnic-cultural integration' of ethnic minorities, while 'formal participation' is an indicator of 'socio-economic integration'.[2]

The question that crops up in all elaborations of these classifications is to what extent clinging to the ethnic cultural repertoire is detrimental to achieving an established social position. This question is particularly related to the integration of guest workers and their offspring and more recently to the integration of asylees and refugees. Conversely, the question is to what extent 'structural integration' leads to erosion of the ethnic cultural identity. At present no convincing empirical answers have been found to these two questions. There does seem to be a growing consensus – of which Scheffer is a leading exponent – that migrants who have not been socialized in the Dutch language and culture have difficulties achieving a fulfilling social position (cf. Dagevos, 2001).

Dichotomization of the integration process is an improvement on those integration theories that unilaterally put the emphasis on integration through the labour market or the cultural adaptations of ethnic minorities. The distinction between structural and cultural integration, however, is not accurate enough. Following Bernard Peters (1993, pp. 96-143), I will therefore distinguish between three inextricably linked dimensions of social integration: the functional dimension, the moral dimension, and the

---

[2] There are others who distinguish between *social emancipation* (achieving an established social, economic and political position) and *cultural affirmation* (clinging to the cultural practices of the country of origin). This distinction corresponds to some extent with the distinction between the public and private spheres (Van Doorn, 1989).

expressive dimension. The functional dimension involves, in my operationalization, the extent to which citizens are able to participate in the major institutions of a society (especially through work and education). The moral dimension involves the extent to which citizens are able to participate fully and equally in society without any risk to their physical and personal integrity (citizenship dimension). It also involves the extent to which citizens conform and are able to adapt themselves to current social and legal standards. Finally, the expressive dimension involves the extent to which citizens are able to develop their individual and shared identities. If an individual or group is not recognized, the result may be an identity crisis or alienation. Table 4.1 below sums up the three dimensions of social integration and their possible negative expressions (cf. Peters, 1993, p. 105).

Table 4.1 Dimensions of integration

Dimension	Functional	Moral	Expressive
Problem	Social position (labour, education)	Social norms	Cultural expressions
Policy objective	Equality and Equity	Rule of law Citizenship Social cohesion	Development of individual and shared identities
Negative	Social and spatial exclusion	Anomie Disintegration	Alienation Identity crisis

Source: Peters, 1993, Engbersen and Gabriëls, 1995.

With some juggling, the aforementioned dichotomies of integration can also be integrated into this 'three-dimensional' table. The structural dimension corresponds largely with the functional and moral dimensions. The cultural dimension encompasses particularly the expressive dimension. Nonetheless, Peters' integration triad offers a more sophisticated conceptual framework, particularly because it offers the possibility to understand the various 'in built tensions' that are inherent to a multicultural society.

3 Spheres of Integration

Apart from the various dimensions of integration it is important to distinguish several 'spheres of integration'. I agree with Michael Walzer that modern society is characterized by various social spheres with different distribution criterion. However, I prefer to point to 'spheres of integration' rather than 'spheres of justice'. This may seem trivial, but it is not. Anyone who analyses the Dutch policy on minorities of the past forty years will notice that in each differentiated phase different aspects were emphasized. In the first phase of the Dutch policy regarding minorities (1960s and 1970s) the emphasis was on *self-organization, social work* and, partly, *education* (remember the debate on education in the minorities' own language and relating to their culture). In addition, special provisions for minorities were realized. The policy on minorities aimed at 'mutual adaptation in a multicultural society with equal opportunities for Dutch people and ethnic minorities' (WRR, 1979). The central idea of 'integration while preserving ethnic identity' was soon criticized because it would strengthen the isolated position of minorities.

Next (1980s and 1990s), the emphasis was on reducing social disadvantages, especially through improving *labour market participation*. Integration is interpreted as 'equal participation in the major social institutions and sectors' (WRR, 1989). A minorities policy with special provisions was no longer desirable. Selective provisions for ethnic minorities were only justifiable when they contribute to the reduction of socio-economic disadvantages and, more particularly, of unemployment and dependency on benefits.

The mid-nineties brought another change in tone and idiom (third phase). The no-nonsense idiom of the eighties was replaced by an idiom of *citizenship*. Politicians no longer spoke of a 'minorities policy' but used the universal term 'integration policy'. The main goal is now on active citizenship with a strong emphasis on the social obligations of citizens. What is new is that more attention is paid to the moral dimension of integration. On the one hand, the problem of the minorities is related to issues such as crime and peaceful co-existence of citizens in multicultural areas. On the other hand, the Dutch government adopted an integration policy that makes it obligatory for vulnerable groups (particularly those of benefit-dependent people) to take courses in the Dutch language and culture.

The policy shifts from social work, self-organization to labour market participation and to the social obligations of citizenship, demonstrate – in my view – that a *broad integration strategy* is needed. It should be acknowledged that the spheres of work, culture, housing, education, politics and law are *all* of crucial importance for the social integration of migrants. These spheres do, of course, differ in terms of scope. For example, the sphere of law determines in particular the entry regulations, the residence status, and who gets access to the labour market and political and social rights (and to what extent). It is also clear that the government's possibilities of intervention are primarily found in the fields of labour policy, education and housing. Political and cultural participation cannot be enforced, but can be facilitated and encouraged. The crucial question is to what extent ethnic minorities have been integrated into each of the mentioned spheres. The extent to which ethnic minorities have been integrated into various spheres and the way in which this has been done are indicative of the social integration of ethnic minorities into Dutch society. I will now briefly discuss the various spheres.

The *sphere of law* determines the admission policy and the residence status of policy categories (Andreas and Snyder, 2000; Guiraudon and Joppke, 2001). As far as the latter is concerned, there is a wide spectrum of possibilities, ranging from an inviolable residence status to no residence status at all. Exclusion in the sphere of law leads to a culmination of inequalities in the other spheres. Compare, for example, the position of so-called 'undocumented' or 'illegal' immigrants. Illegal immigrants have no right whatsoever to reside in the Netherlands and have no access to public provisions. Some exceptions are made for adult illegal immigrants in the event of acute medical emergencies and for their children who should have access to primary education. For asylum seekers, the situation is more complicated. The pluralization and irregularization of immigration flows has led to a complex system of legal differentiations that has serious consequences for the integration of EU-citizens, temporary labour migrants, asylum seekers, regular immigrants and illegal immigrants into the spheres of labour, housing and education. The increased plurality and complexity of migration flows in combination with the restrictive and selective migration policy has thus led to an *ethnic stratification based on residence statuses*. Firstly, there are citizens and immigrants with full rights of citizenship; secondly, immigrants with practically full social rights and certain political rights (denizenship); and thirdly, there are the categories that have very limited or no social rights (especially asylees and illegal immigrants).

The second sphere is that of *politics*. In a democracy, full citizens are given the opportunity to control their own destinies to some extent through politics. In other words, the citizens themselves create the laws they have to obey. There are two important indicators of the political integration of ethnic minorities. The first consists of the political rights they possess. In the Netherlands ethnic minorities have active and passive voting rights at the local level. Dutch municipalities grant foreign residents the right to vote as well as to run for office after 5 years residing in the Netherlands. However, if you do not have the Dutch nationality you are not allowed to participate actively or passively at the general, national election. The second indicator of political integration of ethnic minorities is, of course, the extent to which they (can) actually make use of their legal rights to participate in the sphere of politics. Only a small but growing proportion of the new generation of minorities have found their way in the Dutch political system. One important question is whether there is a connection between the integration into the sphere of politics and the integration into other spheres. Is political integration a necessary prerequisite for ethnic minorities to integrate fully into other spheres?

The third sphere is the *sphere of work*. In the literature on migration and integration, work is considered a crucial instrument for integration. The American sociologist Gans (1991) stated in this respect that semi- and unskilled immigrants first integrated into American society through the labour market and that subsequently (when there was social mobility across one or two generations) further integration of their children was achieved through education. Gans therefore came to the conclusion that integration policies should first of all be geared to the labour market. Educational policies come second. Gans (1991, p. 232) uses the 'take off' metaphor to illustrate this. It is only when a more or less strong position has been achieved through work that parents and their children begin to explore the possibilities of getting ahead through education. Unfortunately, employment can also be a disintegrating factor when ethnic minorities can rely only on a ghettoised labour market. In that case, work can lead to social isolation instead of social integration. However, the major social problem of today is the high unemployment among ethnic minorities. In the last ten years – even though the number of unemployed ethnic minorities is substantially decreasing – the unemployment figures for ethnic minorities are two to four times higher than those for Dutch people. This raises the question as to what is the integration capacity of the sphere of work.

The income realized through employment has consequences for the *sphere of housing*. In the Netherlands, the increase in wealth of the majority of the population goes hand in hand with a concentration of relative social deprivation among a large minority consisting of ethnic minorities. In the years to come, these groups will make up the majority in the central districts of the large cities. At present, the Dutch government is neither willing nor able to curb the suburbanization of the Dutch population and the concentration of ethnic minorities (SCP, 1998). This spatial segregation may thwart the social integration of ethnic minorities. On the other hand, some also point out that ethnic neighbourhoods can be a seedbed for the development of ethnic economic activities and thus may lay the foundation for social improvement (Snel and Burgers, 2000).

The fifth sphere is that of *education*. In the past ten to twenty years, the educational position of many groups of migrants has improved considerably. Nevertheless, the paradox of progress and decline manifests itself again and again, particularly in education. The educational position of ethnic minorities is improving, but that of the Dutch population is also improving, and perhaps even faster. By the way, this is no new phenomenon, but merely a persistent mechanism that has been described in detail in the literature on the chances of improvement for working-class children (Boudon, 1974; Bourdieu and Passeron, 1977). We know how long it took for Dutch society to become more open. Perhaps we should be more patient with groups that are more difficult to integrate. It should be noted that the persistent inequality might cause some disenchantment and demoralization. This can eventually lead to a situation in which more and more young people drop out of school (Bourdieu et al., 1999). There is a real risk for young ethnic minorities when their efforts at school do not yield the desired results, while they grow up in an environment in which many people are unemployed and had the same demoralizing experiences. This pessimistic view on the significance of education policy may be counterbalanced by the experiences of ethnic minorities who did benefit from the educational system.

The sixth relevant sphere is the sphere of *culture*. It was Gowricharn (1992) who, in the Netherlands, repeatedly drew attention to the cultural factor. In his opinion, integration problems and integration possibilities arise partly from the ethnic minorities cultural baggage colliding with the Dutch culture. Gowricharn also speaks of the 'ethnic factor'. He is also of the opinion that integration is a cultural process, in which the dominant society uses 'cultural normative images' that may hinder the integration of ethnic minorities into the spheres of labour, education and housing. Ethnic minorities who do not measure up to these normative images have less chance of getting a job, a house or a positive recommendation at school with regard to further study. In addition to this debate on the existence of excluding cultural normative images, a new debate arose as to the significance of transnational networks and loyalties. This debate points to the limited nature of the discussion about whether migrants should stay or return. Many 'established' migrants still maintain close links with their country of origin, especially economically and in the cultural sense.

Acknowledgement of the significance of these 'transnational societies' and corresponding 'transnational identities' puts into perspective the presupposition that social integration in the Netherlands can only be successful if the ethnic minorities are willing to give up specific cultural identity and loyalties (Glick Schiller et al., 1995; Portes et al., 1999).

The seventh relevant sphere is that of *religion*. Durkheim and Weber pointed to the social integrative function of the sphere of religion. In the Netherlands, the religious 'pillars' played an important role in the simultaneous integration and emancipation of groups of citizens. Not surprisingly, in the debate on the integration of ethnic minorities, some pointed to the possible significance of the pillarization model, particularly with respect to Islam. The number of Muslims in the Netherlands is increasing. The significance of Islam is reflected in the building of mosques, the existence of national Islamic broadcast organizations, Islamic shops, and Islamic primary schools. Nevertheless, the degree of organization of Islam is limited. There are no Islamic political parties or trade unions, no Islamic housing corporations or hospitals, and the participation of Muslims in the provisions of the welfare state does not involve a religious intermediary structure. Nevertheless, the question as to the significance of the sphere of religion for the integration of ethnic minorities keeps cropping up. In the recent past attempts to self-organisation were viewed rather positively as a possible channel of emancipation (compare the pillarization model), nowadays – especially after the tragic event of September 11th and the rise of populist political movements in Europe – Islamic institution building is viewed with anger and fear.

There are, of course, still other 'spheres of integration', for example, health care. And one should also not forget that there are 'informal spheres' of integration. In the next section I will give a brief description of the relevance of these informal spheres of integration.

4 Bastard Spheres

Informal spheres of integration form a sort of shadow cabinet of the spheres that I have discussed here. For example, Peters (1993) states that each society has spheres with 'undersides' that are not visible to many of us, such as illegal types of trade and social organizations. Behind their official facade, legitimate institutions and social systems conceal an unofficial and informal hidden character (Scott, 1990). With regard to the informal side of formal spheres, Everett Hughes (one of the founding fathers of the Chicago

School in sociology) introduced the term *bastard institutions* in the fifties.
Bastard institutions are illegal distributors of legitimate goods and services,
but they also cater for needs that cannot be considered legitimate such as
irregular lotteries, prostitution, black markets (of labour, goods, people,
organs, etc.), organized crime, and also illegal forms of settling conflicts
and providing credit facilities. Hughes says: 'All take on organized forms
not unlike those of other institutions. (...) These bastard institutions should
be studied not merely as pathological departures from what is good and
right, but as part of the total complex of human activities and enterprises. In
addition, they should be looked at as orders of things in which we can see
the processes going on, the same social processes perhaps, that are to be
found in the legitimate institutions' (Hughes, 1994, pp. 193, 194).

These bastard institutions, or to stick to my terminology, these bastard
spheres are particularly important to people whose residence status is not
very clear, such as illegal aliens. The better the Dutch territory and the
access to formal labour market and collective provisions are guarded, the
more the informal institutions gain significance for immigrants who do not
have a valid residence permit. One may think in this respect of smuggling
networks, the informal housing sector, the informal economy, and the
sphere of crime (Engbersen, 2001a, Engbersen and Van der Leun, 2001).
These bastard institutions play a role in the transport and stay of illegal
migrants. Smuggling networks offer illegal migrants an illegitimate way to
enter the country, while the informal spheres of labour and housing offer
them an alternative to the formal labour market and housing market,
particularly now that these markets have become less accessible for illegal
immigrants as a result of various measures. In addition, the sphere of crime
offers an alternative source of income.

A second important factor is the informal practices of public or semi-
public institutions. They play a key role in the passive and active toleration
of *illegal* immigrants (Cornelius et al., 1994). There is a great discrepancy
between the restrictive legislation concerning illegal immigrants and the
policy practice. The policy freedom that institutions in the fields of the
control of aliens, education, housing and healthcare claim for themselves –
on the basis of capacity problems, control problems and for humanitarian
reasons – also leads to a situation in which illegal migrants can become
semi-integrated into Dutch society without being formally part of the
political community. Walzer speaks of the existence of an intermediate
class of illegal immigrants: 'We have our own resident aliens, who live
within the political community, but are not part of it ...' (Walzer, 1994,
pp. 181, 182). What makes this intermediate class so interesting is that they
are integrated in some of the spheres (for example the informal labour

market), but not in a legal sense.

Informal institutions can also be of interest to legal immigrants, particularly the informal economy and the sphere of crime (Engbersen, 2001b). The informal sphere of labour offers unemployed migrants an alternative to the formal labour market. There are indications that immigrants engage in informal, economic activities on a large scale in western cities (Portes et al., 1989; Mingione, 1991; Sassen, 1991). It involves to some extent the invisible and informal activities that are not, or hardly, perceived in official policy, or tolerated passively or actively. The American literature on this subject showed that crime offers an opportunity for social improvement and integration. For example, Bell (1960) stated that ethnic participation in crime is closely related to migration processes. Through crime, newcomers acquire a place in society, and their old positions on the bottom rung are subsequently taken up by new migrants. It is more common, however, to regard participation in the sphere of crime as an indicator of social disintegration.

5 Tensions Within and Between Spheres of Integration

The question is how the dimensions and spheres of integration relate to each other. A central question is to what extent these dimensions are *not* in harmony with each other. The differences between the three dimensions of social integration make it possible to clarify the internal tensions within a sphere. This is possible when, within one sphere, the principle of one dimension is not in harmony with the principle from another dimension. Let me give you three simple examples relating to the spheres of employment, education and religion.

With regard to the *sphere of employment*, one may ask whether the moral and functional dimensions in this sphere are compatible. Or is there an insoluble tension between the social right to a decent legal minimum wage (moral dimension) and the functional demand for an efficient labour market? In the sphere of employment, wage reduction may have a positive influence on the employment chances of semi- and unskilled ethnic minorities, but the consequences in terms of income will be such (poverty!) that they will not be able to participate fully in society. We stumble here on the question of the possible incompatibility between the 'functional' dimension and 'moral' dimension of integration.[3]

---

[3] Another example of incompatibility between the functional dimension and the moral dimension within the sphere of politics can be derived from the debate on the number of refugees that the Netherlands would accept. On the grounds of international agreements

The debate on *education* in the migrants' own language on the other hand points towards a possible incompatibility between the functional dimension and the expressive dimension of integration. There are many people who think that instruction in the Dutch language is more important than paying attention to the identity-reinforcing and culturally enriching functions of the ethnic minorities own language (van Doorn, 1989). Others disagree and argue that education on culture, together with support in their own language is essential to reach higher educational levels (cf. SCP, 2002).

A third example comes from the sphere of *religion*. It involves the circumcision of girls from Somalia (a growing group in the Netherlands), which is usually done secretly. This ritual is prohibited in the Netherlands. The parents' right to religious freedom (expressive dimension) is limited by the child's right to physical integrity as elaborated in the provisions of the Dutch penal code (moral dimension). It should be mentioned here that the right to clitoridectomy is not advocated in public by anyone. A related example are the recurrent 'headscarf cases' in Western-European countries. Sometimes employers refuse to employ Muslim women wearing headscarves. Their dress code for employees who work in visible places in their organizations does not allow them to wear headscarves. Some argue that it is unlawful (moral dimension) to refuse employment to women for wearing a headscarf as a sign of being a Muslim woman (expressive dimension).

Of course, these social tensions within one sphere are obviously apparent within bastard spheres like the informal economy, the informal housing sector or crime. These parallel institutions are built on the tension between the moral dimension and the functional dimension of integration.

In addition to these recurrent tensions between different dimensions of integration within one sphere, there are also incompatibilities between the different social spheres. One example of this can be derived from the current European debate on illegal immigration. In the sphere of politics, there is a strong tendency to develop a more restrictive policy to reduce the number of illegal aliens and to prevent unwanted immigrants from coming in. Politicians refer to the principle that nation states and the European Union decide for themselves who they allow to live on their territory and who may get access to the labour market and public provisions (Bolkestein, 1995, pp. 205, 206). They also point out that an excessive flow of illegal aliens would endanger the social integration and labour market position of

---

and driven by the functional demand of an efficient control of the flow of refugees, the politicians did not want to accept more refugees than agreed upon. However, many citizens objected to this attitude and criticized the politicians on the grounds of moral principles such as internal solidarity and the protection of the personal integrity of people.

legal immigrants. However, many employers are not in favour of a restrictive policy towards illegal migrants, because they regard these illegal migrants as cheap labour, which could make an important contribution to crucial sectors in the European and Dutch economy (e.g. in agriculture and market gardening). They refer to the liberal, economic principles of free movement of people and goods for a free market. Thus, economic cross-border principles are diametrically opposed to national, political principles.[4]

Another example of possible incompatibility between spheres involves the current segregation tendencies in the large cities of the Netherlands. Spatial segregation in the sphere of housing has serious consequences for the sphere of education and also for the sphere of labour. Segregation stimulates the further growth of 'black' schools and can eventually lead to problems in the sphere of employment (due to the territorial stigma attached to certain neighbourhoods). Furthermore, policy instruments that are used in one sphere may be detrimental to the other. Thus, on the one hand, an intensive educational policy has been developed to create equal chances and promote the social and geographical mobility of young ethnic minorities, while, on the other hand, the neo-liberalization in the housing sector, i.e. the limitation of the public housing sector, leads to more segregated, low-income districts with black schools. It goes without saying that this has serious consequences. In other words, policy in one sphere can have unintended negative effects on another sphere.

This analysis shows that a multicultural society experiences 'in built' tensions that are connected with the various dimensions and spheres of integration (Engbersen and Gabriëls, 1995). It is also clear that particularly the moral dimension is of crucial importance in a multicultural society. The moral dimension determines which social standards – which bind each of us – enable the integration of citizens into a multicultural society. These social standards therefore limit the ways in which groups can express their identity and also lay down the conditions for the integration of ethnic minorities. In other words, some things are allowed, and some are forbidden (e.g. circumcision of girls from Somalia, and paying wages that

---

[4] Saskia Sassen (1999, p. 4) writes in this respect: 'Today we see a combination of drives to create border-free economic spaces and drives for renewed border control to keep immigrants and refugees out. The context in which today's efforts to stop immigration assume their distinct meaning for me is the current transnationalization of flows of capital, goods, information, and culture. Governments and economic actors in highly developed countries are increasingly seeking to reduce the role of national borders in such flows, to create transnational spaces. Current immigration policy in developed countries is increasingly at odds with other major policy frameworks in the international system and with the growth of global economic integration'.

are too low). Maintenance of these social standards (regarding freedom, equality, separation of church and state, physical integrity, justice, solidarity, etc.) should be enforced, and individuals should be given the opportunities to integrate functionally. In many cases, this will cause migrants to adopt important parts of the Dutch culture, and also enable them to express their own cultural values, orientations and practices (cf. Dagevos, 2001). Thus, they will influence the cultural landscape of the Netherlands. Dutch culture can use a bit of extra drama. However, the dominance of the secular Western pattern, with its emphasis on individual development, has not fundamentally changed in the Netherlands, and in the public domain one can scarcely speak of multiculturalism (SCP, 1998).

6 A Differentiated and Reflexive Policy in Respect of Ethnic Minorities

The integration of ethnic minorities in the Netherlands is nowadays often discussed in terms of assimilation. The underlying idea is that social integration requires that ethnic minorities adapt themselves to the culture of the Dutch. Paul Scheffer wrote: 'Integration while preserving the ethnic minorities identity is a white lie that should not be encouraged by the government'. The importance of the social integrative function of values were also stressed in an earlier debate on the growing decline of moral standards in Dutch society. On this occasion, Dutch politicians like Hirsch Ballin (1995) and Bolkestein (1995) agreed that Christian and humanistic values were of great importance for social cohesion. This point of view made the representatives of Islamic movements raise the question of whether, in a multicultural society, the State may rely exclusively on Christian values.

The debate on assimilation is not a specifically Dutch debate. Until today, heated debates are held in the United States between the 'assimilists' and 'pluralists' (Waters, 1990, pp. 4-6). The former are convinced that integration is impossible without full adaptation to the culture of the dominant society. The latter assume that a plurality of cultures is possible and that maintaining a specific ethnic identity does not need to obstruct integration. Empirical reality shows that assimilation – also among European migrants – has only taken place to a limited extent (cf. also Portes and Zhou, 1994). This is even more true for groups of migrants from Mexico, Cuba, and Puerto Rico. Portes and Rumbaut (1990, p. 141) state: 'Assimilation as the rapid transformation of immigrants into Americans "as everyone else" has never happened (...) Ethnic resilience has been the rule among immigrants, old and new, and represents simultaneously a central part of their process of political incorporation'. The assumption that immigrants who abandon their own ethnic culture are easier integrated is also put into perspective by Portes and Rumbaut. They point to the importance of ethnic identification and transnational communities for integration into American society (cf. Waters, 1990; Portes et al., 1999).

The integration model that I am discussing here shows why the proposal for an assimilation policy is deficient. Supporters of the assimilation policy do not fully take account of the difference between the moral dimension and expressive dimension of integration. The moral dimension relates to the standards that enable human interaction, and the expressive dimension to the lifestyles that express the identity of people. In a multicultural society, it is important that, for social integration, *standards* are developed that enable interaction between people with very divergent and rapidly changing *(transnational) orientations and lifestyles.* These standards must have the approval of all the citizens that belong to the political community. Rawls (1989) therefore also stresses the importance of an 'overlapping consensus' on the standards that should enable social integration in a multicultural society. In a democracy, these standards need to be determined within the sphere of politics.

The model of social integration developed here presupposes a differentiated and reflexive policy in respect of ethnic minorities. By this I mean a policy that takes account of the extent to which ethnic minorities have been integrated into various spheres of integration as well as of the tensions and incompatibilities that exist within and between spheres of integration. The model presented fulfils two functions of social policy.

First of all, the model can be used to *localize* excluded persons and groups. Those who fall outside any or most of the spheres can be identified as non-integrated. Localization of this category subsequently raises questions as to its social composition. Differentiations according to class, ethnicity and gender (and their interrelatedness) will play a role in this. In this way, it is possible to arrive at a more specific identification of excluded groups and prevent wrong ethnic classifications of groups. After all, the current classification of target groups in the policy regarding minorities proves much too rough. The accuracy of the minorities policy is not improved when whole groups of the population (such as the Surinamese and Turks) are labelled as target groups, while many members of a certain group succeed in achieving an integrated position independently. Localization of excluded persons and groups also offers the opportunity to further examine the sources of exclusion and the relations between the spheres. Walzer himself recently pointed to the consequences when groups fail within the spheres of education and social provisions: 'failure in these areas has spread to the spheres of market, politics, and family, where it caused an accumulation of failures that together led to exclusion' (Walzer, 1994, p. 191). However, other chronologies of segregation are also visible, for example, the problems of illegal immigrants and asylum seekers as a result of a total exclusion or semi-exclusion from the spheres of politics and law, or the problems of established migrants as a result of exclusion from the sphere of labour.

Secondly, the model provides an *analytical framework* for a systematic inventory of the integration and disintegration processes and possible tense relations. However, no unequivocal policy recommendations can be inferred from it. A harmonic, functional relation within and between various dimensions and spheres of integration is rarely visible in social reality. Nevertheless, despite all normative and pragmatic objections, the ideal of functional cohesion may be a worthwhile goal for the policy in respect of ethnic minorities. The position of many minority groups shows that social disadvantages and segregation processes can be identified in various spheres. To paraphrase Walzer: segregation follows them from sphere to sphere (Walzer, 1994, p. 186). A worthwhile objective for the Dutch policy in respect of ethnic minorities might therefore be to find a *new balance* between the functional, moral and expressive dimensions of integration, and between the various spheres of integration. For a country that – despite its immigration history – has only recently acknowledged that it *de facto* has become an immigration country, the American ideal of *E Pluribus Unum* is much too ambitious. The Netherlands would do wise to seek that balance with the help of institutional arrangements that were developed when the Dutch welfare state was given shape. Given the current signs of an imminent crisis, those institutional examples are, of course, no longer sufficient, but they do offer reference points for an integration policy.

References

Andreas, P. and T. Snyder (eds), (2000), *The Wall around the West. State Borders and Immigration Controls in North America and Europe*, Rowman & Littlefield Publishers, Lanham, Boulder, New York and Oxford.

Bell, D., (1980), [1960], Crime as an American Way of Life: A Queer Ladder of Social Mobility, in: 'L.A. Coser (ed.)', *The Pleasures of Sociology*, New York.

Bolkestein, F. (1995), *Het heft in handen: essays*, Prometheus, Amsterdam.

Boudon, R. (1974), *Education, Equality and Social Opportunity*, Wiley, New York.

Bourdieu, P. and J.C. Passeron (1977), *Reproduction in Education, Society and Culture*, Sage, London.

Bourdieu, P. et al. (1999), *The Weight of the World: Social Suffering in Contemporary Society*, Polity Press, Cambridge.

Cornelius Wayne et al. (1994), *Controlling Immigration: A Global Perspective*, Stanford University Press, Stanford.

Dagevos, J., (2001), *Perspectief op integratie. Over de sociaal-culturele en structurele integratie van etnische minderheden in Nederland*, WRR, Den Haag.

Doorn, J.A.A. van (1989), *Rede en macht*, VUGA, Den Haag.

Engbersen, G. (2001a), 'The Urban Palimpsest. Urban Marginality in an Advanced Society', in: *Focaal - European Journal of Anthropology*, no. 38, pp. 125-138.

Engbersen, G. (2001b), 'The unanticipated consequences of panopticon Europe: residence strategies of illegal immigrants', in: V. Guiraudon and Ch. Joppke (eds), *Controlling a New Migration World*, Routledge, London, pp. 222-246.

Engbersen, G. and J.P. van der Leun (2001), 'The Social Construction of Illegality and Criminality', *European Journal on Criminal Policy and Research*, Vol. 9(1), pp. 51-70.

Engbersen, G. and R. Gabriëls (1995), *Sferen van integrate: Naar een gedifferentieerd allochtonenbeleid*, Boom, Amsterdam.

Gans, Herbert J. (1991), *People, Plans and Policies: Essays on Poverty, Racism, and Other Naional Urban Problems*, Columbia University Press, New York.

Glick Schiller, N. et al. (1995), 'From Immigrant to Transmigrant: Theorizing Transnational Migration', *Anthropological Quarterly*, Vol. 68(1), pp. 48-63.

Gordon, M.M. 1964, *Assimilation in American Way of Life: the Role of Race, Religion and National Origin*, Oxford University Press, New York.

Gowricharn, R. (1992), *Tegen beter weten in: een essay over de economie en sociologie van de onderklasse*, Garant, Leuven.

Guiraudon, V. and Ch. Joppke (eds.), (2001), *Controlling a New Migration World*, Routledge, Londen.

Hirsch Ballin, E.M.H., (1995), 'Staatsburgerschap als roeping', in: Th. Geurts et al (red.), *Burgerschap in een vergruizelende samenleving*. Damon, Best.

Hughes, E.C. (1994), *On Work, Race, and the Sociological imagination* (edited and with an introduction by Lewis A. Coser), University of Chicago Press, Chicago and London.

Miller, M. J. (2001), 'The Sanctioning of Unauthorized Migration and Alien Employment', in: D. Kyle and R. Koslowski (eds.), *Global Human Smuggling. Comparative Perspectives*, The John Hopkins University Press, Baltimore, pp. 318-336.

Mingione, E. (1991), *Fragmented Societies: A Sociology of Economic Life Beyond the Market Paradigm*, Blackwell, Oxford.

Peters, B. (1993), *Die Integration Moderner Geselleschaften*, Suhrkamp, Frankfurt/Main.

Portes, A. and R.G. Rumbaut, (1990), *Immigrant America: a Portrait*, Berkeley: University of California Press.

Portes, A and M. Zhou (1994), 'Should Immigrants Assimilate?' *Public Interest*. No. 116, pp. 18-33.

Portes, A., M. Castells and L. Benton (eds), (1989), *The Informal Economy: Studies in Advanced and Less Developed Countries*, John Hopkins University Press, London.

Portes, A., L.E. Guarnizo and P. Landolt, (1999), 'Transnational Communities', *Ethnic and Racial Studies*, vol. 22, no. 2 (special issue), pp. 217-477.

Sassen, S. (1999), 'Craked Casings: Notes toward an Analytics for Studying Transnational Processes', in: J. L. Abu-Lughod (ed.), *Sociology for the Twenty-first Century*, The University of Chicago Press, Chicago and London, pp. 134-145.

Sassen, S., (2001), *The Global City: New York, London, Tokyo*, Princeton University Press, Princeton.

Scheffer, P. (2000), Het multiculturele drama, *NRC-Handelsblad*, 29 januari 2000.

Scott, J. C., (1990), *Domination and the Arts of Resistance: Hidden Transcripts*, Yale University Press.

Snel, E. en J. Burgers, (2000), 'The Comfort of Strangers: Etnische enclaves in de grote steden', *Amsterdams Sociologisch Tijdschrift*, Vol. 27 (3), pp. 292-313.

Sociaal en Cultureel Planbureau, (1998), *Sociaal en Cultureel Rapport* 1998, Den Haag.

Sociaal en Cultureel Planbureau, (2001a), *Rapportage minderheden: Meer werk*, SCP-publikatie, Den Haag.

Sociaal en Cultureel Planbureau, (2001b), *Rapportage minderheden: Vorderingen op school*, SCP-publikatie, Den Haag.

Sociaal en Cultureel Planbureau, (2001c), Onderwijs in allochtone talen, Sociaal en Culturteel Planbueau, Den Haag.

Sunier, T. (1997), 'Islam in beweging', *Migrantenstudies*, Vol. 13(2), pp. 80-89.

Veenman, J. (1995), 'Langzaam voorwaarts: ontwikkelingen in de sociaal-economische positie van zes allochtonencategorieen', *Migrantenstudies*, Vol. 10(4), pp. 230-243.

Veenman, J. (red.), (1996), *Keren de kansen: De tweede-generatie allochtonen in Nederland*, Van Gorcum, Assen.

Vermeulen, H. en R. Penninx (red.), (1994), *Het democratisch ongeduld: de emancipatie en integratie van zes doelgroepen van het minderhedenbeleid*, Amsterdam.

Walzer, M. (1983), *Spheres of Justice: a Defence of Pluralism and Equality*, New York: Basic Books.

Walzer, M. (1994), 'Uitsluiting, onrecht en de democratische staat', in: P. van den Berg and M. Trappenburg (red.), *Lokale rechtvardigheid: de politieke theorie van Michael Walzer*, W.E.J. Tjeenk Willink, Zwolle.

Waters, M.C., (1990), *Ethnic Options: Choosing Identities in America*, University of California Press, Berkeley.

WRR (1979), *Etnische minderheden*, Sdu Uitgevers, Den Haag.

WRR (1989), *Allochtonenbeleid*, Sdu Uitgevers, Den Haag.

WRR (2001), *Nederland als Immigratiesamenleving*, Sdu Uitgevers, Den Haag.

Chapter 5

New Forms of Britishness: Post-Immigration Ethnicity and Hybridity in Britain[*]

Tariq Modood

Introduction

Out of an immigration process which was conceived primarily as the importing of labour to take up jobs in the British economy which white people did not wish to do, there have emerged, for at least some of the migrants and their descendants, new communities capable of and perhaps wanting to maintain themselves as communities. New cultural practices, especially to do with the family and religion, have become a feature of the British landscape; skin colour, identities, place of origin or cultural community continue to shape the personal lives and relationships of even British-born individuals. The importance of cultural and ethnic differences, however, runs much deeper. Ethnic identity, like gender and sexuality, has become politicized and for some people has become a primary focus of their politics (Young, 1990). While not as prominent as in the United States, yet more so than on the European mainland (Baldwin-Edwards and Schain, 1994), there is in Britain an ethnic assertiveness, arising out of the feelings of not being respected or of lacking access to public space, consisting of counterposing 'positive' images against traditional or dominant stereotypes. It is a politics of projecting identities in order to challenge existing power relations; of seeking not just toleration for ethnic difference but also public acknowledgement, resources and representation.

For some time ethnic minority identities were studied by two rival, indeed hostile, approaches. The older approach derived from anthropology and emphasized differences between what were sometimes regarded as

---

[*] This paper has been published in Ronit Lentin (ed.) 1999: *The Expanding Nation: Towards a Multiethnic Ireland*, Department of Sociology, Trinity College, Dublin. We thank Ronit Lentin for the permission to reprint the paper in this volume.

discrete cultures, usually studied in terms of their own internal logic and traditions, and worried about an 'identity clash' for those of Asian descent but born and brought up in Britain, who were supposed to be 'between two cultures' (Watson, 1977). Partly in reaction to this form of anthropology, a neo-Marxian approach was developed which understood the formation of 'blackness', indiscriminately encompassing all non-whites, in terms of societal racism, cultural oppression and anti-racist struggles (CCSS, 1982). More recently, new perspectives have been sketched. Stuart Hall has argued that from the mid- to late 1980s 'a significant shift has been going on (and is still going on) in black cultural politics' (Hall, 1992, p. 252). Not only does this entail a recognition of a diversity of minority identities, 'a plural blackness', but also an understanding that ethnic identities are not 'pure' or static. Rather, they change in new circumstances or by sharing social space with other heritages and influences. Moreover, this also challenges existing conceptions of Britishness (Gilroy, 1987). For, if ethnic minority identities are not simply products of cultures of extra-British origin, but owe something to the stream of British life, then they too contribute to that stream, and so their existence belies the dichotomy of 'essentially black' and 'essentially British'. This has opened the way for talk of 'the black Atlantic' - a shared heritage and experience of blacks in Africa, the USA, the Caribbean, Britain and Western Europe as a basis for a transnational culture and discourse.

In the same period of time there has also emerged an 'Asian' identity based on a hybridic Asianness, rather than a regional, national, caste or religious identity derived from one's parents, and sometimes directly influenced by or modelled on forms of 'black pride' and black hip-hop or rap music (Baumann, 1990). Additionally, and more recently, there has been an increase in Muslim activism and consciousness, giving rise to intense debate about identity and the emergence of new magazines such as Q-News which emphasize a British Muslimness and reject ethnicity as un-Islamic and speak of a global Muslim consciousness (Modood et al., 1994).

What is particularly exciting about these ethnic identity developments is that increasingly 'ethnicity' or 'blackness' is less experienced as an oppositional identity than as a way of being British. Moreover, this is happening at a time when some in the wider British public, including the new Labour Government, is emphasising the plural and dynamic character of British society, and speaking openly of 'rebranding Britain' (Leonard, 1997).

Political Blackness and Asians

I do, however, have some reservations about the 'new blackness' line of Stuart Hall and Paul Gilroy. My three inter-related criticisms are that, firstly, that these socio-cultural theorists invariably focus on the Afro-Caribbeans; secondly, that they speak of a plural 'blackness' which they expect Asians to fit into but in which most Asians are not interested; thirdly, they are guilty of a woeful neglect of religion.

Let me illustrate the last two by offering some findings from The Fourth National Survey of Ethnic Minorities in Britain, of which I was the principal researcher. The survey method, of course, has many limitations, especially in relation to complex topics like those of identity. Nevertheless, if we bear in mind that all research methods have their limitations and cannot be substituted for each other, so that no one is *the* method, then this survey has the potential to offer what small-scale ethnographic studies, armchair theorising and political wishful thinking cannot.[1]

The survey found that South Asians, including those born and raised in Britain, strongly associated with their ethnic and family origins; there was very little erosion of group identification down the generations. Despite the various forms of anti-racist politics around a black identity of the last two decades - an identity which politicians and theorists have argued is *the* key post-immigration formation (Modood, 1994) - only a fifth of South Asians think of themselves as black. This is not an Asian repudiation of 'the essential black subject' in favour of a more nuanced and more pluralised blackness (Hall, 1992) but a failure to identify with blackness at all.

Religious Identities

Rather than skin-colour, which was prominent in the self-descriptions of Caribbeans, it was religion that was prominent in the self-descriptions of South Asians. This owes as much to a sense of community as to personal

---

[1] The survey explored only certain dimensions of culture and ethnicity. For example, it did not cover youth culture and recreational activities such as music, dance and sport. These cultural dimensions are likely to be as important to the self- and group-identities of some of our respondents as the features we gathered data on. Moreover, almost all the questions asked in the survey provided indications of how closely people affiliated to their group of origin. We did not explicitly explore ways in which members of the minorities had adopted, modified or contributed to elements of ways of life of other groups, including the white British. For full details on all aspects of the Fourth Survey see T. Modood et al., 1997.

faith, but the identification and prioritisation of religion is far from just a nominal one. At a time when a third of Britons say they do not have a religion, nearly all South Asians said they have one, and 90 per cent said that religion was of personal importance to them (compared to 13 per cent of whites). While about a quarter of whites attend a place of worship once a month or more, over half of Hindus and seven out of ten Sikhs attend once a month or more and nearly two-thirds of Muslims attend at least once a week. Even amongst the young expressions of commitment were exceptionally high: more than a third of Indians and African Asians, and two-thirds of Pakistani and Bangladeshi 16-34 years old said that religion was very important to how they led their lives compared to 5 per cent of whites (though nearly a fifth of Caribbeans took this view). It is clear, therefore, the presence of the new ethnic minorities is not simply changing the character of religion in Britain by diversifying it, but is giving it an importance which is out of step with native trends.

The centrality of religion to the constitution of South Asian communities and ethnic identities can be further illustrated in a number of ways. Very few Asians marry across religious and caste boundaries and most expect that their children will be inducted into their religion. The demand, especially by Muslims, that children be taught and allowed to hold acts of worship in their parents' religion in state schools, and that the state should fund Muslim schools (on the same basis as the Christian and Jewish schools are funded) has been an object of political activism and conflict. Religious dress codes that require adherents to wear turbans or headscarves or cover their legs continue to be resisted by acts of discrimination and exclusion at schools and workplaces and are the objects of legal rulings. Despite the fact that at least five major South Asian languages are spoken in Britain, and most Asians have some facility in more than one of these languages, each linguistic community is strongly connected to a religious community (Modood et al., 1997, pp. 308-12).

Religion, moreover, is particularly worth exploring in relation to British socialisation. For, firstly, it marks a significant dimension of cultural difference between the migrants and British society. Not only did most of the migrants have a different religion to that of the natives, but all the indications are that they, including the Christians among them, were more religious than the society they were joining. Not only was this likely to have been the case at the time of migration and in the early years of settlement, but it is still true today. Secondly, one of the major social changes that has taken place in Britain during the lifetime of most Asian settlers has been the decline of indigenous religious observance and faith, and so religion among ethnic minorities is an important test case of the effect of British socialisation. Thirdly, generally speaking, most of the cultural practices of migrants and their descendants usually decline with the length of their stay in the society to which they have migrated. This is usually so with language, dress, arranged marriages and so on. It is also the case with religion, though perhaps descendants of migrants are more likely to keep alive a distinctive religion rather than a distinctive language (this has certainly been the case with the Jewish and Indian diasporas, for example, though not with the Chinese diaspora). Rather, what makes religion exceptional is that, if not generally, at least in British society, religion is now strongly correlated with age: the older a Briton is, the more religious they are likely to be. Yet, the longer a migrant has been in Britain, the greater the likelihood of a decline in their original culture. So, in the particular case of religion, age and length of residence in Britain work against each other.

We found, indeed, that while there is not a uniform linear pattern, the more a person's life has been in Britain, the less likely they are to say that religion is very important. Testing for the independent effects of age and length of residence in Britain through an analysis by logistic regression, we found that for Indians and Pakistanis the age and length of residence effects more or less cancel each other out, but among Bangladeshis and African Asians length of residence has about twice the effect as age does. This means that, in the case of the latter-mentioned groups, the decline in religion through British socialisation is being only partially reversed by age.

New Forms of Ethnicity

The Fourth Survey does however offer for the first time some large data-set evidence that ethnicity is coming to mean new things. Distinctive cultural practices to do with religion, language, marriage and so on still command considerable allegiance. The case of religion has already been mentioned. A further example is that nearly all South Asians can understand a community language, and over two-thirds use it with family members younger than themselves. More than half of the married 16-34 year-old Pakistanis and Bangladeshis had had their spouse chosen by their parents. There was, however, a visible decline in participation in distinctive cultural practices across the generations. This was particularly evident amongst younger South Asians who, compared to their elders, are less likely to speak to family members in a South Asian language, regularly attend a place of worship or have an arranged marriage.

Yet, as has been said, this did not mean that they ceased to identify with their ethnic or racial or religious group. In this respect the survey makes clear what has been implicit in recent 'identity politics'. Ethnic identification is no longer necessarily connected to personal participation in distinctive cultural practices, such as those of language, religion or dress. Some people expressed an ethnic identification even though they did not participate in distinctive cultural practices. Hence it is fair to say a new conception of ethnic identity has emerged.

Traditionally, ethnic identity has been implicit in distinctive *cultural practices*, this still exists and is the basis of a strong expression of group membership. Additionally, however, an *associational* identity can be seen which takes the form of pride in one's origins, identification with certain group labels and sometimes a political assertiveness.

The ethnic identities of the second generation may have a weaker component of behavioural difference, but it would be misleading to portray them as weak identities as such. In the last couple of decades the bases of identity-formation have undergone important changes and there has come to be a minority assertiveness. Identity has moved from that which might be unconscious and taken-for-granted because implicit in distinctive cultural practices, to conscious and public projections of identity and the explicit creation and assertion of politicized ethnicities. This is part of a wider socio-political climate which is not confined to race and culture or non-white minorities. Feminism, gay pride, Quebecois nationalism and the revival of Scottishness are some prominent examples of these new identity movements which have come to be an important feature in many countries in which class-politics has declined. Identities in this political climate are not implicit and private but are shaped through intellectual, cultural and political debates and become a feature of public discourse and policies, especially at the level of local or regional government. The identities formed in such processes are fluid and susceptible to change with the political climate, but to think of them as weak is to overlook the pride with which they may be asserted, the intensity with which they may be debated and their capacity to generate community activism and political campaigns.

Some of the differences in culture and identity can be partly explained by place of birth, period of residence in Britain, occupational class or by a combination of these and related factors, but underlying them was an irreducible difference between groups. Easily the strongest influence on South Asians' identity was their age at the time they came to Britain. Getting on for half of those who migrated after they had reached the age of 35 exhibited a 'strong' behavioural identity; one eighth of them were in the 'weak' group (Modood et al., 1997, pp. 334-36). In contrast, half of the

South Asians who had been born in Britain were members of the 'weak' behavioural category. An important contrast between groups, perhaps related to the influence of religion, is between African Asians and Indians (about 90 per cent of whom are Sikhs and Hindus), and Pakistanis and Bangladeshis (over 95 per cent of whom are Muslims). On a range of issues to do with religion, arranged marriages, choice of schools and Asian clothes, the latter group take a consistently more 'conservative' view than the former, even when age on arrival/birth in Britain and economic position are taken into account. The fact that the Pakistanis and Bangladeshis are more likely to come from rural backgrounds, and, in particular, from poorer rural backgrounds, is bound to be relevant, and perhaps also the attitudes and practices in relation to gender-roles, marriage and ties of kinship (Ballard, 1990). The sense of 'siege' and 'threat' that some Muslim peoples have historically felt in the context of Western colonialism and cultural domination, and to which rural peoples in particular responded through a 'defensive traditionalism' may also be a factor (Modood, 1990).

Britishness

A misleading picture would be conveyed if I did not add that besides colour and religion, other ethnic identities too were mentioned by Fourth Survey respondents, and indeed, that ethnic/racial/religious identification was of course not universal. For East African Asians, for example, their job was as important an item of self-description as any other.

The Fourth Survey also uniquely allows us to explore British national identity by bringing a large data-set to bear on the question. It is quite clear that the identities discussed above, various as they are, do not necessarily compete with a sense of Britishness. More than two-thirds of Asians said that they felt British, and these proportions were, as one might expect, higher amongst young people and those who had been born in Britain. The majority of respondents had no difficulty with the idea of hyphenated or multiple identities (see also Runnymede Trust, 1998). But there was evidence of alienation from or a rejection of Britishness. For example, over a quarter of British-born Caribbeans did not think of themselves as being British. In separate in-depth interviews we found that most of the second generation did think of themselves as mostly but not entirely culturally and socially British. They were not however comfortable with the idea of British being anything more than a legal title, in particular they found it difficult to call themselves 'British' because they felt that the majority of white people did not accept them as British because of their race or cultural background; through hurtful 'jokes', harassment, discrimination and violence they found their claim to be British was all too often denied (Modood et al., 1994, ch. 6).

Yet at the same time, the trend in all groups, however, is away from cultural distinctness and towards cultural mixture and intermarriage. The trend is not equally strong in the various groups. For example, among the British-born, of those who had a partner, half of Caribbean men, a third of Caribbean women, a fifth of Indian and African Asian men, a tenth of Pakistani and Bangladeshi men and very few South Asian women had a white partner. In our survey, 40 per cent of Caribbean children who were living with two parents had one white parent. The Caribbean-white, the black-white, social, cultural, sexual and generational mix is now so deep in Britain that it is bound to soon have a profound impact on the idea of a black identity, a black community, though these matters are not yet being discussed in public. What is openly discussed by leading black analysts is the vibrant strength of a black British cultural identity in the mid-1990s. Darcus Howe has spoken of black people having 'a social ease and confidence now that we have not had before' (Younge, 1995); Henry Louis Gates Jnr. believes that 'a culture that is distinctively black and British can be said to be in full flower' (Gates, 1997, p. 196), and Stuart Hall has argued not only that 'black British culture could be described as confident beyond measure in its own identity' (Hall, 1998, p. 39) but also that young black people have made themselves '*the* defining force in street-oriented British youth culture' (Hall, 1998, p. 40).

Some, indeed, have argued that the hope for multiculturalism lies in the development of new syncretic and hybrid youth cultures centred on black musical forms like rap and hiphop, and their Asian equivalents (Gilroy, 1987). There however is a real danger in identifying transatlantic music with hybridity. It sets up an ideal of integration that all minorities, regardless of their distinctive character and aspirations, are expected to, indeed pressured to conform to. Such pressure may usually take the form of peer conformity, media and fashion messages, but can also be a matter of policy, as in Berlin, when social and youth workers are employed to teach Turks rap in the hope that they may become more like American and British blacks. It is important that hybridity or youth is not assumed to produce just one kind of cultural formation. The current popularity of the new Islamic identities among the young is indicated by the many Muslim student societies found in British universities and colleges. Different minorities will wish to and come to relate to the mainstream in their own way, and while some ways may prove more prevalent than others, an approach characteristic of one group should not be elevated to a paradigmatic status.

Nor should we assume that groups which are most culturally distinct or culturally conservative are least likely to feel British and vice-versa. It has already been mentioned that the Caribbeans, of all non-whites the culturally and socially closest to the white British, had the highest proportion who dismissed identification with Britishness - more than the Pakistanis and the Bangladeshis, the most culturally conservative and separate of these groups. This certainly should not be taken to imply that the cultural conservatism consists in simply wanting to be left alone as a community and not making political demands upon the public space. For example, half of all Muslims wanted state funding for Muslim schools. The political demands of Muslims such as these are not akin to conscientious objections, to principled exemptions from civic obligations, but - akin to other movements for political multiculturalism - for some small degree of 'Islamicisation' of the civic. Not for getting the state out of the sphere of cultural identities, but for an inclusion of Muslims into the sphere of state-supported culture.

My emphasis that different minorities will and should be allowed to relate to British society in their own way, to connect to different parts of society, to make their own linkages and syntheses is not to deny that the black achievement in youth music, and indeed youth and popular culture in general, including sport, is something quite extraordinary. A group that comprises less than 2 per cent of the population has, both in terms of quantity and quality, established itself as a leading-edge presence in urban youth culture in the face of racism, social deprivation and relative exclusion from positions of power and wealth. From being pariahs many black people have become objects of desire, with many young whites envying and imitating their 'style' (cf. Hall in Gates, 1997, p. 196). It is worth emphasising that this black British cultural success, like some other aspects of Caribbean settlement in Britain, has been highly inclusive. For while born of an assertiveness and a search for dignity, and while sometimes oppositional, it has also been a movement of integration, of wanting to be included into the British mainstream, of sharing and mutual respect (Phillips and Phillips, 1998, and Part 4 of the BBC television series, *Windrush*, to which this book is an accompaniment). It has, inevitably, been largely a black-white relationship but some young Asians and others have been drawn into it too. Black music, then, has indeed played an important role in the development of contemporary British multiculturalism, but it is not the whole picture. Consider, for example, some of the larger sources of the multicultural character of London.

An Open and Plural Britain

Over one and a half million of London's population of seven million are not white, easily the largest single presence of non-whites in Europe, and forming nearly a quarter of the city. Additionally, about 10 per cent of the whites are not born in England, and there are communities of over 10,000 from thirty-four countries, including about a quarter of a million from Ireland (Storkey, 1997). London is a leading centre of world communications, finance, trade and tourism, all these flows contributing to its cosmopolitan character and further reinforcing it, as business and tourism is attracted to London by its distinctive multicultural character and its ability to cater to diverse groups.

Among the many factors that could be cited to explain these features of London, let me just emphasise one factor that does not focus on ethnic minority groups but contrasts the kind of openness found in Britain with the kind of openness found in continental Northern Europe. Northern Europe has come to develop the most extensive and generous form of the welfare state and a related political culture has played a major role in defusing the nationalistic conflicts within Europe of the early last century. Yet multicultural thinking, including amongst the progressive opinion, is weak. The Northern European city in which multiculturalism is most a matter of debate and fact is surely Berlin, the city in the region which has a marked recent American and British influence. The history of Northern Europe has been a regional one and so its contemporary political openness is focused on the constituent parts of the region. In contrast, Britain has had an oceanic or maritime history that has brought it into contact, for good or for ill, with many parts of the world. The Empire brought the British into contact with a degree of cultural hetrogeneity not experienced by Northern Europeans. French history does have parallels with the British, though the comparison only highlights that both in imperial and contemporary settings the French are less tolerant of cultural plurality than the British. It is these different histories of contacts and tolerance that is part of the explanation of why today it is the case that London is not simply an English or a British or even an European city, but a world city. And why a characteristic of British culture, despite its self-image of insularity, is the readiness to borrow and mix ideas and influences, as supremely exemplified in the English language.

This has particular relevance to Britain's relations with its European neighbours and to European political integration. It is often said that Europeanism and multiculturalism are contemporary developments out of a common politics. Now, there may be some people in Britain who are equally enthusiastic about both developments but this is not generally true in Europe as a whole.[2] For Britons and mainland Europeans are open to outsiders in different ways. Europeans have sought to put the excesses of nationalism behind them by seeking rapprochement with their neighbours but see no inconsistency in requiring cultural assimilation from non-European origin migrants. The British, especially the English, are less open to their European neighbours but are less hostile than most Europeans to multiculturalism and to international exchange. This I think gives Britain and especially British multiculturalists a 'mission' in Europe, that is to make Europe more open to the world and to multicultural situations, perhaps to be a bridge between Europeans and non-Europeans.

Conclusion

While there is, then, much empirical support for those theorists who have emphasised the fluid and hybridic nature of contemporary post-immigration ethnicities in Britain, Stuart Hall's suggestion that groups are so internally complex that they have become 'necessary fictions' (Hall, 1987, p. 45; 1992, p. 254) is much exaggerated. Moreover, the theoretical neglect of the role of religion reflects a bias of theorists of 'difference' that should be urgently remedied. British race theorists had assumed that there was a deep racial/colour divide. Contemporary developments suggest that ethno-religious divisions will prove more persistent.

The new emphasis on British mixedness, on ethnic hybridity, however, is important. For it helps to highlight that ethnicity is very different from nationalism - a fact that is sometimes obscured when we talk about 'minorities'. Hybridity is clearly not a sub-state nationality (in the way of Scottishness or Catalan), it is a form of complex Britishness. This is particularly worth emphasising because in Britain there are people who want not just to be black or Indian in Britain, but positively want to be black British or British Indians (Hall, 1998; Jacobson, 1997). They are less seeking civic rights against a hegemonic nationality than attempting to politically negotiate a place in an all-inclusive nationality. The contrast between ethnicity and nationality is politically important. Right-wing commentators used to worry about the threat that Commonwealth migrants and their descendants posed to Britishness. It is clear now that many in

---

[2] Indeed, even in Britain, the career of Roy Jenkins, the Home Secretary who led the way on racial equality and went on to become the Head of the European Commission, suggests that the more deeply involved in European politics one becomes, the less sympathy one has for British multiculturalism.

these ethnic minority groups think of Britain, appropriately reimagined and restructured, as a unifying identity. It is in fact those groups that have a national-territorial base in the British Isles and a historical grievance with the British state who today most shrink from the label 'British'. While Pakistanis in Bradford have been coming to an understanding of themselves as British, it is the Scots and the Irish - both within and outside their territorial nations - that are in denial about being British, who see one national identity as incompatible with another.[3]

In Britain at the moment a unitary British identity no longer looks feasible. This is not a cause for panic. For, contrary to what Enoch Powell and some radical anti-racists predicted, there is a desire for a hyphenated Britishness amongst 'immigrants' and their descendants. At the same time a new non-right wing discourse of Britishness led by Tony Blair has recently emerged. These two developments can be brought together. Each development is somewhat embryonic, and certainly multiculturalism, which so far has been largely a social, a bottom-up movement, requires greater mainstream political commitment and leadership than it has received hitherto. The change in attitudes that is required amongst the white British is a real political challenge. Equally important is the right kind of multiculturalism: a multicultural Britishness that is sensitive to ethnic difference and incorporates a respect for persons as individuals and for the collectivities that people have a sense of belonging to. That means a multiculturalism that is happy with hybridity but has space for religious identities. Both hybridity and ethno-religious communities have legitimate claims to be accommodated in political multiculturalism; they should not be pitted against each other in an either/or fashion as is done all too frequently by the celebrators of British Asian hybridity (e.g., Rushdie, 1991; Kureshi, 1995) and by some liberal political philosophers (e.g., Waldron, 1992). Hanif Kureshi in his novel, *The Black Album*, suggests that British Asian youth is being pulled by 'sex, drugs and rock an' roll', on the one hand, and by communal religious solidarity on the other hand. It is fascinating that the incompatible but separately attractive polarities identified by Kureshi amongst Asians resonate with Prime Minister Tony Blair's thinking about Britain. On the one hand, there is a celebration of stylish, creative hedonism (London as a world leader in *couture*, pop music, restaurants, night clubs and so on), on the other hand there is a passionate plea to renew the ethical springs of community and to put duty and high-minded responsibility back into citizenship. The making of British Asian

---

[3] Interestingly, non-whites in Scotland and Wales do often have a sense of identification with these nations (Saeed et al., 1996) but non-whites in Britain rarely think of themselves as Europeans (Runnymede Trust, 1998).

identities thus, no less than the black culture that is already so prominent, has the potential to influence and be shaped by the remaking of Britishness.

References

Baldwin-Edwards, M. and M. A. Schain (eds), (1994), *'The Politics of Immigration in Western Europe'*, West European Politics, 17(2), special issue.

Ballard, R. (1990), 'Migration and kinship: the differential effect of marriage rules on the process of Punjabi migration to Britain', in C. Clarke, C. Peach and S. Vertovec (eds), *South Asians Overseas*, Cambridge University Press.

Baumann, G. (1990), 'The re-invention of *bhangra*: social change and aesthetic shifts in a Punjabi music in Britain', *The World of Music*, 2, Berlin.

Centre for Contemporary Cultural Studies (CCCS) (1982), *The Empire Strikes Back: Race and racism in 70s Britain,* Hutchinson.

Donald J. and A. Rattansi (eds), (1992), *'Race', Culture and Difference,* Sage, London.

Gates Jnr., H. L. (1997), 'Black London', *New Yorker*, 28 April-5 May.

Gilroy, P. (1992), 'The End of Anti-Racism', in Donald and Rattansi *op.cit.*

Hall, S. (1987), 'Minimal Selves', in L. Appiganesi (ed.) *The Real Me: The Question of Identity and Postmodernism*, London, Institute of Contemporary Arts.

Hall, S. (1992), 'New Ethnicities' in Donald and Rattansi *op.cit.*

Hall, S. (1998), 'Aspiration and Attitude ... Reflections on Black Britain in the Nineties', *New Formations*, Frontlines/Backyards Special Issue, 33, Spring.

Kureshi, H. (1995), *The Black Album* Faber.

Leonard, M. (1997), *Britain TM: Renewing Our Identity*, Demos.

Modood, T. (1990), 'British Asian Muslims and the Rushdie affair', *Political Quarterly*, Vol. 61(2), pp. 143-60; reproduced in Donald and Rattansi (eds), pp. 260-67.

Modood, T. (1992), *Not Easy Being British: Colour, Culture and Citizenship,* Runnymede Trust and Trentham Books.

Modood, T. (1994), 'Political blackness and British Asians', *Sociology*, vol. 28(3).

Modood, T., Beishon, S. and Virdee, S. (1994), *Changing Ethnic Identities*, London, Policy Studies Institute.

Modood, T., R. Berthoud, J. Lakey, J. Nazroo, P. Smith, S. Virdee and S. Beishon et al (1997), *Britain's Ethnic Minorities: Diversity and Disadvantage*, London, Policy Studies Institute.

Phillips, M and Phillips, T (1998), *Windrush: The Irresistible Rise of Multicultural Britain*, London.

Runnymede Trust, in partnership with the Commission for Racial Equality (1998), *Young People in the UK: Attitudes and Opinions on Europe, Europeans and the European Union*, London.

Rushdie, S. (1991), 'In Good Faith', in S. Rushdie, *Imaginary Homelands*, London.

Saeed, A., N. Blain and D. Forbes (1996), 'Scottish National Identity: its relevance to different ethnic groups', *British Psychological Society Annual Conference*, University of Strathclyde.

Storkey, M., J. Maguire and R. Lewis R (1997), *Cosmopolitan London: Past, Present and Future*, London Research Centre.

Waldron, J. (1992), 'Minority Cultures and The Cosmopolitan Alternative', *University of Michigan Journal of Law Reform*, 25(3+4).

Werbner, P. and T. Modood, (eds), (1997), *Debating Cultural Hybridity: Multi-Cultural Identities and the Politics of Anti-Racism*, Zed Books, London.

Young I. M. (1990), *Justice and the Politics of Difference*, Princeton University Press, Princeton.
Younge, G. (1995), 'Black in Britain: Where Are We Now?', *The Guardian*, 20 March.

Chapter 6

Religious Traditionality in Multicultural Europe

Ursula Apitzsch

Introduction

The experiences of forced as well as voluntary migration in Europe tell us that the migrants' search for social and cultural belonging in the receiving society is connected with biographical work performed in order to reconstruct a symbolic space of traditionality which creates the possibility of defining one's own position in the new society. The ability of subjects to elaborate this type of biographical knowledge seems to be becoming more and more a basis of mutual recognition in European multicultural societies, with their paradoxical concepts of declared religious secularism and simultaneous state recognition of Christian privileges. In my paper I firstly want to briefly reconstruct some difficulties in the arguments put forward up to now on multiculturalism in European nation states. Secondly, I want to discuss the meaning of traditionality in the light of Antonio Gramsci's arguments on folklore. Thirdly, I will discuss the meaning of religion in the European tradition of secularism and its consequences for multicultural Europe. In conclusion I want to present a new type of religious traditionality in migrant biographies in Europe, considered under the pressures of both integration and belonging. In each of these cases, 'biographical work' had to be activated by the subjects in order to overcome situations of crisis. In analysing this 'biographical work' one can identify types of traditionality representing both trajectory potentials and potential resources that can be used to control the dynamics of the crisis and to re-elaborate a biographical action scheme. It is my hypothesis that religious traditionality does not automatically lead to processes of ethnization but, on the contrary, potentially generates post-national, post-ethnic biographical reflexivity. New forms of individual autonomy can be reconstructed within processes of the biographical construction of self-esteem as elements of emerging new social practice.

1 The Meaning of Tradition in Multicultural Societies of Europe

The concept and the politics of the 'multicultural society' in European countries within the three last decades have contained a strange mixture of tendencies that have been both friendly and hostile towards migrant traditions. It has involved the basic acceptance of the 'inside views' of the respective ethnic groups, on the one hand, while at the same time it affords European societies a variety of cultures 'free of charge', so to speak, without their having to concern themselves either with the problems that gave rise to migration or with the consequences within the immigration societies as a whole. The symbolic representativeness of traditional cultures of origin within the diversity of immigrant cultures made it seem feasible to conceive of these 'ancestral' cultures as the real territory to which migrants can withdraw in both the economic and the mental sense. Awareness that such a multicultural model of society was essentially ambivalent did not develop until attention was drawn to the 'New Racism' debate in France. Only then was the contribution of social science to the creation of the model critically described as 'intellectual articulations of the segregation deception' (Balibar, 1989, p. 369) and the plea for each people to be allowed its own cultural peculiarities and each culture its own system of moral values and political traditions finally unmasked as involving essentially the same arguments as those used by the 'New Right' in France in exploiting the notion of 'cultural differences' to pursue its political objective of discrimination against migrants. In Germany, leading parties have only very recently started to consider their country as a justified and normal destination for immigrants.

The definitive features of the multicultural society - the acceptance of mere physical proximity and the emphasis on cultural differences - are quite obviously not in a simple way compatible with the principle of universalist morality as it has developed within the Enlightenment tradition in Europe. 'Right' (*Recht*) is either founded on universalist principles, or 'culture' has the last word, and - as Marx wrote in his critique of Hegel's 'Philosophy of Right' - the feudal serf who suffers under the knout must suppress a cry of rebellion, 'once the knout is time-honored, ancestral, and historical' (Marx, 1977, p. 132).

This critique of culturalist concepts points the way back to the 'constitutional patriotism' of the democratic social and legal order in the French revolutionary tradition as the sole foundation for a multicultural society which is also capable of intercultural discourse. But can such a synthesis of the general and the particular actually succeed without more precise knowledge of the relations between cultures in the immigration society? Does the French example, or the example of Great Britain, not show instead that granting civil rights to immigrants from former colonies is no protection against social exclusion and marginalization? As soon as nationality no longer functions as the criterion for exclusion, the ethnic and cultural dimension is constructed as the main determinant instead. Academic disciplines with a humanist ethos, such as pedagogy, have aided this process for years by offering their services as mediators between the supposedly 'indigenous' and the supposedly 'foreign'. The problematic nature of multicultural thinking thus seems to reside not only in its defining the main differences in society in cultural terms, but also in the fact that it is liable to underestimate those social forces in society that distinguish not only between 'different' cultures but also between the 'indigenous' and the 'foreign'. Such distinctions and demarcations also involve elements of domination, coercion and subordination, disguised behind the label of culture or 'ethnicity'. The famous study entitled 'The Empire strikes back', which was published by the Centre of Contemporary Cultural Studies (CCCS) in 1982, argued that coloured immigrants in particular were only able to form their so-called 'cultural identity' in a position of marginality, in other words in those sections of society that are excluded from positions of social power (CCCS, 1982).

The pluralist understanding of the 'many cultures' in society, which developed out of the protest against the ethnocentricity of western universalism, has led insidiously to paradoxical results with respect to the discussion of cultural traditions. Individual developments and crises of migrants not only of the first, but also of the second generation, were purposely explained in terms of the closed cultural context of the society of origin in order to arrive at a 'better understanding'. Especially in studies conducted in the fields of education, sociology and cultural anthropology, the society of origin was interpreted unquestioningly in the name of cultural identity as something 'immutable'. A contrast is thus constructed, creating two clinically separated worlds in which there is an opposition between each of their respective central components. Once this polarity has been established it will control subsequent perceptions, thus reinforcing the prejudice and vice versa. The migrant is locked within the ideological structure of his/her society of origin, while at the same time western values are assumed to be superior.

Existing approaches to multicultural policymaking, as could be observed in some German cities in recent years, seek to promote legal equality and rational discourse. But this does not do away with the problem that the debate on the multicultural society is barely able to include the question of societal sub- and superordination. As long as the population of rich, industrial countries continues to be underclassed by immigrants, the stress on cultural identity can have a certain functional utility, in the sense of subordination under the dominant culture.[1] The question of cultural relations cannot be discussed without referring it back to the question of hegemonial structures.

2 Migration and Culture: The Familiar From Afar and the Alien in Ourselves

Is it possible to learn from traditional cultures in a modern country? The most common opinion or concept regarding the diversity of cultures in modern democratic societies is based on pluralism: we owe equal respect to all cultures because we know (e.g. from anthropologists like Lévi-Strauss) that all human cultures have something important to say to all human beings. But this at once raises two questions: Are not there some cultures that have done much more for universal humankind than others? And are not there cultures undergoing phases of crisis and collapse? We may remember the famous sentence attributed to Saul Bellow, 'When the Zulus produce a Tolstoi we will read him'.

This sentence was considered by the Canadian philosopher Charles Taylor - defender of the 'Politics of Recognition' - to be 'a quintessential statement of European arrogance', regardless of whether or not it was Saul Bellow who actually made the statement (Taylor, 1992, p. 42). Bellow's or anyone else's error here would not have been an error in evaluation, 'but a

---

[1] A number of studies on this have been produced since the 1970s - the CCCS study in Great Britain mentioned above, as well as a series of American studies. Poor achievement in school, for example, can be due to other factors than those typically cited by way of explanation (loss of one's own culture, cultural differences, lack of resources in schools). In the USA, children from social minorities which had not been able to establish any links to structures of social power through the development of social networks developed low school achievement as a strategy of adaptation to the prevalence of discrimination and the barriers to success in working life and society generally in later adult life (Ogbu 1974).

denial of a fundamental principle', namely the 'acknowledgement of the equal value of all humans potentially' (Taylor, 1992, p. 42). For Taylor this is a fine example of what many critics of the universal idea of formal equal dignity call Western ethnocentrism. 'The claim is that the supposedly neutral set of difference-blind principles of the politics of equal dignity is in fact a reflection of the one hegemonic culture. As it turns out, then, only the minority or suppressed cultures are being forced to take alien form. Consequently, the supposedly fair and difference-blind society is not only inhuman (because suppressing identities) but also, in a subtle and unconscious way, itself highly discriminatory' (Taylor 1992, p. 43).

This sentence reminds one of Antonio Gramsci's critical conception of studies on traditional cultures which he elaborated in his Prison Notebooks. According to his analysis, so-called 'folklore research' cannot be conducted in isolation from 'official' world views in the dominant society.

His concept leads to an understanding of culture that is far removed from any ascriptive totalizing tendencies, on the one hand, or any 'atomistic' view of individuals, on the other. It seems appropriate to link it with the tradition of George Herbert Mead's symbolic interactionism, or John Dewey's critical pragmatism (for the pragmatist view of multiculturalism see Amy Gutmann 1992, 7).

What Gramsci's analysis has in common with the concept of recognition in a deliberative democracy is the fact that he does not reduce the social problems associated with differing degrees of modernity to the relationship between native people and foreigners, but defines these differences as a problem of modern consciousness generally. Modern consciousness is characterised for him by the fact that only through traditionality, in often 'folkloristic' distortions, is it able to retain certain moments of its rural pre-history and the counter-knowledge rooted in and dominated by the process of modernisation. The relationship of such sedimented collective experience to industrial society is by no means identical to the relationship between traditional and modern societies; this difference in degree of modernity is rather a crucial defining aspect of modern society itself.

Folklore should ... be studied as a 'conception of the world and life' implicit to a large extent in determinate (in time and space) strata of society and in opposition (also for the most part implicit, mechanical and objective) to 'official' conceptions of the world (or in a broader sense, the conceptions of the cultured parts of historically determinate societies) that have succeeded one another in the historical process. (Hence the strict relationship between folklore and 'common sense', which is philosophical folklore.) This conception of the world is not elaborated and systematic because, by definition, the people (the sum total of the instrumental and subaltern classes of every form of society that has so far existed) cannot possess conceptions which are elaborated, systematic and politically organised and centralised in their albeit contradictory development. It is, rather, many-sided - not only because it includes different and juxtaposed elements, but also because it is stratified, from the more crude to the less crude - if, indeed, one should not speak of a confused agglomerate of fragments of all the conceptions of the world and of life that have succeeded one another in history. In fact, it is only folklore that one finds surviving evidence, adulterated and mutilated, of the majority of these conceptions. Philosophy and modern science are also constantly contributing new elements to 'modern folklore' in that certain opinions and scientific notions, removed from their context and more or less distorted, constantly fall within the popular domain and are 'inserted' into the mosaic of tradition (Gramsci, 1988, pp. 360, 361).

This permits us to base our analysis not only on *one* but on *many* cultures within a given national society. Important elements of the 'pre-history of the present' are *not* eliminated within the dominant culture. 'Different cultures live side-by-side within the same society, and the locations of identity are the locations where there is mutual recognition of the social groups' (Di Carlo, 1986, pp. 28f.). At the same time, however, it is clear that the 'many cultures' cannot be separated from the context that binds them to the structures of domination in both the country of origin and the country to which they emigrate. The concept of 'national culture' takes effect at this point, as a hegemonial framework in which dominated and subordinate cultures encounter each other (Gramsci, 1977, pp. 1660f.).

Thus it is possible to recognize the gesture of submission that these elements entail, but also to identify the universal or the global in the particular, in the subaltern, in the 'traditional'.

3 The European Concept of Secularism and 'Declared' Religion

Can the discourse on multicultural tolerance be connected in a justified way with the discourse on religious tolerance? The discourse on religion is regarded by its participants and by the concession of constitutional rights as a discourse on truth, while the discourse on culture may also be described as a discourse on affinity and prejudice - as the Italian philosopher Norberto Bobbio has remarked (Bobbio, 1986). Nevertheless, in the traditions of European Enlightenment and Idealism, religion has already lost its dignity as a form of truth that might be respected from a philosophical perspective. For Hegel the true religion was no longer the ethical description of the good life, and holiness was no longer connected with sacred cultural objects. The social realization of a good life for the citizens was to be expected from the 'ethical state', while the discourse on truth was restricted to philosophy itself. With Napoléon Bonaparte's secularization, formerly holy Christian objects became part of a universal art market. At the same time, however, the Christian churches were recognized as social institutions and privileged subjects of public law. In this way, through secularization again - as it had already been carried out in the 16th century in England and in 1648 in the act of the so-called 'Westfälischer Friede' of Münster and Osnabrück after the great European religious wars - the role of the churches in the public sphere did not diminish but actually increased. Religion was no longer a matter of objective or subjective truth but just 'declared religion', a matter of bargaining and contracting between state and religious institutions with juridical consequences for the - voluntary or non-voluntary - declared members of the churches. Today we have to ask whether official religion may be treated as an object of the 'politics of recognition', which Charles Taylor defined as the adequate politics of a multicultural society. On the one hand, we cannot respect a religion that we regard as oppressive but that still has a privileged public status, and on the other hand we cannot critically discuss a religious individual or group in order to change dogmas and attitudes.

What is interesting, however, is that the Christian religion is, under the conditions of secularization, reforming itself from inside. The separation of the religious and the cultural sphere, mainly in Protestant churches, allows a critique of practices that are not compatible with fundamental human rights such as individual freedom and integrity. At the same time secularization connected with the public role of the churches sees as its consequence the predominance of the male-dominated reformulation of the 'Great tradition' - the dogmatic and political sphere of religions - and the continuous dissolution of what researchers like Mary Douglas and Barbara Myerhoff have called the 'Little Tradition' or the 'Domestic Religion'.

'Domestic Religion' is the specific way in which religion has been passed on from generation to generation by families - and mainly the female members of families - as an everyday practice. In her book 'Number Our Days' Barbara Myerhoff has documented as a study on 'domestic religion' the everyday life of Jewish survivors of the Holocaust in a center for elderly people in California (Myerhoff, 1980). Referring to Robert Redfield's distinction between Little and Great Traditions she defines the 'domestic religion' of 'Yiddishkeit' as a form of religious life that can be found predominantly in the culture of women at a specific distance from the Great Tradition.

'Robert Redfield's distinction between Little and Great Traditions points to a similar interpretation. The latter, referring to the abstract, eternal verities of a culture, are usually controlled by literati from a distance, interpreted and inforced by official institutions. The Little Tradition, in contrast, is a local, folk expression of a group's beliefs; unsystematized, not elaborately idealized, it is an oral tradition practised constantly and often unconsciously by ordinary people without external enforcement or interference. Domestic Religion, Little Tradition - whatever term one prefers - have in common the potential of providing a sacredness that issues from its being thoroughly embedded in a culture' (Myerhoff, 1980, pp. 256f.).

The 'Little Tradition' and its significance for the creation of symbolic spheres in everyday life has never been the object of special attention by the liberal critique of religion. Facing migration processes, however, we have to ask whether not only the male-dominated 'Great Tradition' of religion but also the integrity of a special form of religious socialization within the family has to be respected. This question may be connected with Will Kymlicka's claims for the recognition of the cultural aspect of the integrity of each and any person in a multicultural society (Kymlicka, 1995). The European tradition of enlightenment and secularism, however, creates enormous difficulties for anyone wishing to endorse this view. Liberals may accept churches, altars, processions and many other forms of territorial claims in the name of religious freedom (Vianello and Caramazza, 1998, pp. 56ff.), but they mostly reject traditional forms of life in modern societies which are merely understood as forms of underdevelopment and lack of modernity (Apitzsch, 1999).

Religious freedom in the understanding of European secularism is connected to state recognition of religious institutions, not to the recognition of a specific religious way of life. The separation of religion and culture leads to a gender-blind negation of symbolic ways of the constitution of belonging. The liberal discussion on tolerance has been simplified by only emphasizing personal integrity as setting the limits of religious freedom. This is just a claim that has to be taken for granted in a democratic society, where the equal treatment of diverse cultural groups within the society and personal freedom within a group are the clear consequences of respect for the declaration of human rights (Kymlicka, 1997). Therefore it is of course impossible within liberal traditions to justify the oppression of women, for example in the name of any religious tradition. European secularism, however, mostly goes far beyond this critique and discriminates against forms of religious everyday-life practice such as Muslim practices of celebrating, praying and dressing. I suppose that it is this context blindness in liberal theory that leads Bhikhu Parekh to his rethinking of multiculturalism in contemporary liberal responses to diversity. Bhikhu Parekh, however, leads the discussion back to the dichotomy between a desirable practice 'in general' and the society's 'operative public values' (Parekh, 2000, p. 267), and this means for me back to the endless discussions between universalist and relativist positions. Instead, I would propose to confront operative values and their reflexive reconstruction by different social subjects.

In the following, I want to present some examples of traditionality in diverse religious contexts that show how domestic religion may in a very reflexive way create a symbolic sphere of belonging by criticizing the 'Great Tradition' in a family-centered and gendered perspective.

4 New Forms of 'Domestic Religion' as a Challenge for 'Secular' Europe

4.1 The 'New Shtetl' in Antwerp

Lena Inowlocki studied for several years the process of tradition-building in European Jewish communities after the Holocaust. She found an astonishing process of re-constructing traditional Jewish life in the course and by the mediation of three generations (Inowlocki, 1993). The first generation, survivors of the Nazi concentration camps, had suffered a total interruption of Jewish traditions and were mostly unable to live 'domestic religion'. The second generation, born immediately after the war as displaced persons, tried to rebuild their own Jewish educational institutions in order to create a new community life. The third generation lived within these institutions and at the same time created a new traditional Jewish life - which seems to be a contradiction in itself. This third generation is creating a new symbolic sphere of Jewishness, which means for their parents and grandparents that it made sense to survive the Holocaust. However, the members of the second generation often speak about 'brainwashing' when they try to describe what has happened to their children and what they themselves had wanted to develop for their children. Neither the second nor the third generation lives a life outside of the modern secular world. What they want to establish is a background of 'thinking as usual' (in the sense in which Alfred Schütz introduced this term into sociological theorizing) for their very special group which would enable them to start with a discourse between the three generations (Schütz, 1962).

4.2 The New Type of the Intellectual Muslim Girl

In German universities we often meet female Muslim students wearing impressive big scarves, the 'türban', which cover not only their hair but also part of their foreheads. Mostly they are daughters of Turkish immigrants from secular families who came twenty or thirty years ago. Their scarf is not their grandmother's rural headgear but a symbol of belonging in the modern receiving society. In their new dress the girls feel themselves respected by their own community as well as by the receiving society which - despite acts of discrimination - often regards them as experts in the culture attributed to them. They discover that they are becoming to be recognized as 'bargaining partners' between their own group and the receiving society. They finally feel that they have found their 'style of life'.[2] They are creating their own traditional female style while choosing consciously and individually which Imam and which religious school they want to follow. 'Great tradition' for them has become a sort of 'bricolage'. Sigrid Nökel in her study on the daughters of guest workers and Islam gives empirical examples of this new 'style of life' being regarded as a form of 'nobilitation' of a person (Nökel, 2002).

4.3 Assyrian Religious Tradition and Beyond

In her essay on 'Bread, Book and Monument. Ethnic Memory and Beyond' Aleksandra Alund tells us about the 20 year-old student Hanna. Hanna studies international political science and the rights of minority peoples at a Swedish university. Her parents came from Turkey to Sweden as migrant workers when she was a very young girl. They are Assyrians, whose ancestors are said to have lived in the region of the present south of Turkey for 2000 years with their own Christian church and their own Assyrian language. This language has been conserved by the study of the

---

[2] I refer here to a lecture by Yasemin Karakaşoğlu on 'Zwischen Moscheeverein und Universität' [Between mosque and university], organized by the Landeszentrale für Politische Bildung in Kiel on November 2, 1996. See also Karakaşoğlu, 1999.

holy texts and everyday communication in Turkey as well as in the diaspora.

Hanna wants to feel 'at home' in Swedish society, and therefore she has to do biographical work which concerns her family's tradition. It is the Swedish receiving society that made it possible for Hanna to learn the Assyrian language and to know more about her Assyrian Christian religion. At the same time she recognizes the decline of tradition in her own community, and she sharply criticizes this.

> The decline of tradition means that good customs are getting weaker and bad ones stronger. Marrying the young people off seems more important than what one has taught them. They hold on hard, in the wrong way, and they haven't really understood that they're in Sweden. ... They keep their children away from Swedish friends. Their world is authoritarian and hierarchical. Children and parents can't talk with each other in a reciprocal fashion. Everything is decided from above and down. ... I don't mean that they should forget about food or about weddings. But you don't do your daughter a favour by marrying her off too early. ... Those who've married early and had kids are considered Assyrian – wholly and completely. Just because they've done that. In fact, however, they disappear. ... I want my younger siblings to grow up without feeling divided or being forced into paralyzing choices. That's why I'm needed at home. They must become both Assyrians and Swedes. If they don't learn Assyrian, they won't learn Swedish either (Alund, 1997, p. 150).

Why is it so important for Hanna to be considered as a member of the Assyrian community? Why is she fighting so hard against what she calls the 'decline of tradition'? Hanna explains her concept of an 'ingrained tradition', which makes it possible for her to feel a full member of Swedish society. On the other hand, Hanna explains that Assyrian tradition outside Swedish society would never have had the same importance for her that it has today.

> In Turkey I wouldn't feel such responsibility and concern. Here in Sweden there are many opportunities, and I demand my right to become myself, with all that that means. In Turkey, others would take the responsibility, not me (Alund 1997, p. 148).

Here Hanna makes it clear that the new importance of the old tradition has to do with her own role in Sweden, with the 'many possibilities' offered by this country. Her tradition has become something like a resource to help her find her place within Swedish society.

Without Sweden I would never had been educated, or been able to know so
much or to find myself. In Turkey I wouldn't have cared about Assyrian things.
There I would have lived like everyone else. But here I have become myself
(Alund, ibid., p.148)

It seems as if her own tradition provides Hanna with something like the
'transformation formula' (as Alfred Schütz wrote in his famous essay on
The Stranger, Schütz, 1972, p. 62) which can turn new experiences in the
country of assumption into habitual knowledge and traditional routine. But
the formula would also work for Hanna in the opposite direction: it would
turn troubled experiences of 'authoritarian' and 'hierarchical' ways of
living in her traditional community, the 'ghosts of tradition' (Alund, 1997,
p. 149), into alternative ways of understanding and recognition.

The others can't read and write our language. My education means I must help
the others, so that they, too, can understand how they are Assyrians (Alund,
1997, p. 149).

The reconstruction of Hanna's biography shows that tradition is neither
something which is essentially given, nor accidental biographical
patchwork. Traditionality as the reconstruction of a symbolic space of
tradition in everyday life is not necessarily restricted to the belief in a
common ethnic origin (as Max Weber defined ethnicity). Instead, it
reveals the possibility of common resources of meaning constructed by
biographical work.

5 Some Conclusions

In the three examples of religious traditionality in Europe presented in the
context of displacement and migration, biographical work does not mean
idiosyncratic 'identity history' in the way which has been criticized by
Eric Hobsbawm (1998). It seems to be, instead, the discovery of belonging
in the context of the framing conditions of the receiving country. This
reflexive cultural creativity, however, creates new problems in the
multicultural societies of the new Europe.

As I mentioned above, Christian religions in Europe after their forced
'secularization' have rarely been nourished by group traditions or hybrid
new cultural forms, but they survived as religious forms with a 'declared'
and privileged official status which became more and more separated from
religious and everyday life practice. Against this background secularism
does not always guarantee tolerance, but it may also develop into

something like an everyday-life religion forming the prejudice of superiority in relation to the so-called traditional religions of immigrant groups. We may speak here about the 'dialectics of enlightenment', which Adorno and Horkheimer discovered in relation to technological development and the culture industry.

What seems remarkable in this context is the fact that the religious development of immigrant groups is also affected by these dialectics of the modernization process. Tariq Modood and others show in a survey on Britain's ethnic minorities that, while minorities like Moslem and Hindu groups as a whole still show a much higher level of religious adherence than native British groups, the second and third generations have begun to assimilate to the British secular model of 'declared' religiosity. While the young people are increasingly abandoning prayers at home and in the mosque or temple, they are starting to claim an official status and public rights for their declared religious group in the state and in civil society in order to get equal rights to Christian churches (Modood, 1997). In Germany, too, members of the Turkish communities have started to claim an official status in public life.

It seems to me that the rising importance of religious traditionality in Europe has not been imported only from outside. Rather, and on the contrary, the dialectic of the European model of secularization may itself give birth to these new developments. European societies have to decide whether to abolish the non-secular official status of 'declared' religions or to offer an official status also to the many other forms of religious belonging in immigrant societies.

References

Alund, A. (1997), 'Book, Bread and Monument. Continuity and Change Through Ethnic Memory and Beyond', *Innovation*, Vol. 10(2), pp. 145-60.

Apitzsch, U. (1993), 'Gramsci and the Current Debate on Multicultural Education', *Studies in the Education of Adults*, Vol. 25(2), October 1993, pp. 136-45.

Apitzsch, U. (1999), *Migration und Traditionsbildung*, Opladen/Wiesbaden.

Arendt, H. (1990), *Eichmann in Jerusalem*, Leipzig.

Balibar, E. (1989), 'Gibt es einen "Neo-Rassismus"?' *Das Argument* 175.

Bobbio, N. (1986), 'Le ragioni della tolleranza', in C. Boni (ed.), *L'intolleranza: uguali e diversi nella storia*, Bologna, pp. 243-57.

Bourdieu, P. (1979), *Entwurf einer Theorie der Praxis*, Frankfurt (Orig. ed.: Esquisse d'une théorie de la Pratique, précédé de trois études d'ethnologie kabyle, Geneva 1972).

Bredella, L. (1992), 'Towards a Pedagogy of Intercultural Understanding', *American Studies*, Vol. 37(4), pp. 559-94.

Bubner, R. (1983), 'Ethnologie und Hermeneutik', in G. Baer and P. Centlivres (eds): *Ethnologie im Dialog*, Fribourg, pp.183-196.

CCCS (eds.) (1982): *The Empire Strikes Back*, Birmingham.

Di Carlo, A. & S., (1986), *I luoghi dell'identità*, Milano.

Di Carlo, S. (1987), 'Die Kultur der Emigration in Europa', in Apitzsch et al. (eds): *Emigration und kulturelle Identität*, Frankfurt/Main, pp. 19-25.

Finkielkraut, A. (1989), *Die Niederlage des Denkens*, Reinbek.

Gramsci, A. (1977), *Quaderni del carcere*, ed. V.Gerratana, 4 vols., Torino.

Gramsci, A. (1988), *Gramsci Reader*, ed. D. Forgacs, London.

Gutmann, A. (ed.), (1992), 'Multiculturalism and "The Politics of Recognition"' (Introduction), Princeton.

Habermas, J. (1993), 'Anerkennungskämpfe im demokratischen Rechtsstaat', in: C. Taylor and A. Gutmann (eds), *Multikulturalismus und die Politik der Anerkennung*, Frankfurt/M.

Hobsbawm, E.J. (1998), 'Identity History is not enough', in *On History*, London, pp. 351-66.

Inowlocki, L. (1993), 'Grandmothers, Mothers, and Daughters'. Intergenerational Transmission in Displaced Families in Three Jewish Communities, *International Yearbook of Oral History and Life Stories*, Vol.II, New York, pp. 139-53.

Karakaşoglou-Aydin, Y. (1999), *Muslimische Religiosität und Erziehungsvorstellungen*, Frankfurt/Main.

Karakaşoglou-Aydin, Y. (2000), 'Studentinnen türkischer Herkunft an deutschen Universitäten unter besonderer Berücksichtigung der Studierenden pädagogischer Fächer' in: Attia, I. und H. Marburger (eds): *Alltag und Lebenswelten von Migrantenjugendlichen*, Frankfurt/Main, pp. 101-26.

Kristeva, J. (1990), *Fremde sind wir uns selbst*, Frankfurt/M.

Kymlicka, W. (1995), *The Politics of Multiculturalism – A Liberal Theory of Minority Rights*, Oxford.

Kymlicka, W. (1997), *States, Nations and Cultures*, Assen.

Leggewie, C. (1990), *Multi Kulti*, Berlin.

Lyotard, J.F. (1988), *The Different: Phrases in Dispute*, Manchester.

Marx, K. (1977), 'A Contribution to the Critique of Hegel's "Philosophy of Right"', Introduction, in K. Marx, *Critique of Hegel's 'Philosophy of Right'*, Cambridge.

Modood, T. et al. (1997), *Britain's Ethnic Minorities: Diversity and Disadvantage*, London.

Myerhoff, B. (1980), *Number Our Days. A Triumph of Continuity and Culture among Jewish Old People in an Urban Ghetto*, New York.

Nökel, S. (2002), *Die Töchter der Gastarbeiter und der Islam*, Bielefeld.

Ogbu, J.U. (1974), *The Next Generation: An Ethnography of Education in an Urban Neighbourhood*, New York.

Parekh, B. (2000), *Rethinking Multiculturalism. Cultural Diversity and Political Theory*, Basingstoke, London, p 267.

Schütz, A. (1962), 'Collected Papers', in 'The Problem of Social Reality', The Hague.

Schütz, A. (1972), *Gesammelte Aufsätze*, vol. 2, Den Haag.

Taylor, C. (1992), 'The Politics of Recognition', in Gutmann, A. (ed.), pp. 25-73.

Taylor, C. and A.. Gutmann (eds) (1993), Multikulturalismus und die Politik der Anerkennung. Frankfurt/M.

Vianello, M. and E. Caramazza (1998), *Donne e metamorfosi della politica. Verso una società post-maschilista*, Rom.

Walzer, M. (1992), 'Comment', in Gutmann, A. (ed.), pp. 99-103.

PART II
THE SELF-LOCALIZATION OF MIGRANTS

Chapter 7

Custom Tailored Islam?
Second Generation Female Students of Turko-Muslim Origin in Germany and Their Concept of Religiousness in the Light of Modernity and Education

Yasemin Karakaşoğlu

Introduction

This paper will present some observations on changing religious attitudes of young Turkish women with a Muslim family background. To some extent, young female Muslims of the second migrant generation apparently redefine an ethno-religious identity in a non-Muslim society vis-à -vis both the majority's concept of secularism and their parents' traditionalist Muslim beliefs. This process inevitably affects their views towards integration in the majority environment. A substantial part of the discussion will be devoted to individuals who, while adhering to Muslim orthodoxy, strive for increased visibility and recognition as an integral part of Germany's public life. I will, however, also touch upon similarities and differences between Alevi and Sunni female students, as they represent two different strands of ethno-religious orientations from Anatolia.[1] The former consider themselves representatives of a truly modern version of Islam which does not require any change to blend with western life-style.[2] The

---

[1] The Alevi can be described as a heterodox Islamic minority from Turkey, with strong Shi'i influence on the one hand, and non-Muslim Anatolian religious traditions on the other. Strong emphasis is laid on the esoteric meaning of the faith. Alevis feel themselves freed from observance of the formal religious laws and rites. The group includes 15 million Turkish and Kurdish-speaking members, i.e. approximately 20% of the citizens in Turkey and of the migrants in Germany with Turkish/Kurdish background (for further information see Kehl-Bodrogi 1988 and 2000).

[2] Kehl-Bodrogi characterizes this as 'the new self-image of the Alevis, which represents a universally valid and modern form of faith' (Kehl-Bodrogi, 2000, p. 23).

latter try to combine modern life with the Muslim faith, some of them through the discovery of 'true Islam' – which they regard as compatible with modern life. Nevertheless, my focus will be on the veiled students, because their struggle for public recognition earned them symbol status with both the majority and the Muslim minority activists alike. To the former they are perfect examples of the Muslims' unwillingness to integrate, while the latter see them as heroines of emerging Muslim presence in a secular public environment.

Turkish Islam in Germany

It may be useful to precede my research findings with a brief account of Islam in Germany. Social circumstances have been rather favourable to the development of Islam and the articulation of Muslim demands. In the early days of labour migration there was scarcely any Muslim infrastructure in Germany. Issues of culture seemed irrelevant when in 1961 representatives of the German and Turkish governments negotiated the recruitment of cheap and willing *Gastarbeiter* for a prospering German industry. Prior to this official beginning of Turkish migration to Germany only a few hundred Muslims lived in Germany. Their number increased quickly. Today about 3 million Muslims are living in Germany. They account for 3.4 per cent of the country's population. Almost 80 per cent of them are migrants from Turkey, mostly descendants from the 'guest-workers'. Turks (including Kurds) make up the largest non-German community in Germany. This is why the presence and image of Islam in Germany can be classified as (a) strongly dominated by traditional Turkish or Kurdish folk culture, and (b) the religion of an urban subproletariat.[3] While more than 75 per cent of today's young migrant population from Turkey were born in Germany, the heritage of their families' status as former guest-workers more often than not still results in restricted access to education, political power, the labour market, housing, etc. Integration thus continues to be impeded. Evidence is readily provided by recent surveys done with Turks and other migrants in Germany.[4] Even 40 years after the first wave of labour migration from the Mediterranean to post-war Germany, issues like the construction of mosques (especially if a dome and minaret are planned), *helal* slaughtering, establishing Muslim schools and kindergartens, veiling

---

[3] Esser pointedly characterizes the Turks in Germany as an 'ethno-religious subnation' (Esser, 1998, p. 8).

[4] See for instance the surveys of the Friedrich-Ebert-Stiftung 1996, Diehl and Urbahn, 1998, 13. Shell-Jugendstudie 2000 or Waidacher, 2000.

of female students and Muslim teachers, or devoting university chairs to Muslim theology seldom fail to raise emotions in both public debates and legal proceedings.[5]

Contrary to what several sociologists and educators expected in the 1980s,[6] the significance of religion among the youth of Muslim origin in Germany has obviously not declined. The Muslims' call for public representation, their wish to be visible amidst the Christian majority, seems to become stronger as new generations of Muslims are growing up who include a rising minority of well educated elites. Rather than fading away through assimilation in the course of three generations, Islam as a factor of identity for Mediterranean Muslim migrants has developed new approaches. Today 80 per cent of the Turkish population, but only 45 per cent of the Germans, regard religion as being very important for a meaningful life. At the same time 90 per cent of both Muslim and non-Muslim believers consider religion as a matter of privacy that should not be interfered with by the state. It is particularly second-generation Turkish Muslims in Germany among whom Islam appears to loom large as a constituent of personal identity. These Muslims are, however, strongly inclined to develop their own approach to religion – an approach which is often quite different from the traditional popular Islam their parents adhered to. We can see a process of rising self-consciousness in every field of public life and the struggle for access to public space, articulated both individually and collectively. Recent surveys showed that young Muslims are more affiliated to their religion than their Christian peers in Germany (Shell Jugendstudie 2000; pp. 157-80; Waidacher, 2000, pp. 125-27).

Students – the New Muslim Elite

On the fringes of this framework a small but steadily rising group of socially successful Muslim Turks, these are the 24,000 university students of Turkish origin, have worked their way through the institutions and found access to higher education. They have begun to voice their own demands and the needs of their community in a more elaborate way than their parents and grandparents were able to. Some of them do so in the name of Islam. When veiled and unveiled Muslim students of this ethnic origin enrolled in German universities, the discussion of Islam's religious and

---

[5] For more details about the development of Turkish Islam in Germany see Karakaşoğlu, 1996.

[6] For an example of those predictions see Thomä-Venske, 1981, p. 130.

social impact gained fresh momentum and a different quality.[7] In search of a reason why the Turkish community seems to be less integrated than other migrant communities in Germany, Islam is often described as a segregative factor. The following chapters will outline some of these new Muslim actors' concepts of the relationship between religion and modernity, education and integration.

Findings have been taken from my own study of students of education. From 1996 to 1999 I conducted research on the religious orientations and educational attitudes of both Sunni and Alevi female students of education, mostly involved in teacher-training. My research was based on 26 in-depth interviews with ten veiled, nine unveiled and seven Alevi female students at universities in the Ruhr area.[8] My aim was to show that obvious attributes like outward appearance, the use of religious symbols, or formal affiliation with a certain denomination fail to reveal the actual diversity of religious orientations and practices. In fact religious orientations among Turkish student teachers, or, more generally, Turkish students of education, who have Sunni or Alevi backgrounds, appeared far from homogeneous. Personal views and attitudes rather than formal denominations provided the key concepts of classification. From Glock's five dimensions of religiousness (religious faith, religious knowledge, social consequences of religion, religious practice, religious experience, see Glock, 1969) four general types of religious disposition could be derived to categorise my sample: atheists, spiritualists, secularists and ritualists (see Table 6.1). Two of these include subtypes: the secularists can be divided into Alevi and Sunni secularists, while the ritualists seem to favour either a pragmatic or an idealistic outlook. Alevi students are either spiritualists or secularists. Sunni students were represented in all categories, with all the veiled ones, however, appearing among the ritualists.

---

[7] Esser (1998) stresses that the most important investment for access to key positions in the majority-society is investment into higher education. For an ethnic or religious minority higher education is the only means to gain access to the core culture of the majority-society, and thus to key positions (p. 10). From this point of view integration is seen as constituting an equal likelihood of benefitting from the opportunities which the society is offering to its members (Esser, 1998, p. 14).

[8] For more details of my research see Karakaşoğlu-Aydın, 2000.

Table 7.1.1 Types of religiousness occurring in the sample

	Atheists	Spiritualists	Alevi Secularists	Sunni Secularists	Pragmatic Ritualists	Idealistic Ritualists
1) Ritual Dimension (religious practice)	*No significance*	*Very low significance*: Acquisition of religious knowledge as a form of religious practice	*Very low significance*: Acquisition of religious knowledge as a form of religious practice	*Significant*: Reciting of the Koran, reading of Koran-translations, feasting, prayers (individually performed)	*High significance*: Ritual practice as important but not dominating part of everyday life (feasting, praying, reading of Koran and Koran translations, headscarf)	*Very high significance*: Ritual practice as prime guide-line for everyday life (fasting, praying, reading of Koran and Koran translations, headscarf)
2) Ideological Dimension (religious faith)	*No significance*	*High significance*: Belief in God, belief in miracles, no ties with mainstream religion	*Significant*: Belief in the Alevi religion	*Significant*: Belief in Allah, prophethood of Mohammed, Koran, the other world	*Very high significance*: Belief in Allah, prophethood of Mohammed, Koran, the other world	*Very high significance*: Belief in Allah, prophethood of Mohammed, Koran, the other world

Table 7.1.1 Types of religiousness occurring in the sample (continued)

	Atheists	Spiritualists	Alevi Secularists	Sunni Secularists	Pragmatic Ritualists	Idealistic Ritualists
3) Intelletual Dimension (religious knowedge)	*Only as part of common knowledge*	*Low significance:* Knowledge only as part of common knowledge	*High significance:* As an important way of strengthening Alevi identity	*Low significance:* Religious knowledge as necessary for education of children	*Very high significance:* Religious knowledge as part of ritual practice and to strengthen the belief in Islam, distinction from tradition	*Very high significance:* Religious knowledge as basis for a conscious belief, a means to get access to 'true Islam', important for life, distinction from tradition
4) Dimension of religious experience	*No significance*	*High significance:* Gives a feeling of security, happiness, gives life a meaning, emotional need, satisfaction	*Significant:* Identification with ceremonies, symbols, gives the feeling of specialness	*High significance:* Support in critical life events, makes life meaningful, trust in the existence of the other world	*Very high significance:* Makes life meaningful, feeling of security, happiness, help. God's nearness, widening of personal scope	*Very high significance:* Makes life meaningful, feeling of security, happiness, help, God's permanent nearness
5) Dimension of social consequences of religiousness	*No significance*	*Low significance:* Basis of individual ethic, help in life-crises, strengthening of character	*High significance:* Basis of individual ethic, strengthening of human understanding	*High significance:* Basis of individual ethic, guidance in social behaviour	*High significance:* Help in life-crises, basis of individual ethic, achieving authenticity	*Very high significance:* Religiousness dominates private and partly public life, social commitment, authenticity

Why do They Wear Headscarves?

One of my main points of interest was the question of why some of these young academics have taken to wearing the headscarf. At first sight, at least, wishing to share in important social functions such as teaching is not easily reconciled with the use of a symbol which the majority regards as a concealment of the woman behind. In the discussion of my findings I will show how such religious orientations interact with the young women's educational ideals, i.e. with their concepts of contemporary education in general, and of their own roles as future educators in schools and similar institutions. Conclusions which perhaps contribute to this volume's overall concern may be summarised in the following three paragraphs. Wherever appropriate I will use quotations from the interviews to illustrate my suggestions.

Religious orientations of people with a Muslim family background are not limited to the kind of 'visible' religiousness indicated by a headscarf. There are in fact many different nuances which also include variants of spiritualism and even a sort of atheism based on Muslim culture. Boundaries between the different orientations are fluid: some believers have left their Muslim roots behind (these are the 'spiritualists', most of whom come from an Alevi background), whereas secularism does not necessarily preclude the wearing a headscarf. The symbolic garment in these latter cases seems to serve as a token of 'externalised' religiousness. It does not affect the wearers' fundamentally secular ideas of religion as a private individual matter, and of religious freedom as a basic human right. The decision to wear a headscarf thus does not always reflect a desire to gain a reputation for personal religiousness in all areas of life. It may also express completely different and quite individual views of what makes up an Islamic way of life.

Though religious orientation stresses an allegedly Muslim style of clothing, it is still not necessarily related to a conservative and dogmatic world-view. The religious orientation of the veiled young women is quite different from that of their parents (see also Nökel, 1996, 2002; Karakaşoğlu-Aydın, 1998; Klinkhammer, 1999; Swietlik, 2000). The religious orientation of the ritualists in my sample can be characterised as an intellectual approach through cognition. It is important for them to claim that their way of life complies with the rules of the one and only 'true' Islam, as opposed to traditional Turkish Islam, which they regard as a culturally estranged religious hybrid. I quote from one of my interviews to demonstrate how the young women put it:

I try to see everything in terms of my religion. Although when I say that, I know that a lot of what we've been taught as religion is wrong. For example, that men and women must be separated from each other, are not allowed to sit in the same room. Anyway, I've found out for myself that there's no harm in it when a woman dresses in a particular *tesettür* [Turkish for a certain kind of correct Islamic costume, YK]. I mean, real Islam would have it that way. Or, the case of sex education. That's forbidden in Islam, it's really indecent, how can anyone just teach it? That's what we were taught. But in fact it isn't like that, in Islam it is given very high status, it is a necessity, that is what our religion teaches us. I believe that, making allowances for this false knowledge, I can learn everything through my religion, of course from the true correct religion that hasn't got so much to do with tradition (...). Culture, customs and usage change, but religion doesn't. In Turkey lots of cultural matters are considered to be linked to religion, but they aren't, it's just wrong (Nermin).

No Break With the Parents' Generation

I follow Olivier Roy's statement (ISIM-Newsletter 5, 2000, p. 1) that in the context of immigration 'there are no social constraints or even inducements to behave as a good Muslim; praying, fasting, eating *helal* require personal involvement'. One has to re-create an individual basis, the patterns of an everyday life for a Muslim'. My findings, however, do not entirely support his conclusion that 'to be a 'true' Muslim is an individual choice, because it usually means a double break; with a too traditional familial environment and with the dominant secular society'. My own research seems to suggest a different interpretation. Claiming to live according to 'true' Islam means sticking to the common – religious – basis of the family while trying to reconcile it with more modern life styles. This is achieved by re-interpreting religious norms in terms of a more intellectual approach to the Islamic sources. The desired outcome is to be able to live in Germany as a believing Muslim who plays an important role in the secular public sphere. So while this brand of 'true' Islam avoids abandoning the tradition, it does not shun secular society either. It is a synthesis of both.[9]

	To illustrate this combination of the parent generations' religious tradition and concepts of modern urban ways of life I would again like to quote from one of my interviews. In the following sequence we listen to a veiled student of education who tries to explain why at the end of her school career she decided to wear a headscarf. Along with religious motives, her reasoning shows similarity to feminist arguments on equal

---

[9] These findings about the development of islamic identities in the turko-muslim commun-ties in Germany correspond to those on the muslim-pakistani communities in Britain which Modood presents in several articles. Modood, 1997, pp. 157-58.

career-opportunities for women:

> My mother considers clothing very important, she always wanted us to be well-dressed so that the teacher would say, you come from a modern family! But when my mother came to the parents' visiting day the teacher made a 180 degrees turn because my mother had her head covered. Afterwards the teacher treated me somewhat differently, or at least I had the impression she did. That was when I began to understand what it was all about, and that's what made me finally decide to wear a headscarf. Of course the prime reason was that I am firm in my beliefs, and that they are right. But it was also because I believed that women who wear headscarves should never take second place. And that a woman with a headscarf can be at least as modern as one without, and can have a career just the same. This I believed from the bottom of my heart, and I wanted to prove it. That's another reason (Fatma).

Ethnic Revival Among the Young Alevi

These developments within the Sunni section of my sample are somewhat distortedly mirrored among the young Alevi women. It is not only the struggle for recognition by both their parents and the non-Muslim majority which shapes the Alevis' personal approach to religiousness. Their reconstruction of Alevi identity also reflects Sunni prejudice against the Alevi's 'lack of religious practice' and 'lack of morality between the sexes'.

> As I grew older, particularly when I started further education and entered the *Gymnasium*, but also now at the university, I realised these, well, religious wars. And this of course changed my attitude. I wanted to get to know more about Alevis because I had heard these prejudices like 'They do such and such, and they are unbelievers' and this really changed my personal attitude. But I must say I'm still not a fanatic Alevi, because I am against this – from both sides. I sometimes think I still don't know enough about all that, I still have to deepen my knowledge. But in doing so I know I changed myself very much so that I know now I am Alevi, and how Alevis behave, what our tradition is, and how Alevi worship is supposed to be performed. And I know all this is good for me (Yeşim).

In arguing against these prejudices they draw a clear line between their understanding of Islam and that of the Sunni. This clear distinction is an important means of fostering their ethno-religious identity. On the sample students the 'ethnic revival' established in Alevi literature, which is characterised by a marked dissociation from orthodox Islam, was certainly not lost. However, they also have something in common with the Sunni, although this is not immediately apparent. The lay Alevi and the ritualists agree on distinguishing between the Turkish tradition, which to them has been a predominantly negative experience, and the 'genuine' nature of their acquired religion. Thus both groups manage to rid themselves of what they perceive as the traditional religious orientation of their parents. They confront their parents' traditionalism with the 'true religion' they discover in the specialist literature, in lectures and in their further education. Both groups also dissociate themselves from what they depict as the 'typically Turkish' education of their parents. The lay Alevi tend to claim so-called Western 'modern' ideas such as tolerance, sexual equality, non-aggression and humanism as genuine Alevi values. It is not German society but their own religious background which therefore entitles the Alevi students to present themselves as representatives of 'modern' values. Since their own religio-cultural background demands no outward signs of religious affiliation, the Alevi can step forward as representatives of a view of religion which is compatible with Western ideas on women's emancipation, thereby emphasising their religious orientation's independence from the Sunni framework.

Intellectual Approach to the 'True' Religion

With the exception of the atheists, each of the different orientations relies on an internalised ethico-religious model to guide social behaviour. These models have precedence over ritual practice, since for all of the groups ritual practice is inconceivable without the internalisation of its inherent ethics, moral intention and social meaning. The emphasis is again on the difference from the parents' generation, which lacked comparable intellectual access to religion. The intellectual approach to religion as a prerequisite of 'true' religiousness emerges as the most conspicuous common characteristic of the (Sunni) ritualists – of pragmatic and idealistic outlook alike – with the lay Alevi. To all of them, the acquisition of knowledge about the fundamental principles of their religion constitutes a crucial factor in strengthening both their religious sense of belonging and their personal religious identity. In both cases the acquisition of knowledge has become associated with ritual practice. The underlying meaning is, however, not the same.

For the ritualists, acquisition of knowledge opens a 'new' approach to ritual practice, because knowledge of its essential religious intention is the only means of its deliberate and 'true' reinterpretation. This group shows characteristics of the 'scriptualism' that Geertz described as a reaction to the demands of Western 'modernism'.

For the lay Alevi, acquisition of religious knowledge does not derive from an obligation to strictly observe religious practice, since their attitude towards the formal aspects of religion is a much more flexible one. The students themselves report that in fact even their parents would perform the rites but rarely, and not expect the children to do otherwise. The gap was instead filled by an increased emphasis on 'internalisation'. Besides, my interviews confirm certain tendencies towards 'erosion' and 'ethnic revival' inside the Alevi community, which have been described in the literature. Whereas the religious orientation of the spiritualists illustrates the effect of 'erosion', the lay Alevi women's interest in the Alevilik's approach to religious ritual and religious knowledge certainly comes with an 'ethnic revival' flavour. Equipped with thorough knowledge the students would feel more capable to represent the religious community-spirit in the outside world and, if necessary, to defend it. From a more practical point of view, in-depth knowledge of the fundamental principles of the Alevilik is, of course, also useful to reject Sunni criticism. For most of the interviewed Alevi women, ritual practice consists of acquiring knowledge.

What is Modern, What is Contemporary Religious Education?

If 'modernisation' implies an agreement on basic concepts such as social pluralism, democracy, tolerance and individual freedom, then my findings confirm what the literature reports on other sections of the Turkish Muslim community: even an individual whose religious orientation has the strongest intensity and widest scope in all dimensions may feel quite at ease sharing 'modern' views. According to earlier research, migrant Muslims' religious beliefs are remarkably changeable and not necessarily opposed to social integration (Diehl, Urban and Esser, 1998, pp. 30-32). Apparently female students of education are no exceptions. In addition, the present conclusions suggest that for members of the second migrant generation religious belief can be a resource which they rely on to actively shape their process of integration.

As we could see with the group of Alevi students, the young women's educational ideals reveal similarities to western concepts of individual freedom, tolerance and acceptance of social pluralism. On the other hand, some of the Sunni students, notably among the 'ritualist' subgroup, seem to cling to 'older' ideas of education. Their understanding of education diverts from the common dichotomies of individualism vs. collectivism, independence vs. family ties, ritualism vs. internalisation. In their concept of family education seemingly contradictory ideals are merged to inform new ones.

As future educators, however, more than anything else they expect to be professional mediators of knowledge and general concepts of contemporary education. Although 'education' for Muslims – and especially Islamists in Germany – is one of the main issues they have to deal with, nothing in my interviews suggested that this group of more or less 'Islamist' young women might cherish a specific view of Islamic pedagogy or style of education. The recent call of Nimat Hafez Barazangi and other Islamic pedagogues for a contemporary approach to an Islamic theory of education still seems to go unheeded with the newly emerging group of Muslim pedagogues in Germany. Although one group of orthodox students – the 'idealistic ritualists' as I called them because of the role religious rites play in their everyday life – prefer religious values and norms as a framework for the education of their own children, they do not transfer this concept of Islamic education onto their professional life as teachers. They make a clear distinction between the family, where Islam rules the whole of life, and the public sphere where they are supposed to act as teachers in secular institutions. I could not find evidence in their statements of a missionary orientation as far as their pupils are concerned (see Karakaşoğlu-Aydın, 2000). But they make it perfectly clear that within their own families, and for their children in particular, conversion to other religions or opposing the religious life style of the family will not be accepted. As one of my interviewees put it, when asked if she would grant her children the right for self-determination and independence:

> In some respects yes, they should be open minded, they should be able to care for themselves and do as they please, but only as long as all this is kept within the borders of Islam (Aynur).

Still most of them said they were not going to distinguish between the education of boys and girls:

> I would treat them equally. For instance I wouldn't allow my son or my daughter to go to the discotheque or to have sexual intercourse with the other sex before marriage.

In this case, equality in education of the sexes is seen as equality of restrictions. All these young women are convinced beyond doubt that their respective approaches to Muslim education will bring up their children to become good citizens and valuable members of society.

From the point of view of the ritualists, 'Islamic education' requires that the entire process be based on Muslim norms and values. The non-orthodox Muslim female students, on the other hand, would surely teach Islam, or at least its 'basics', but not accept it as an overall educational framework. Against this difference it seems striking that ritualists as well as secularists usually appreciate the establishment of private Muslim schools (in terms of equality with existing Christian ones) but do not want their children to attend them, since they fear disintegration from the non-Muslim German majority and, hence, slackening career options for their children.[10]

Individuality Through Religion

In wearing their Islamic dress in public the ritualists are demanding acceptance of a religious life-style as one among the many patterns a pluralist society deems admissible. The point was made perfectly clear by one of my interviewees who compared her headscarf to the green hair of punks: 'Some people like to dye their hair green, and I'm wearing my headscarf, so what's the difference?'. They want both their religious and their professional identities to be accepted at school without being suspected of infiltrating the secular German educational system with Islamist ideas. As one of the Secularists put it with a laugh, 'And religion, well I'd like to be accepted the way I think, I mean with my religious views, which are not Christian, but Muslim. Still I don't think it'll matter all that much at school. I mean, I won't teach Maths and Turkish as a Muslim theologian' (Ayten).

One of the veiled orthodox interviewees stresses that for her, tolerance involves both sides alike. She definitely refuses to conform to the majority view as far as ethnic or religious orientation is concerned. She behaves as a self-confident individual, a full member of the surrounding society with equal rights and demands:

> Yes, well I want to be accepted with my nationality and my religion. That is, I don't want to adapt to their ideas at all, but to be accepted the way I am, because otherwise I wouldn't feel accepted. Yes, just as I accept them, the way they are, that's what I expect as well (Hidayet).

---

[10] These findings correspond to those from a study on Pakistani Girls in British schools. In stressing the importance of integration with other cultures the girls interviewed disagreed with setting up Muslim schools. 'They know that their futures are in Britain, and they do not want to be isolated from the rest of British society', Shaikh and Kelly, 1989, p. 18.

The Public Role of Religion in Germany and New Demands of Muslims

Perhaps it is useful to connect my research findings to a more general political discussion on the public role of Islam in Germany. A young Muslim teacher was at the centre of a controversy about whether Muslim women teachers should be allowed to wear an 'Islamic dress' in German schools. I am talking about the case of Fereshta Ludin, a young woman of Afghan origin who was trained as a teacher in Baden-Württemberg. It was the State Ministry of Cultural Affairs rather than the school's headmaster who, at the beginning of her two years practical training (which follows the university examination), demanded she take off her headscarf. According to the ministry the headscarf was at variance with basic Christian values and constitutional secularism alike. As a symbol of backward, fundamentalist Islamic attitudes its message was opposition to the principles of freedom of thought and of the equality of the sexes.[11] Against this image of the headscarf, Ludin emphasised in interviews that she would always defend those two principles of the society, that it was her own decision to wear it as a personal symbol of what Islam meant to her, and that she did not consider it a way of putting under pressure Muslim girls who did not wish to wear a headscarf. While public debate is still going on, the case has been brought before the Supreme Administrative Court (*Bundesverwaltungsgericht*) in Berlin. The final decision of the Supreme Administrative Court confirmed in 2002 the opinion of the State Ministry of Cultural affairs in Dade-Würtemmberg, so that Ludin is forbidden to work as a teacher at public schools if she insists in wearing her headscarf. Ludin now works as a part-time teacher of English at the Islamic Grammar School in Berlin (a private school with state support), the only one of its kind existing in Germany. Each of the federal states has its own approach to the issue of veiling. Whereas in Baden-Württemberg the headscarf is forbidden, in Northrhine-Westfalia (NRW) the Ministry leaves it up to the school directors to decide individually. So in the NRW city of Wuppertal, the veiled deputy head mistress of one of two neighbouring schools hopes for improved communication with Muslim pupils and their parents, while at the other teachers are not permitted to wear headscarves lest the children's religious freedom should be impaired.[12]

---

[11] It is not merely in the case of Germany where this view of Islam applies. Carens and Williams found a similar stereotyped image of Islam, which they consider dangerous to Western democracies (Carens and Williams, 1996, p. 158).

[12] For more details of the 'Ludin case' see Karakaşoğlu-Aydın, 1999.

The Ludin case demonstrates that German state authorities, much like a considerable part of the population, still tend to regard the headscarf as evidence of an undemocratic, theocratic and thus dogmatic world view. Veiled teachers are suspected of imposing a backward world view on their pupils. They are considered a potential danger for a democratic and tolerant education. From this perspective it seems entirely impossible to be veiled and still meet the demands of secular professionalism.[13]

My interviews include examples to the contrary. They illustrate the wish of young Muslims to play an important role in public life in Germany, to have a position in the community without neglecting their specific approach to Islam. It even seems that being visible as a Muslim in the secular non-Muslim environment is not only a matter of personal preference, of life style, or of searching for individual or collective identity, but perhaps also an important and effective way for members of a minority to be recognised with their special religious demands and their distinct identities, both individually and as a Muslim lobby. This is especially the case when, like in Germany, religion is not separated from the state as clearly as the term secularism would have us believe.

The German concept of secularism is not a radically lay one. It has never been effectively severed from the society's Christian roots. Freedom of religion, as guaranteed by Article 4 of the German constitution, does not only imply the right to believe or not to believe, to practise or not to practise one's faith in public and to maintain religious institutions and organisations, but religion may also interfere with individual and communal freedom. Religion is both a private and a public issue because it is free to act as a social power (Böckenförde, 1996, p. 93) or enter the field of politics. Very often the need for separation of religion and state in Western democracies is misunderstood to mean separation of religion and politics (Walzer, 1998, p. 304). In Germany there is no such strict separation between religion and politics. As a result the Christian churches and also the Jewish community have their own official representatives; they are entitled to membership of various social and even political committees like the Radio and Television Committee (an institution which serves as kind of a self-regulation body). As a result in some of the *Länder* the churches are a major provider of social services. A typical case is Northrhine-Westfalia, where 80 per cent of the kindergartens are run by the churches. In all *Länder* church taxes are collected by the state, and in most of them religious education is part of the state schools' regular curriculum. Teachers of religious education are needed by both the state and their

---

[13] For a more detailed account of politicians' and other public actors' comments on this case see Karakaşoğlu-Aydın, 1999.

church. No such thing is possible for Muslims in Germany, because the immigrants' Islam lacks the hierarchy which is so characteristic of the churches' organisational structures.

Muslim immigrants and their increasing demands for equal participation in every realm of society have done much to revitalise the debate on the role of religion within the German state. Extremely controversial views are held concerning the way religion relates to modernity. In this respect the position of Islam in a basically Christian yet secularised society is one of the most crucial issues. One of the questions is, to what extent Islam will be offered the opportunity to achieve a social position similar to that of the Christian churches. At least we may safely expect that the churches, given their many social and economic ties with the German state, will not willingly surrender their privileges in favour of a radically laicist separation of state and religion.

It is this special German secularism of sorts which encourages officials, lawyers, managers of welfare organisations and church authorities to ask for 'the spokesman', 'the one and only top representative of Islam', when Muslims call for recognition of their special religious demands. By doing so, German officials force the migrant Islam to present itself – for all its internal diversity, which my interviews amply demonstrate – as a homogeneous unit which to deal with seems sufficiently easy. In the long run this approach is, of course, almost bound to encourage fundamentalist claims of speaking on behalf of the 'very truth' of Islam. I agree with Walzer's conclusion that 'within constitutional limits, religious and ideological movements can mobilise whatever passion they can mobilise: democratic politics can and should be permissive in this regard' (Walzer, 1998, p. 305).

In this process only those groups which are successful in presenting themselves as a powerful unit, as an effective pressure group or as visible individuals can expect recognition of their particular needs and demands. An effective and powerful strategy is to make sure those demands and needs are a permanent issue of public debate. The use of symbols and of symbolic legal proceedings are important tools for young Muslim activists to gain visibility and recognition as a new religious, political and cultural element in society. Muslim university students, especially the female ones, are key figures in the struggle for recognition of Islam as a social factor in Germany because they combine visibility, intellectuality and institutional knowledge of German society. According to Esser's sociological dimensions of integration (Esser, 1999, p. 24) their academic status is an additional advantage. They are culturally integrated because of their knowledge of the German language and their level of education, they are structurally integrated because of their knowledge of German institutions, and they are socially integrated because of their interaction with the mainstream society. Their emotional integration – as reflected in feeling alike with Germans or being proud of Germany – is ambiguous. They wish to be considered equal and permanent citizens of Germany and still preserve their distinct religious identity.

Conclusion

Young women who follow their ideals of an Islamic life style are not inclined to hide away from the public, or to be submerged in an anti-modernist ethnic community. To them an Islamic life style is a means of developing an independent self inside Western society. A good example of this intention is the following statement by one of my veiled interviewees:

> What does my religion give me? First of all an identity. It gives me an answer to 'where am I, who am I?'. How can I put it? I'm not just anybody, I have a personality, I have standards, a life-style. And since I do all this consciously, I feel safer and more secure (Nükhet).

This attitude is connected to a concept of integration as opposed to assimilation. The latter is equated with losing one's ethnic, cultural and religious roots, and thus with losing an integral part of one's personality. Integration and assimilation are two key concepts of the Muslim discourse on how to relate to the non-Muslim majority. Even the most recent annual congress of the youth organisation of the Islamic Community of Milli Görüş (IGMG)[14] which was held at Essen in November 2000 had a decoration of posters on which the IGMG proclaimed 'Integration yes, Assimilation no' and 'We are Muslims, and we are Europeans'. These slogans seem quite defiant expressions of not wishing one's identity to be tampered with, even if it includes belonging to a common European culture. The following statement shows that, to some extent at least, this defiance might derive from a fear of losing one's identity at the end of a forced process of assimilation. This is expressed by the interviewee as the fear of having to give up her name, a very important part of the modern individual's self-identification:

---

[14] According to official reports of the German secret service Milli Görüş is an extremist and islamist organization which aims at preventing young muslims from social and cultural integration into the German society (Verfassungsschutzbericht 1999, p.164, Verfassungs-schutzbericht 2000, p. 207).

No doubt integration is a must, but assimilation means total Germanisation, in appearance too, as far as clothing and so on are concerned, behaving completely like a German. But then it's no longer multicultural but pure German, maybe you'll even have to change your name (Fatma).

Policy makers in Germany still need to develop a code of practice for religious equality that will meet the challenge of religious pluralism which de facto already exists. Such efforts are, however, bound to fail as long as the Muslims themselves are not regarded as equal partners in the discussion. Thus in Germany the acceptance of Islam and of Muslim claims will depend on the extent to which these young academics will be able to enter key positions inside the German democratic system. If they succeed they might develop and articulate fresh approaches to Islam as an integral instead of an alien element of German society.

References

Barazangi, N. H. (1995), 'Educational Reform', Esposito, John L. (ed.), *The Oxford Encyclopedia of the Modern Islamic World*, vol. 1, New York, pp. 420-25.

Bundesministerium des Inneren (ed.) (2000), *Verfassungsschutzbericht 1999*, Berlin/Bonn.

Bundesministerium des Inneren (ed.) (2001), *Verfassungsschutzbericht 2000*, Berlin/Bonn.

Carens, J. H. and Williams, M. S. (1996), 'Muslim Minorities in Liberal Democracies: The Politics of Misrecognition', in R. Bauböck, A. Heller and A. R. Zolberg (eds), *The Challenge of Diversity. Integration and Pluralism in Societies of Immigration*, Avebury, Aldershot, pp. 157-86.

Diehl, C. and Urbahn, J., in cooperation with H. Esser (1998), *Die soziale und politische Partizipation von Zuwanderern in der Bundesrepublik Deutschland*, Abteilung Arbeit und Sozialpolitik des Forschungsinstituts der Friedrich-Ebert-Stiftung (ed.), Bonn.

Esser, H. (1998), 'Ist das Konzept der Integration gescheitert?', unpublished Paper presented on the occasion of the opening of the Landeszentrum für Zuwanderung NRW on January 8th 1998 in Solingen.

Esser, H. (1999), 'Inklusion, Integration und ethnische Schichtung', *Journal für Konflikt- und Gewaltforschung*, vol. 1, pp. 5-34.

Glock, C. Y. (1969), 'Über die Dimensionen der Religiosität', in J. Matthes (ed.), *Kirche und Gesellschaft. Einführung in die Religionssoziologie II*, Hamburg, pp. 150-68.

Karakaşoğlu, Y. (1996), 'Turkish Cultural Orientations in Germany and the Role of Islam', in Kolinsky, E. and D. Horrocks (eds), *Turkish Culture in German Society Today*, Berghahn Books, UK, pp. 158-80.

Karakaşoğlu-Aydın, Y. (1998), 'Das Kopftuch gibt mir meine Identität als muslimische Frau zurück'. Zum Selbst- und Fremdbild kopftuchtragender Studentinnen in Deutschland, in *Frauen in der Einen Welt*, no. 1.

Karakaşoğlu-Aydın, Y. (1999), 'Religionsfreiheit für Muslime? Die Kopftuchdebatte im Fall Fall Ludin', in T. Müller-Heidelberg, U. Finckh, W.-D. Narr and S. Soost (eds), *Grundrechte-Report 1999. Zur Lage der Bürger- und Menschenrechte in Deutschland*, Hamburg, pp. 72-7.

Karakaşoğlu-Aydın, Y. (2000), *Muslimische Religiosität und Erziehungsvorstellungen*, IKO-Verlag, Frankfurt am Main.

Kehl-Bodrogi, K. (1988), *Die Kızılbaş/Aleviten. Untersuchungen über eine esoterische Glaubensgemeinschaft in Anatolien*, Klaus-Schwarz-Verlag, Berlin.

Kehl-Bodrogi, K. (2000), 'The New Garments of Alevism', *ISIM-Newsletter* vol. 5, p. 23.

Klinkhammer, G. M. (1999), 'Individualisierung und Säkularisierung islamischer Religiosität: zwei Türkinnen in Deutschland', in Jonker, G. (ed.), *Kern und Rand. Religiöse Minderheiten aus der Türkei in Deutschland*, Das Arabische Buch, Berlin, pp. 221-36.

Modood, T. (1997), '"Difference", Cultural Racism and Anti-Racism', in P. Werbner,/T. Modood (eds), *Debating Cultural Hybridity. Multi-Cultural Identities and the Politics of Anti-Racism*, ZED Books, London and New Jersey, pp. 154-72.

Nökel, S. (1996), '"Ich hab ein Recht darauf, meine Religion zu leben', Islam und zweite Migrantengeneration in der Bundesrepublik Deutschland", in Schlee, G. and K. Werner (eds.), *Inklusion und Exclusion*, Rüdiger Köppe Verlag, Köln, pp. 275-303.

Nökel, Sigrid (2002), *Die Töchter der Gastarbeiter und der Islam. Zur Soziologie alltagsweltlicher Anerkennungspolitiken. Eine Fallstudie*, transcript Verlag, Bielefeld.

Roy, O. (2000), 'Muslims in Europe: From Ethnic Identity to Religious Recasting', *ISIM-Newsletter*, vol. 5, pp. 1-29.

Shaikh, S. and Kelly, A. (1989), 'To mix or not to mix: Pakistani girls in British schools', *Educational Research* vol. 31, no. 1, pp. 10-19.

Shell Jugendstudie (2000), *Jugend 2000*, Band 1, Leske und Budrich, Opladen.

Swietlik, B. (2000), 'Als ob man zwei verschiedene Köpfe in einem hätte ...' – Religiöse Sozialisation zwischen Islam und Christentum', in I. Attia and H. Marburger (eds), *Alltag und Lebenswelten von Migrantenjugendlichen*, Frankfurt am Main, pp. 139-56.

Thomä-Venske, H. (1981), *Islam und Integration: zur Bedeutung des Islam im Prozeß der Integration türkischer Arbeiterfamilien in der Gesellschaft der Bundesrepublik*, Hamburg.

Thränhardt, D. (1999), 'Integrationsprozesse in der Bundesrepublik Deutschland – Institutionelle und soziale Rahmenbedingungen', Friedrich-Ebert-Stiftung, Gesprächskreis Arbeit und Soziales (ed.), Nr. 91, *Integration und Integrationsförderung in der Einwanderungsgesellschaft*, Bonn, pp. 13-46.

Walzer, M. (1998), 'Drawing the Line: Religion and Politics', *Soziale Welt*, vol. 49, pp. 295-308.

Chapter 8

Post-Migration Islam: Negotiating Space in Dutch Society

Thijl Sunier

Introduction

> In the Netherlands, elderly Turkish Muslims say: 'We'll go back to Turkey'. But in fact they won't. They invest money in a beautiful house over there, instead of spending money on securing a better future for their children in the Netherlands. Among people of my age there are more and more who realize: 'We are Muslims and we remain so. But we are Muslims in the Netherlands'. We struggle and negotiate with local authorities to have our voices heard and to defend our interests. At the next elections of the administrative board of the mosque I will let the members choose: either keep the situation as it is and pretend that a chairman is okay when he sells cheap olives and cheese in the shop of the mosque, or take a new road and face the questions young boys and girls ask our leaders. In that case we need leaders who can cope with the new situation.

This statement made by the young chairman of a Turkish mosque in the city of Rotterdam illustrates strikingly clearly the kind of discussion which is going on among leading circles of Islamic organizations in the Netherlands. Since the early 1990s, an important shift seems to have taken place in the thinking about the strategies, working procedures and in the articulation of interests of Turkish Islamic organizations. These developments come down mainly to a greater focus on the position of Muslims *in* Dutch society, or rather of Muslims as *Dutch citizens*.

The question how and in what direction Islam and its institutions in the Netherlands and elsewhere in Europe will develop and what ideas and attitudes its followers have, seems to occupy politicians, journalists, scientist and the public for well over a decade. But also among Muslims themselves, ideas about political agendas, strategies, operating modes and the attitude vis-à-vis Dutch society are apparently contested and topics of serious debate.

In the eighties the number of Islamic organizations and institutions, especially mosques, grew relatively quickly.[1] It turned out that this growth could not simply be explained by pointing at the growing number of immigrants from Islamic countries such as Turkey and Morocco. Especially after the so-called Rushdie affair, the question arose as to the factors accounting for this growth. A considerable number of people feared that a growing number of Muslims had a very negative attitude towards Dutch society and that 'fundamentalism' was gaining support among them. The idea exists that Islamic organizations have a kind of double political agenda. Towards the host society, they act cooperatively, but internally radical discourses are spreading rapidly and gaining support.

Islam in Scientific Literature

In spite of the growing number of publications on Islamic institutions and organizations in Western Europe, organizational development is a rather neglected theme. Islamic organizations are viewed either as *migrant organizations*, or as *associations of people with the same religious (Islamic) background*. Although these approaches are relevant to a certain extent, they are inadequate as an analytical tool in the attempt to understand why, how, and to what extent Islamic organizations have managed to improve their position. There is hardly any analysis that goes beyond mere description of existing organizational activities and the desires of the Muslim population.

If we consider Islamic organizations solely as organizations of migrants, we should therefore consider them as temporal phenomena. One of the implications is that the foundation, persistence and development of these organizations is almost entirely based on their function as intermediary between the migrant 'community' and the host society. Their *raison-d'être* is supposed to be related to the fact that migrants do not yet fully participate in the new society.

In such an *immigration approach* no fundamental distinction is made between Islamic institutions and organizations and any other organizations founded by migrants. Activities and services performed by these institutions are related to the migrant background of their members. It is assumed that these organizations function as a kind of sanctuary in a strange and sometimes hostile environment. As the process of integration

---

[1] For an extensive overview of Islam in the Netherlands see N. Landman (1992), *Van mat tot minaret. De institutionalisering van de islam in Nederland,* and J. Rath et al. (1996), *Nederland en zijn islam.*

will take place anyhow, it is assumed that the significance of Islamic organizations as organizations of migrants will gradually diminish.

If they, however, persist, this is because migrants are not yet fully integrated. This image of Islamic organizations and institutions is widespread. Islamic schools in the Netherlands, for example, are mainly seen as 'black schools' (schools with a disproportionate number of 'foreign pupils'). The debate about these schools is in fact a debate about integration of migrants. But in addition to that, the image of Islamic schools has also to do with specific images about Islam itself. This brings us to the second approach, the so-called *culturalist* approach (Vermeulen, 1992).

This approach is based on the assumption that Islamic organizations are associations of people with the same religious background. Islamic principles and prescriptions and religious-ideological images and affiliations require specific types of organizational activities. It also assumes that these images and affiliations are contributions by migrants as cultural baggage from the country of origin. Cultural continuity is therefore an important aspect of this approach. While this may explain their persistence to a certain extent, this approach demonstrates the failings of an essentialist perspective. For example, it does not account for the fact that Islamic organizations increasingly perform duties and services which go beyond strictly religious matters. In general this type of approach implicitly fails to distinguish between Islam and organizations of Muslims. Although the two have much in common, they are certainly not the same. In this approach Islam is disconnected from the social context in which it is embedded, and it is assumed that this is also more or less the case with Islamic organizations, irrespective of the social setting. Again we can immediately recognize elements of the present-day debate about the position of Islam.

Muslim Organizations as Interest Organizations

The argument I want to put forward here is that organizational development has its own dynamics which requires a specific analysis. We should not only look at the characteristics of the various Muslim communities as such, but also at the aims and operational modes of organizations. Instead of paying attention to internal characteristics only, we must particularly analyze the relations between Islamic organizations and the surrounding society and the developments which take place in these relations. When looking at the literature on Islam in Europe, this seems to be a neglected theme.[2]

The analysis of organizational development among Muslims requires an alternative approach in which *interest struggle* and *emancipation* are central themes. To a certain extent Muslim organizations can be characterized as *interest organizations*. They have been set up in order to gain certain goals and to change the political structures. Muslims in Europe do not organize themselves because Islam prescribes this, but because they want to achieve certain goals which are related to the circumstances in which they find themselves (Nielsen, 1992). Organizational activities and the articulation of interests are therefore confined to the specific context in which they take place. Developments which take place are to a large extent the result of well-chosen rational strategies by collective actors, bound by a specific social and political context (Eisinger, 1973; Hechter et al. 1982; Jazouli, 1986; McAdam, 1982; Tarrow, 1994). This implies that there is no need for specific theories applicable to only Muslims or migrants when analyzing organizational development and interest struggle among Muslims. Although the characteristics of a conflict of interests among Muslims are specific to a large extent, the mechanisms underlying a conflict of interests are general and applicable to any interest group. Interests of Muslims are not self-evident, that is to say based on Islamic principles, as is often assumed. They are contextual and dynamic and change according to changing circumstances.

When we examine the way in which Muslims, by organizing themselves, try to gain access to decision-making processes and defend their collective interests, Islamic organizations can be depicted as *social movements*. At least they perform activities characteristic of social movements. Specific theories on social movements offered me a useful framework, particularly for the analysis of the recent developments in the articulation of interests among Turkish Muslims in the Netherlands. Social movements must be considered as rational attempts by excluded groups to obtain sufficient political leverage to advance collective interests through non-institutionalized means. Successful collective action is the result of a favourable interplay of both internal and external factors.

In the early 1990s I conducted research among Turkish Islamic organizations and young Muslims. The focus of my research was to analyze how Islamic organizations had developed since the early 1980s and what factors accounted for that process. The research has been carried out in the city of Rotterdam because this city offered me a relevant environment. In

---

[2] For a discussion of the literature on Islam in Europe, particularly the Netherlands, see Sunier 1996.

the 1980s some important changes in municipal policies took place which affected the position of Islamic organizations. Especially Turkish Islamic organizations played a crucial role in the establishing of an intensified cooperation in a variety of fields between municipality and government.

After an initial exploration of the organizational infrastructure in the city, I directed my attention to three neighborhoods with a relatively high number of Muslim inhabitants and a correspondingly large number of Islamic institutions. On the one hand, I tried to get a clear picture of the internal affairs of the Islamic organizations: what kind of activities are carried out towards the own rank-and-file, who is officially and actually in charge in the organizations, how are members recruited and how is the mutual solidarity reinforced. In talking with people involved, I concentrated on the young male members and leaders. It turned out that young people in many cases initiated discussions within the organizations about the status quo.

On the other hand I investigated external relations between Islamic organizations and the surrounding society. With what kind of Dutch institutions do Islamic organizations have contacts, what is the character of these relations, and what kinds of ideas exist about cooperation with the municipality, social welfare institutions, and other societal and political institutions such as churches, political parties, etc.

Towards the end of the 1990s I went back to those organizations for a short follow-up of my initial research.

Organizational Development

When we consider the ways in which Turkish Muslims in the Netherlands defended their collective interests in the past decades as an ongoing organizational process, there are some developmental phases to be distinguished.

Between the end of the sixties and the mid-seventies, the main form of collective action among Muslims was to acquire suitable room for prayers. Initially they were seeking temporary accommodation during important religious occasions such as Ramadan. In this phase Dutch intermediaries played a crucial role, especially the churches. In fact it was no collective action *by* Muslims but collective action *for* Muslims. At that time Muslims themselves did not even ask for this. Among Dutch intermediaries the idea existed that Muslim 'migrant workers' might need such facilities for the time they stayed here. Only after some time did Muslims show the first forms of cooperation in order to create areas for prayer.

It was clear that the need for prayer rooms among ordinary believers was, at that time, closely connected to their orientation towards their country of origin. The created accommodation was not just a religious facility; it functioned as a gathering place for people who felt themselves temporary passers-by, who would return to their country of origin soon (Landman, 1992).

Not only Muslims themselves, but the government and policymakers as well as Dutch society in general were convinced that their stay would be temporary. The creation of religious facilities was therefore considered to be something which should be completely left to private initiative. No special policies were needed. As such, both migrants and policymakers had in fact the same intentions.

The Seventies

In the course of the seventies some important developments took place. The number of immigrants, especially Turks, increased considerably, because of family reunions. These families settled in the old quarters of the town centres. For the vast majority of the Muslims, however, returning to the country of origin was still a fact. The actual return was postponed, because of family reunions. Many migrants had no other alternative than staying here due to financial problems. For a variety of reason Muslims were confronted, more than before, with many dilemmas and problems, prompted by living in a non-Islamic country. As a consequence the need for religious facilities increased likewise, especially the need for qualified religious personnel. At the same time organizational structures improved and the variation in activities increased. Many mosque organizations developed into real centres for migrants. There were teahouses, shops and other facilities. Also in this period the first coordinating structures came into being among Turkish Muslims.

Organizational development and the articulation of interests among Turkish Muslims got a new dimension when several religious-ideological movements began to operate among Turkish Muslims in Europe. The origin of these movements was related to the political situation in Turkey, where Islam has a highly political significance. Not only could these movements act more freely in Western Europe, but the thousands of Turkish migrants in Western Europe were also considered as a means to develop the movements in general. For the leadership it was of crucial importance to build up a rank-and-file among the Turkish migrants.

It comes as no surprise that the creation of religious institutions became the single most important strategy of these movements. Ordinary religious needs among Muslims were now used as a means to increase their influence. The foundation of mosques and other religious institutions now also became an expression of the competition between these movements.

Although this organizational development was a clear continuation of the political climate in Turkey, there was also a breach with the past. The several movements were confronted with each other in a completely different way. Not only had these movements a different position in society as compared to Turkey, the rank-and-file also had a different position, and a different background as compared to the rank-and-file in Turkey itself. Whereas the political struggle in Turkey largely takes place in the more urban areas, the potential rank-and-file in Europe mainly has a rural background. As a consequence these movements 'ruralized' more or less in Europe.

Apart from these internal aspects, also with respect to the socio-political context in the Netherlands, important developments took place that influenced the position of Islamic organizations and organizations of migrants in general. In the early eighties the Dutch government changed its policies towards migrants. Permanent residence became the central focus. Organizations of migrants gained more significance in the process of integration of migrants. They were politically and ideologically incorporated into government policies. Islamic organizations were also considered important organizations of migrants, and their activities were judged according to their functions in the process of integration. I call this the 'migrantization' of Islamic organizations.

As a result, a new type of leadership appeared on the scene. These leaders had lived in the Netherlands for a relatively long time, they knew society quite well and had acted as an intermediary between Muslim migrants and Dutch society. They were entrepreneurs rather than 'ideologists' and were oriented towards mobilizing as many resources as possible. They successfully made use of their contact with Dutch policymakers and institutions. They emphasized that Islamic organizations must be considered as the main forms of 'self-organization' among migrants. These leaders increasingly took part in discussions on the position of migrants and as opinion leaders they gained influence on 'defining of the situation'. Towards society they represented the Muslim populations and articulated what needs existed among Muslims. They also articulated what it means to be a Muslim in a non-Islamic society.[3] By stressing the 'foreign' character of the Islam, as something which is part of the cultural heritage of a specific group of migrants, they were able to convince policymakers that certain facilities were required. As these leaders were at the head of the umbrella organizations, the initiative in interest struggle therefore gradually shifted from a local level towards a national level.

As far as most Muslims were concerned, they were still very much orientated towards the countries of origin. They still considered their stay in the Netherlands as being of a temporary nature.

The Eighties

In the course of the eighties new developments took place. These developments did not only make the above-mentioned strategy increasingly obsolete, it also put the legitimacy of the leaders under pressure. Three issues were especially important: greater orientation towards the position of Muslims *in* Dutch society, the position of youths within Islamic organizations and the relation between local organizations and national umbrella organizations.

Towards the end of the eighties, a part of the leadership of Turkish Islamic organizations at least realized that establishing enduring relations and cooperation with Dutch institutions such as welfare organizations and local political authorities and paying more attention to all kinds of social issues was crucial for their future. The leaders who were inclined to change the strategy thought that Islamic organizations until then had adopted an attitude of being the weaker party vis-à-vis the Dutch society. This strategy had proven to be beneficial in the past, but it turned out to be increasingly counterproductive in the present.

These leaders wanted to correct the image that Muslims are not willing to take part in neighbourhood development and other important social issues. At least a part of the younger participants in the organizations considers good relations with the surrounding society more important than strong ties with the country of origin. Relatively more energy has to be put into good relations with the surrounding society. This is especially the case on a local level. Two important issues are at stake. Firstly, the recognition that Islamic organizations are local organizations which form a part of the local neighbourhood community, and secondly that Muslims are very well

---

[3] Schierup (1992) has called this emphasis on cultural boundaries the 'enclavization of culture'.

able to adapt themselves to new circumstances without giving up their religion. They want to be recognized as equal citizens of society.

The articulation of interests is gradually shifting towards matters concerning recognition. A growing number of young Muslims has the feeling that the foreign connotations linked to Islam and the image of Islamic organizations as organizations of foreigners or migrants perpetuate their position rather than improve it. It hinders them in their efforts to participate in society. Recognition is therefore linked to the question whether and to what extent Muslims can be considered a part of the Dutch 'imagined community' (Anderson, 1991).

The Nineties

While the 'migrantization' of Muslims was an important and effective strategy of integration in the eighties, a new strategy seems to be necessary now. According to these young leaders who are inclined to change their strategy, the policies concerning Islamic organizations should be disengaged from policies with regard to migrants. They are of the opinion that there should be a discussion about the question how Dutch society should be defined. According to them, full integration is only accomplished when this redefinition has taken place.

A shift in strategy not only concerns the position of Islamic organizations in Dutch society, but internally changes have to be introduced as well. In recent years young people gained more influence within Islamic organizations. The number of young people and youth organizations within Islamic organizations grew rapidly. As a consequence the activities offered by the organizations changed likewise. But young people also gained more influence in the administration of Islamic organizations recently, not only because the intensified negotiations with Dutch institutions required more qualified personnel than before, but also because the increase of young people within the organizations influenced the balance of power. In short, a shift occurred from achieved to earned leadership (Nielsen, 1992).

It is obvious that these developments did not occur without many discussions, controversies and a power struggle. In a large number of organizations the power is still firmly in the hands of the first generation of Muslims, but as mentioned before the legitimacy of their power is increasingly being questioned.

One important aspect of this power struggle is the role and influence of umbrella organizations. I stated before that the initiative in negotiations and a promotion of one's interests within Dutch society in the eighties shifted towards the national umbrella organizations. Apart from that, Turkish Islam is organized along religious-ideological lines. According to many young leaders, both this centralized decision-making structure and the ideological fragmentation impedes the successful establishment of local contacts and cooperation between all types of institutions. The young leaders want to bring back the initiative to promote their interests on a local level. I saw many examples of young active members of Turkish Islamic organizations from different ideological background, working together on neighbourhood level, while at the same time their national leaders are fighting each other for influence.

In short, it seems to me that religious-ideological controversies are increasingly being replaced by controversies between two generations of migrants. The young generation of Muslims within Islamic organizations is trying to develop the organizations from organizations *for* Muslims into organizations *of* Muslims. Until the late eighties organizational development and promotion of interests was a matter of representatives and managers. There was a huge gap between leaders and the rank-and-file. In recent years this situation of imbalance seems to have altered gradually. Young people want to be a member of an Islamic organization out of conviction and not out of tradition.

Factors

The very reason that changes occur in the strategy towards the surrounding society is closely related to both the structural as well as the ideological context in which Turkish Islamic organizations operate. Both can be considered as 'openings' or else as impediments for Muslims in their interest struggle (Duyvendak, 1997; Eisinger, 1973; Sunier et al., 2000). This political opportunity structure partly consists of previous formulated policies of the government, but political opportunities are also partly the result of present struggle and negotiations between two or more parties.

In general the above-mentioned recent developments are closely related to the changes in the political and ideological context in which Islamic organizations operate. These changes became manifest at the end of the eighties when the Dutch government realized that the position of migrants in the so-called 'hard' sectors such as education, employment and housing, was far weaker than among native Dutch people. The integration into these sectors was emphasized. Preservation of specific cultural elements by the migrants was tolerated as long as it did not impede structural integration. These policies were sometimes phrased in such a way as if a preservation of one's culture would inhibit a full-fledged participation in the central institutions of society.

The ideological climate towards Muslims and Islam also changed at that time. The Rushdie affair functioned as a kind of catalyst. The media showed an exaggerated interest in the sometimes extreme statements of some Islamic leaders. The image of Muslims seemed to shift from non-integrated migrants to Muslims as a 'fifth column'. This shift in ideological climate had as a result that many young Muslims started to reconsider their position in Dutch society. This may explain to a certain extent why so many young Islamic leaders insist that their organizations focus on social issues.

Apart from these more general contextual developments, the main changes in the structure of political opportunities are to be found on a local level. In general local governments have to carry out policies formulated by the national government, but in big cities where the municipal administration is subdivided into local 'borough' administrations, the local level becomes all the more relevant for Islamic organizations. Previous research has showed that there is a great variety in actual policies between municipalities. I carried out my research in Rotterdam, partly because this city has, in recent years, adopted rather new and, according to Dutch standards, unique policies on Islam and Islamic organizations. It is the first and as yet only Dutch city which developed a specific 'mosque' policy. It is also the only city with a subsidized council of Islamic organizations (SPIOR). Apart from these important accomplishments, the extensive urban renewal programme and subsequent opportunities for neighbourhood management and regeneration projects offered Islamic organizations starting-points to emphasize their local character and local function. Although the situation in Rotterdam is far from ideal, it is nevertheless a fact that Muslims gained a greater access to political decision-making procedures than elsewhere in the Netherlands.

A very crucial factor in explaining the recent developments in the promotion of interests among Muslims is the changing perspective among young Muslims. This is so important because it can be considered as the very beginning of recent organizational development and change. I call this factor a *cognitive shift*. Young Muslims increasingly realize that they have to orientate themselves towards Dutch society for their future and that they have to break away from the status of their parents.

Consider the following statements by young members of Islamic organizations:

We have much more attention to what's going on in Dutch society. The municipality is busy elaborating a mosque policy in the city, but they do not ask us what we think about it and what we want. The organization of inhabitants in this neighbourhood, together with the social workers for migrants are discussing about improvement of the neigbourhood, but they do not invite our organization to the meetings, despite the fact that we have a lot of contacts with Turkish people here. Dutch inhabitants are afraid of Muslims and do not know what we do in the mosque. When we do not raise our voice now and make clear that we are bound to stay in the Netherlands, then they decide for us. [...] Our parents only think about a beautiful mosque inside, while the outside is even more important.

Look, we have come to the Netherlands as migrants. We have families in Turkey, our fatherland. But in fact most of the young people will stay in the Netherlands forever. We are already a little bit Dutch, although we will always stay Turkish. Our children become real Dutch. They have been born here. When they are Muslims, they are Dutch Muslims. But what happens? The government still treats us as migrants after all these years. In fact, our leaders are to blame for it. They think that you can achieve more when you always say I am a migrant. Elderly people do not bother what happens outside. They live with their eyes closed. They do not look at the future. They do not understand that cooperation is the only way to survive.

As we saw before, the attention in Islamic organizations already shifted towards the young generation in the eighties. Activities for young people increased considerably. Young members made it clear that the leadership of the organizations must accept the fact that their social position is completely different from that of their parents. They must be approached in a different way, with different means. It turned out that most young people in Islamic organizations had completely different motives to participate in activities of Islamic organizations as compared to elderly Muslims.

For the majority of elderly first generation members, premigration circumstances and their own community constitute the single most important points of reference in the development of their Islamic identity. Dutch society hardly plays a role as a point of reference. Ethnic and religious categories seem to merge. For a growing number of young people, however, the host society, that is to say Dutch society, forms an important point of reference. This is especially the case with those who have a relatively good social position. Many have broken away from the position of their parents. To them returning to the country of origin is not a viable option anymore. Their future is situated in the Netherlands and not in Turkey, not only from a practical viewpoint but also increasingly from a mental perspective. It seems to me that the psychological effects of the 'return-to-the-country-of-origin' option have been underestimated in literature. The practical feasibility of returning does not have to coincide with the psychological function it can perform. For many first generation migrants, returning is still an essential aspect of their future perspective, although the actual decision is postponed again and again. It functions, to a certain extent, as a survival strategy. It makes them more or less immune to stigmatization and discrimination.

For a growing number of young people these psychological functions have disappeared. Just because returning to the country of origin can no longer function as a release, their orientation towards Dutch society becomes stronger and their expectations of society become higher. This can make them more sensitive to mechanisms of real or perceived exclusion and they are ready to fight this.

This changing perspective influences the way in which they give meaning to the Islam. Those who have lived in the Netherlands for quite a long time speak Dutch well, have mastered social skills, and interact, either at school, at work or in leisure time, intensively with Dutch people, attach a clearly different meaning to Islam as compared to those who do not posses these qualities. They tend to emphasize the dynamic changeable aspects of Islam. In doing so they more or less move away from the 'traditional' Islam of the elderly milieu. Among some of these young Muslims, due to their long stay in the Netherlands, the significance of their own ethnic and regional background has diminished in the construction of Islamic identity. This of course does not mean that their own community and the country of origin are not important anymore. What is at stake here is that the Netherlands have become the main point of reference in constructing Islamic identity. Many have the feeling that they treat Islam more consciously and that they are able to formulate more clearly what it means to be Muslim in the Netherlands. Islam is for them an alternative rather than something which is self-evident. The fact that Islam is just one of the religious denominations in the Netherlands is not just something which has to be accepted, it rather should play a role in the development of one's identity, *provided that Dutch society accepts Muslims as being equal to other people!* Among this category I met the most 'converts'; youths who stated that they had neglected Islam for a long time, but now they thought better of it and embraced Islam on new terms.

A typical characteristic of this cognitive shift is that these youths wanted to 'rewrite history' and render a new interpretation of Islam, of which the gradual disassociation of Islam from its ethnic connotations was the main aspect. The concepts of 'Turk' and 'Muslim' as important identity markers are dissociated from each other by them. Although most of the youths consider their Turkish background as an important part of their identity, they thought it 'complete nonsense' to single out the Turks as a specific category in Islamic history. Consequently, every society could finally become an Islamic society, provided certain conditions had been fulfilled. Although the history of Islam was related to the history of specific countries and peoples, Islam itself was considered a universalist and inclusive religion. The message was directed towards every living soul, and there were no countries and no peoples for whom Islam could be more suitable or appropriate than for others. For a Turk it is as difficult or as easy as for any other person to become a good Muslim. Every view of Islam as a kind of national ideology was an attack on the very nature and message of Islam itself. Islam therefore renders a more inclusive meaning.

According to these young Muslims, the introduction of an Islamic way of living together with a permanent residence in the Netherlands is not just a simple matter of compromises between Islamic principles and principles of the Dutch society. This shifting significance manifests itself primarily as a shift from Islam as a tradition to Islam as a conviction. Religious 'community' does not necessarily run parallel anymore with other social bindings and the Islam becomes a matter of individual choice. Islam becomes significant as an ethic system in which one's fragmented life experiences are symbolically linked together in a new discourse. Religious 'community' is constantly being reproduced within the context of changing circumstances.

Recent Developments

The tendency described above manifests itself clearly, amongst other things, in the increasing number of 'multinational' or rather 'non-national' Islamic organizations in the Netherlands. In Rotterdam and surrounding areas, there are already initiatives among young Muslims to found a 'Dutch' mosque. Friday sermons should be held in Dutch and the administration should be completely independent from the existing ethnically divided structures. Also the discussion about a Dutch Islamic academy for training imams has to be mentioned in this respect.

It is, however, first and foremost the discussion about the place of Islam in a rapidly secularizing Dutch society that is the most striking feature of recent developments. This discussion is in itself not new, but it is not anymore a discussion *about* Muslims, but one in which Muslim intellectuals, politicians and professionals increasingly take issue themselves.

Conclusions

In this article I have tried to sketch briefly under what circumstances changes within Turkish Islamic organizations take place and which factors account for it. The crucial issue at stake in these changes is the extent to which Islamic organizations should develop into Dutch organizations. The changing orientations among young Muslims are to a large extent connected to an interplay of internal and external factors, of which a changing orientation to the future among young people is rather essential. Although in my view these changes are being influenced by religio-ideological differences among Muslims, it is a development which, at the same time, reaches beyond these ideological fragmentations.

Of course, we are still in a initial phase. In many cases there is only discussion, but in my view it is clear that Islamic organizations are in general acting more openly and this influences the internal power relations within Islamic organizations. When looking at these developments five years later, it seems that internal developments and controversies within the established Islamic organizations must be considered, more or less, as a stage in a process. It paved the way for new initiatives that are coming up at a rapid pace.

What I have tried to show is that Islamic organizations increasingly enter the normal political arena. The outcome of this process depends on a lot of factors. It not only influences internal power relations, but, more importantly, also Islamic discourse itself. A growing number of young people orientate themselves towards Dutch society, which implies that they expect more from that society, especially with regard to their socio-economic position. When society is willing to treat Muslims as equal citizens and when there is an 'open' structure of political opportunities, then young Muslims will increasingly emphasize that Islam can become an integral part of Dutch society and they will be willing to cooperate. If, however, they are confronted with a closed political structure, it likely produces a radical discourse which leaves no room for further integration and cooperation. Dutch society and policy makers should thus be aware of the active role they play in the process.

References

Anderson, B. (1991), *Imagined Communities. Reflections on the Origin and Spread of Nationalism*, (Revised edition), London, Verso.

Duyvendak, J.W. (1997), 'Gelegenheidsstructuren en gelegenheidsargumenten. Nederland en de ruimte voor islamitische organisaties', *Migrantenstudies*, 14/2, pp. 103-6.

Eisinger, P.K. (1973), 'The Conditions of Protest Behaviour in American Cities', *The American Political Science Review*, vol. 67, pp. 11-28.

Hechter, M., D. Friedman and Appelbaum, M. (1982), 'A theory of Ethnic Collective Action', *International Migration Review*, vol. 16/2, pp. 412-34.

Jazouli, A. (1986), *L'action collective des jeunes Maghrébiens en France*, Paris, l'Harmattan.

Landman, N. (1992), *Van mat tot minaret. De institutionalisering van de islam in Nederland*, Amsterdam, VU Uitgeverij.

McAdam, D. (1982), *Political Process and the Development of Black Insurgency 1930-1970*, Chicago, University of Chicago Press.

Nielsen, J.S. (1992), *Muslims in Western Europe*, Edinburgh, Edinburg University Press.

Rath, J., Penninx, R., K. Groenendijk, K. and Meyer, A. (1996), *Nederland en zijn islam*, Amsterdam, Het Spinhuis.

Schierup, C. (1992), *Multiculturalism, neo-racism, and vicissitudes of contemporary democracy*, paper for Nordic Seminar for Migration Research, Esbjerg.

Sunier, T. (1996), *Islam in beweging. Turkse jongeren en islamitische organisaties*, Amsterdam, Het Spinhuis.

Sunier, T., Duyvendak, J. W., Saharso, S. and Steijlen, F. (2000), *Emancipatie en subcultuur. Sociale bewegingen in België en Nederland*, Amsterdam, IPP.

Tarrow, S. (1994), *Power in Movement. Social Movements, Collective Action and Politics*, Cambridge, Cambridge University Press.

Vermeulen, H. (1992), 'De Cultura. Een verhandeling over het cultuurbegrip in de studie van allochtone etnische groepen', *Migrantenstudies*, 8/2, pp. 14-31.

Chapter 9

The First Generation of Turkish Male Migrants – A 'Second Hand Image' or a 'First Hand Image'?

Margret Spohn

Introduction[1]

Is research about male migrants really needed? It is certainly unusual to place first-generation male migrants in the focus of research.[2] The reason for this fact could be that in the past researchers had recognized there was a lack of knowledge about the living conditions, the social and sexual behaviour, as well as about the family relations of migrant women and children. This resulted in a huge number of more or less qualified studies. There seemed to be no need to do any research into the male migrant population. But the simple assumption that any research that is not focusing on women must equate to being research on men is a misapprehension, as I will demonstrate later.

But even when there was no special research concerning men, the male Turkish migrants did not disappear from the public eye. The so-called 'first generation' is now reaching the age of retirement. Contrary to the long held belief that – once pensioners – the Turks would return to their country of origin, all statistics and research studies show that even in their old age they remain in Germany. The scientific community as well as the German public in general has long neglected this fact. Then suddenly in the late 80s more

---

[1] The following article is based on the newly published book: 'Türkische Männer in Deutschland. Familie und Identität. Migranten der ersten Generation erzählen ihre Geschichte', Bielefeld, transcript Verlag, 2002.

[2] As far as I am aware there is only one study in Germany dealing primarily with Turkish male migrants, which is the book written by Werner Schiffauer: 'The migrants from Subay' (Die Migranten von Subay, 1991) where he is asking the question how the experience of modernity affects the relationship between the father (still in Turkey) and the son who migrated to Germany. Schiffauer's sons, his second generation, are my first generation migrants.

and more studies about the situation of the now old first-generation migrants started to appear (Scheib, 1995; Schleicher, 1996; Bilal, 1993; etc.). The first studies focused on the question of a future health and care system for the migrants and whether Turkish family networks could be involved. In summary, these studies showed a very deprived situation of these persons:

- Far away from their home country knowing that the dream of going back is over ('the collapse of the illusion of turning back'), they have to spend their last days in a foreign country ('der Fremde') (Dietzel-Papakyriakou and Olbermann, 1996; Dietzel-Papakyriakou, 1990, 1993),
- They suffer from poor health and without family support separated (mentally) from their children, who have accepted the German way of life rather than the Turkish life style of their fathers,
- Now in their old age they have low financial resources, because they did not work long enough in Germany to qualify for full pensions.

As pensioners, the first generation of Turkish migrants reappeared in the scientific community and in public opinion. But we know far more about this group than just this image of an old, ill, lonely and hopeless person. As explained earlier, a lot of studies focus on migrant women and children. In these studies women and children speak about their husbands and fathers. Also most researchers and social workers publish their own point of view of the Turkish husbands and fathers without ever having asked the men themselves. And so, from year to year, from book to book a certain image of the first generation of Turkish male migrants has been handed down. Nauck speaks of a 'Zitierkartell' (Nauck, 1993, p. 367), a 'cartel of quoting' which uses the same images again and again. I introduce in my research the expression: 'second hand image' to give a name to the fact that the image of the first generation of Turks is mainly generated through the German media, researchers, social workers as well as through their women and children. The Turks are seen as:

- Supposedly conservative and not willing to integrate into the German community,
- The main reason for female (daughters' and wives') oppression,
- Tradition holders for a male-centred image.

These images of the first generation were completely contrary to my personal contacts to members of this generation. And just the fact that some

40 years ago somebody from a foreign, mostly rural orientated country decided to come to Germany to work in industry, in an environment where they did not understood a single word, demonstrated to me that these persons must have been in their younger days highly motivated individuals with a certain spirit of adventure. This generation had really lived the experience of different worlds. They had to find their way in Turkey and Germany to feel good and to live in harmony with themselves. I could not believe that all this power they had shown at the beginning of their migration has disappeared and been replaced by depression, loneliness, authoritarian behaviour towards their family and rejection of the German society.

To obtain a 'first-hand image', 20 first-generation Turkish males were interviewed about their own points of view, their experiences, their dreams and fears. The research presented here focuses on family-oriented male identities, which means their experiences of being a son (from a young age in Turkey and also from an older age in Germany), a husband (again both in Turkey and Germany) and a father (once more in both countries). The aim was to find out how the Turkish migrants locate themselves as male human beings within different societies (see figure 9.1). The left-hand section of the figure shows that the men spent important parts of their life both in Turkey and in Germany. In Turkey they spent their childhood, their youth and the first years of adulthood. They came to Germany as adults. In Germany as well as in Turkey they have been confronted with different norms and values from their parents, their spouses, their children and the environment, which they could either have had accepted, rejected or partly accepted or rejected.

Migration could play an important role in this context, as the men will perhaps be confronted with different norms and values. This can lead to:

- Confirmation of their own norms and values from childhood and adulthood and their application in Germany,
- Rejection of the norms and values gained during their own childhood and adulthood and to the application of what is seen as German norms and values,
- Partial rejection of the norms and values gained during their own childhood and adulthood and to the application of a mixture between what is seen as German and Turkish norms and values.

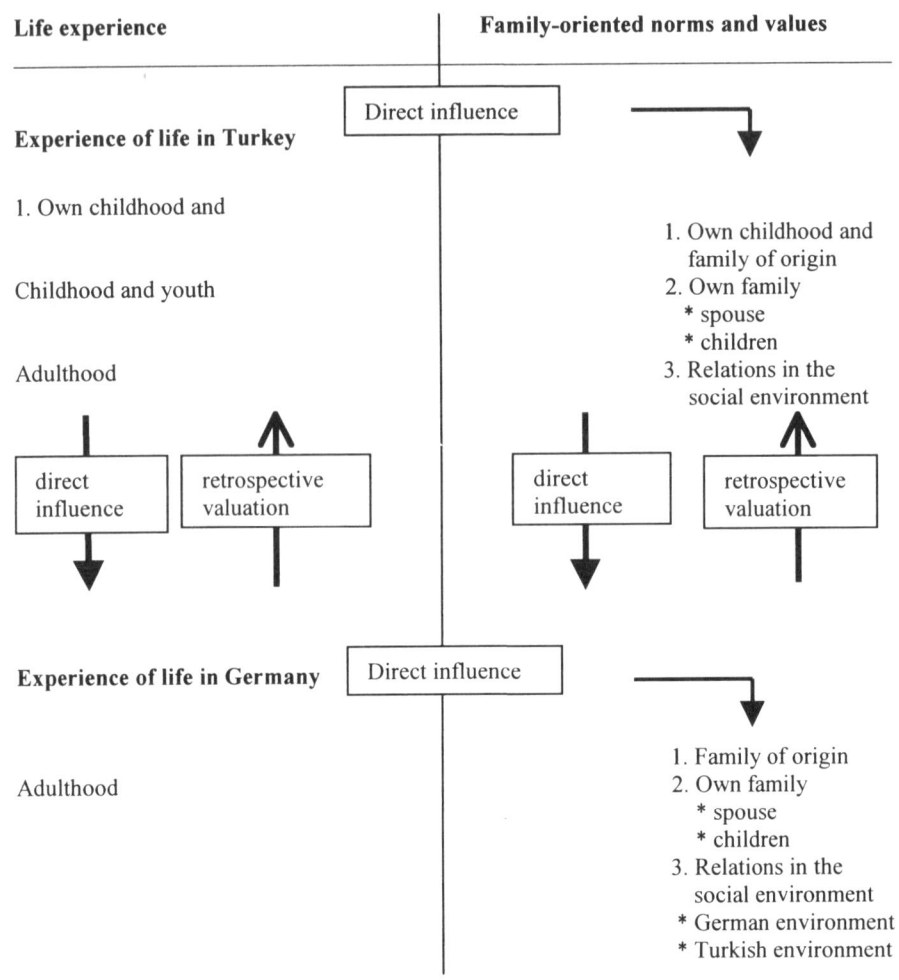

Figure 9.1 Turkish men and family-oriented male roles in migration

In this perception, migration is not defined as *the* turning point of life. Perhaps migration was chosen in order to live a life in Germany which was not possible in Turkey, perhaps the migration had no influence at all on family-oriented male identities. In order to analyse the role of migration it has to be shown whether the interviewee whilst in Turkey had accepted or was in opposition to the family-oriented male norms and values of his family/environment. So the term 'change' becomes a main focus point of the research. The following table helps to underline this approach:

Table 9.1 Family-oriented Turkish male identities in Turkey and Germany

	Family-oriented Turkish male identities in Turkey	Family-oriented Turkish male identities in Germany
Relation to the family of origin	Change No Change Conditional Change	Change No Change Conditional Change
Relation to the spouse	Change No Change Conditional Change	Change No Change Conditional Change
Relation to the children	Change No Change Conditional Change	Change No Change Conditional Change

Çiğdem Kağıtçıbaşı, a Turkish social-scienctist and an expert in cross-cultural psychology who currently works at the Koc University in Turkey, developed three different family models in a cross-cultural research. Her aim was to find a model/models capable of integrating the interaction between family, society and environment also in different countries. Her family models are applied here in a migration context. In her ideal models Kağıtçıbaşı explained interactions in the family. In my research I focused more on the male point of view towards himself, towards his spouse and towards his children.

The model of interdependence:

- Families of this type are mostly found in rural/agrarian societies,
- It shows a high level of relatedness to the family (culture of relatedness – collectivistic),
- The members of a family function in the same time as a production unit – they all work together, mostly in agriculture, in the home production of goods, agricultural production or consumption, child care and so on,
- The loyalty of the individual is oriented toward the collective and is not self-centred,
- The newly developing personality of a child identifies itself with the group,
- Families are characterized by patrilinear family structures,

- Families have little income,
- (A lot of) children, sons are preferred, are seen as a form of old age security,
- Individual education of the children is not important,
- Upbringing is oriented towards obedience of the child and 'respect' of the child towards the parents,
- Women have a low status (Kağıtçıbaşı, 1996, pp. 78ff).

The model of independence:

- Families of this type are mostly found in urban/technologist societies,
- It shows a low level of relatedness to the family (culture of separateness – individualistic),
- The generations live apart,
- Loyalty is oriented towards the individual,
- The newly developing personality of a child identifies itself more as an individual,
- Fewer children (no gender preference),
- The parents invest in the education of their children. They are no longer seen as security in old age,
- Upbringing is oriented towards 'independence' and the child,
- Women have a high status (Kağıtçıbaşı, 1996, pp. 82ff).

The above two models show nothing new. It can be said that they focus on the well-known dichotomy between more rural or industrial countries. But she introduces a third model, which she called: A *model of emotional interdependence* and this model gives a very good opportunity to analyse family structures in a new way. Today, societies are much too complicated to reduce family interaction just to the dichotomy urban-old versus industrial-modern. This third model enables a very effective approach, especially in a migration context. This model, that is typical for more urban areas, is characterized by the following features:

- Interdependence in the emotional realm at both family and individual levels but independence in the material realm (culture of relatedness-collectivistic),
- Loyalties are oriented as well towards the individual as towards the family and group,

- The developing identity of a child defines itself both as an individual as a member of a family,
- The parents have fewer children. They invest in their education and hope at the same time to get something back in old age,
- The preference for male children is less and less important,
- The upbringing of the child is not only oriented towards 'respect' but also towards 'independence' of the child,
- The status of women increases.

Figure 9.2 gives an overview about the features and relationship within the model of emotional interdependence. This theoretical model was applied to the first generation of Turkish migrants. The initial aim was to find out to which family type the family of origin belonged and how the interviewee sees and evaluates his past and what role his past plays in the education and upbringing of his children and in his relationship to his spouse. Different models could be possible:

- His whole life he belongs to the same family type as his family of origin. Even in a retrospective perspective he defends the norms and values of his childhood and he applies the same upbringing also to his children,
- Already in his youth he was against certain norms and values and already in his younger days he showed his disapproval and got into conflict with his parents,
- Already in his youth he was against certain norms and values but could not show his disapproval. This was only possible after the migration to Germany,
- In his youth he accepted the norms and values from his parents and it was after the migration to Germany and his subsequent experience that he started to see things another way, to change under the influence of his environment.

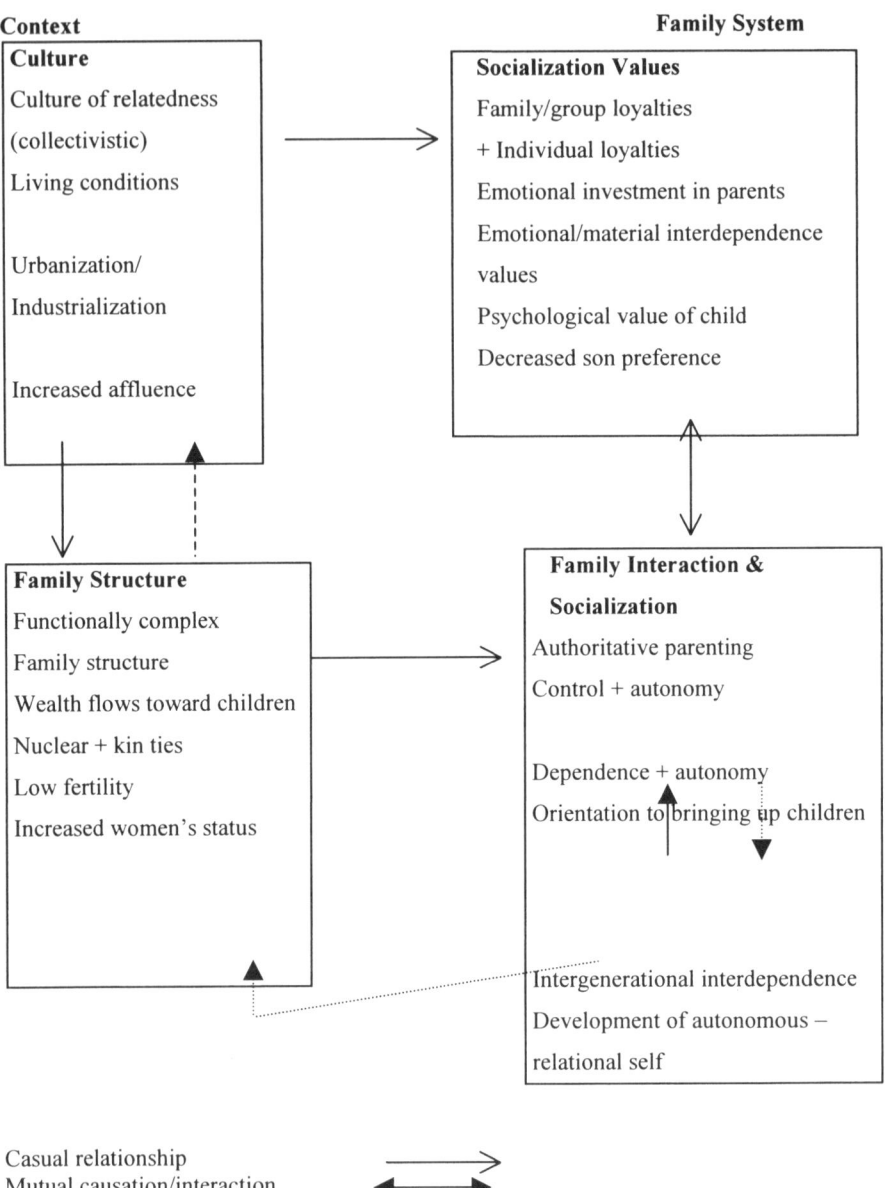

Figure 9.2 A model of emotional interdependence

Source: Kağıtçıbaşı, 1996, p. 88; Kağıtçıbaşı (1990).

The qualitative interviews have been analyzed[3] with help of the family models of Kağıtçıbaşı along research questions that follow the suggestions of these models:

- Situation as a male child in Turkey (relationship to the parents and the social environment),
- Situation as a young man in Turkey (relationship to the parents and the social environment),
- Situation as a young married man in Turkey (relationship to his wife, his parents and the social environment),
- Situation as a father in Turkey (relationship to his children – style of upbringing in comparison with own upbringing),
- Situation as a son, husband and father in Germany,

The main focus was oriented towards the question as to whether the interviewee, within the family models of Kağıtçıbaşı, has undergone a change in his family-oriented male identities. And if such a change was noticeable, was that the result of a conscious decision, or is it an unconscious act? Table 9.2 gives an overview of the first results.

---

[3] A great part of my work is dedicated to methods in intercultural research. To the questions what happens if a (more or less) (young) woman interviews an (more a less) (old) man; if a member of the majority culture interviews somebody of a minority culture; if an academic interviews somebody from the working class; if a single woman interviews a married man, etc. In British research it is much more usual than in German research to take into consideration the researcher's position and its influence on the research process.

Table 9.2 Distribution of the interviewees according to the family models of Kağitçibaşi

Models of masculinity according to the family models of Kağıtçıbaşı	Cases	Numbers
Continuous model of 'interdependence'	M. Hacıoğlu M. Levent M. Inan M. Nazım M. Olgun M. Tufan	6
Continuous model of 'independence'	M. Fener M. Çınar M. Volkan M. Ergin M. Bilen M. Polat	6
Continuous model of 'emotional interdependence'	M. Gür M. Alkan	2
Change from the model of 'interdependence' to the model of 'emotional interdependence'	M. Demir M. Mardın M. Korkmaz M. Uçar M. Sert	5
Mix between the model of 'emotional interdependence' and the model of 'independence'	M. Reyis	1
Change from the model of 'emotional interdependence' to the model of 'independence'[4]		0

The first result is that already in Turkey, long before their migration to Germany, the first generation migrant workers belonged to different types of family forms. They belonged to different social backgrounds with diverse family-oriented male behaviour. Already in Turkey there was a significant differentiation.

Fourteen men lived in Germany by the same model that they already had lived in Turkey. For the six men belonging to the *model of interdependence*

---

[4] Theoretically there could be three further models of a possible change: from the model of 'independence' to the model of 'interdependence' from the model of 'independence' to the model of 'emotional interdependence' and from the model of 'emotional interdependence' to the model of 'interdependence'. These types did not appear in my interviews.

this entails a great balancing act between their favourite life style and the German environment. Much more than in all the other models, religion plays an important role. It provides an anchor in a changing world where also the own children contribute to this change. Especially concerning the children, the fathers of the model of continuous interdependence have to reach compromises again and again between their own norms and values and the world of their children. These fathers have a strong belief into the so-called 'generational-contract'. Now in their old age they wish to 'reap the rewards of their labour' and hope that their children will act in the required way.

In the *model of continuous interdependence*, migration plays a role in two ways: The fact of being in Germany allows being able to hold on to the strong belief that in Turkey everything is as it used to be in their own youth. Since the changes in Turkey are not perceived and even not seen, these men believe that today's Turkey is identical with the Turkey of their young days, where a father had been *the* authority in a family.

This is shown by the very clear example of M. Hacıoğlu, who still believes that he is the master even over the life and death of his children and his wife. His typical sentence was: 'When I say "die" to my wife, she will die'. And even when he is talking about conflicts with his children and grandchildren, who do not want to accept the authority of the absent father, M. Hacıoğlu is neither willing nor able to change his mind about structures in Turkey. I have to say that neither his spouse nor his children had been in Germany at any time. He has been away for 30 years. So the structures he describes are more in his imagination than the reality.

In the original model of interdependence the status of men, as well as of women, is enhanced by age. In Germany, these men make the experience that their status and degree of acceptance does not grow in proportional with their age. It is even the contrary in a society where the power belongs to the young and middle-aged generation. That is why it is understandable from their point of view to hold on a model where old age is the guarantee for respectful treatment.

In the model of continuous interdependence, migration cannot be seen as a break in their life. Most of the men lived their life in continuity and raised their children in the same way, as they themselves had been educated.

The men belonging to the model of independence have fewer problems finding their way in German society because their way of life and thinking is very similar to that of the main group in Germany. But this alleged equality is just a supposed one. The men of this group develop very sensitive feelings towards their unequal treatment by elements of German society. The future of their children is a matter of the highest concern. Their children raised in Germany are educated here in the same way as young Germans, but will nevertheless not have the same rights as their German peers. The treatment of their children gives the fathers a feeling of impotence in face of the German majority. At the same time their integration into the German society is shown very clearly by the fact that in this group in every family at least one son or daughter-in-law is German. By contrast none of the men contained in the model of interdependence has a German son or daughter-in-law.

Concerning the role of migration, it is quite obvious that it is not a break in their lives. The same model that they find in Germany influenced the men belonging to the model of interdependence. But in comparison to Turkey, they lose their social status in Germany. M. Çınar, an engineer, as well as M. Fener, a teacher, talk a lot in the interview about the loss of their status in Germany.

For some of the men it was just the migration, which enabled them to live their life in a model of interdependence and to break with the model of independence of their families of origin. It was only in Germany that was it possible for M. Polat to obtain a divorce from his wife, whom he had never loved and whom he had been forced to marry by his parents. And M. Volkan started to live a very independent life in Germany.

During their lifetime five men made a change from one model to another. This change can be either an active or a passive process.

Table 9.3 Distribution of the analysed cases with regard to an active or passive change of family oriented models of masculinity

Models of family-oriented masculinities in the sense of Kağıtçıbaşı	Active behaviour	Passive behaviour
Change from the model of 'interdependence' to the model of 'emotional interdependence'	M. Demir M. Mardın	M. Uçar M. Sert M. Korkmaz

Most of the men get through this change with awareness. Bad experiences in their youth (no access to education, starting work at a very young age, forced marriages, fear of the father) led them to a conscious change of their life style and to a clear break with the model of their youth. First of all the men changed the upbringing of their own children, which means free access to education, giving them the right to choose their spouses. In this case migration can be seen as a break. Because only in a migration context was it possible for the men to realize that other norms and values exist. In the critical analysis of the norms and values of their youth with the German system, they find their own way and are ready to change.

Apart from the children who profit from the changed norms and values, the wives also profit from this change to a larger extent. The position of the woman improves and the couple acts more in the way of a partnership.

But this change is not an active process in all cases. The example of M. Korkmaz shows that verbally he has not changed at all. In the interview he mentions the family-oriented norms and values from his youth as a good way to live in Germany. And he is proud to educate his children in the same way that he was educated. But by analysing his theory with his living (upbringing) practice it is very obvious that – even though he denies the fact – he had changed from one model into the other. If M. Korkmaz had stayed in Turkey he would have broken under his fear of his father and uncle. Only migration allows him to live in harmony with himself. The difference between his youth and upbringing and the upbringing of his children is obvious.

To conclude it can be said the interviewed men belonged to a group who reacted in a very flexible way to changing life and social environment conditions. Their own male identities are built in the first instance by acceptance or rejection by *the* dominant male identity model of their youth: the father or uncle. Some of the men had already rejected that model in Turkey but, due to the pressure of the family and the social environment, could not find a way to change it. In these cases, migration gives them the opportunity and the freedom finally to live their life the way they wanted.

In all cases, living in Germany led to an awareness of their own position, the differences and common interests applicable to both the German and the Turkish society. The men choose the aspects of both societies which were appropriate to their beliefs and life conditions. Contrary to Nauck, who argues that this utilitaristian way does not need any change of norms or values (Nauck, 1986, p. 286; 1988, p. 506), I found in my research that such a change of norms and values did take place. This becomes very obvious when the interviewees make a clear distinction between the way they have been brought up and how they educate and bring up their own children, or in which way the relation as a married couple changed in comparison to their parents or their own life in Turkey. Nauchk's theory can be applied only for the men belonging to the model of continuous interdependence. In order not to lose their children, these men undergo a utilitarian change without which no real change of norms and values would have taken place.

For all the men, but especially for the men belonging to the model of emotional interdependence, the children are at the centre of their lives. They give them the power to undergo changes and to try new challenges. The definition of what characterizes a successful upbringing is different in all three models. While for the men belonging to the model of interdependence it means that the children accept the norms and values of their fathers, it means for the men belonging to the model of independence that the children are able to find their adequate place in the German society. So they can reach what was not possible for the fathers: Acceptance within German society. Only for the men belonging to the model of emotional interdependence was 'happiness for the children' seen as the aim of a successful upbringing.

But all the men, whatever model they believe in, had in common that the final aim of a child has to be to get married and have kids themselves. The men reacted with sorrow and a lack of understanding if their children did not follow their fathers in that way.

As discussed at the beginning of this paper, the very well known second-hand image of the first generation of Turkish male migrants would start to change if more research with and not about the first generation were undertaken.

References

Bilal, H. (1993), 'Seniorenarbeit mit MigrantInnen in Berlin-Spandau', Informationsdienst zur Ausländerarbeit, vol. 3, p. 58.

Dietzel-Papakyriakoi (1993), 'Ältere Ausländer in der Bundesrepublik Deutschland - Zwischen Ausländersozialarbeit und Altenhilfe', Informationsdienst zur Ausländerarbeit, vol. 3, Frankfurt, pp. 43-53.

Dietzel-Papakyriakoi, M. (1990), 'Das Alter der Arbeitsmigranten: ethnische Ressourcenund doppelte Benachteiligung', Zeitschrift für Gerontologie, vol. 23, Darmstadt, pp. 345-53.

Dietzel-Papakyriakoi, M. and Olbermann, E. (1996), 'Zum Versorgungsbedarf und zur Spezifikälterer Migrantinnen und Migranten', Informationsdienst zur Ausländerarbeit, vol. 3, Frankfurt, pp. 46-51.

Kağıtçıbaşı, Ç. (1996), *Family and human development across cultures: a view from the other side*, Mahwah; New Jersey: Lawrence Erlbaum Associates.

Nauck, B. (1988), 'Inter- und intragenerativer Wandel in Migrantenfamilien', Soziale Welt, vol. XXXIX/1988, Göttingen, Verlag Otto Schwarz & Co, pp. 450-65.

Nauck, B. (1993), 'Dreifach diskriminiert? – Ausländerinnen in Wetdeutschland' in H. Gisela, Nickel, M. Hildegard (eds), *Frauen in Deutschland 1945-1992*, Bundeszentrale für politische Bildung, Schriftenreihe, vol. 318, Bonn, pp. 354-98.

Nauck, B. and Özel, S. (1986), 'Erziehungsvorstellungen und Sozialisationspraktika in türkischen Migrantenfamilien', Zeitschrift für Sozialisationsforschung und Erziehungstheorie, vol. 6, no. 2. pp. 285-312.

Scheib, H. (1995), 'Ältere MigrantInnen und die Altenhilfe. Ergebnisse einer Untersuchung zur Nutzung der Altenhilfe durch ältere MigrantInnen in der', Frankfurt am Main, Informationsdienst zur Ausländerarbeit, vol. 3, Frankfurt, pp. 46-51.

Schleicher, F. (1996), 'Ältere Migrantinnen und Migranten in der Altenplanung am Beispiel der Stadt Köln', Informationsdienst zur Ausländerarbeit, vol. 3+4, pp. 93-4.

Spohn, M. (2002), *Türkische Männer in Deutschland. Familie und Identität. Migranten der ersten Generation erzählen ihre Geschichte*, Bielefeld. Transcript.

Chapter 10

Collective Identities of Turkish Migrants in Germany – The Aspect of Self-Localization

Kathrin Prümm, Rosemarie Sackmann, Tanjev Schultz

Introduction

In the following we present some findings from a research project on the collective identity of Turkish migrants in Germany.[1] This project was initiated against the background of public discussions about the failure of integration in the case of Turkish migrants. A common assumption in these discussions holds that Turkish migrants and their descendants do have a collective Turkish identity and that this identity would foster the existing separation from German mainstream society. However, it is an empirical question whether Turkish migrants actually have got a collective identity and just how significant it is. It was the aim of our research project to help answer this question.

Categories, Groups and Collective Identities

The existence of a collective identity cannot be presupposed. While ethnic population categories usually are a starting point for research, categories should not be equated with collective groups. The ascription of a person to a category of migrants is based upon social statistical criteria such as immigration and ethnic origin. However, these features do not tell us

---

[1] The project was carried out at the Institute of Intercultural and International Studies (InIIS) at the University of Bremen between May 1999 and May 2001. It was financed by the German Research Association (Deutsche Forschungsgemeinschaft, DFG). Supervisors of the project were Prof. Bernhard Peters and Dr. Rosemarie Sackmann, researchers Kathrin Prümm and Tanjev Schultz. An earlier version of this paper was presented at a workshop in Bremen in February 2001.

whether a given person considers him- or herself part of an immigrant community. Moreover, even the existence of social groups which are based on preferential relationships among migrants does not imply that these persons share a collective identity. Social groups can exist without collective identity. Surely, social relationships may have an influence on collective identity formation, but this is not necessarily the case. Since the existence of a group and a collective identity cannot be presupposed, our analysis is based on the subjective beliefs and orientations of individuals.

We understand collective identity as part of the culture of a group (compare Peters, this volume). The culture of a group consists of symbol systems and symbolic contents which play a large part in the lives of the group members. The *shared culture* of a group consists of all the symbolic elements shared by group members, that means elements that are used for orientation in interaction and communication by group members. Among these symbols and interpretation schemes some refer to the character and fate of the group. The totality of these cultural elements is the collective identity of the group.

Within the conceptual framework of our project, collective identity is defined as the ideas of group members about the particularity of the group, ideas about values, references to past and future of the group as well as ideas about the correct behaviour of members of the group. The term 'collective identity' is value-free, that means: it is neither assumed that migrants in Germany need a collective identity in the same way a human being needs an unhampered, unspoiled personal identity, nor is it said that the existence of a collective identity of migrant groups is in itself a threat to successful integration into German society. The aim of the study was solely to discover whether there is a collective identity of Turkish migrants, and how such an identity, if found, is manifested.

Collective identities can be of different variety and solidity. They do not necessarily contain all of the listed elements; they can be vague and diffuse, or highly differentiated and articulated. Moreover, the structural relationships between different collective identities must be considered. There are certain identities which exclude each other; in other cases membership in two identity groups is possible. Finally, there are intertwined structures of identities. It is an interesting question, in what cases there are conflicts of loyalty regarding the membership in different groups and the participation in different collective identities. The issue of highest interest today is probably the relationship between national identification and identification with an immigrant community. Hereby, it can be assumed that the collective identity of most immigrant communities will have a 'hybrid' form. We expect that certain elements of the identification with the country of origin are embedded in an immigrant identity, which also contains elements of identification with the country of immigration.

We did not expect to find that Turkish migrants in Germany form a homogenous group with one extensive collective identity. Rather, it is to be expected that existing lines of social differentiation influence the relation of individuals to constructions of collective identity. For our project, we especially considered two lines of differentiation: *generations* and *gender*.

Data base

Our research was an explorative project with qualitative orientation. Core of the project were guide interviews. Same-sex parent-child dyads were selected for the project. After the interview, all interviewees were given an additional questionnaire. The results presented here are based on 112 interviews and on 122 questionnaires. Same-sex parent-child dyads were selected for the project. All interviewees were at least 18 years old. The parents are called first generation here. They were adults when they migrated to Germany. Their children are called second generation. They either migrated as children or were born in Germany. Most interviews with first generation migrants were held in Turkish. All interviews with second generation migrants were held in German. Women were interviewed by women, men by men.

We won our interview partners by snowball principle, while trying to reach as broad a section of people as possible. For interviews of this type, the influence of self-selection is generally high, therefore our interviews cannot claim to be representative of the entire category in question.

Self-Localizations: The Dimensions of Group and Place

Talk about ethnic groups categorizes the people in question according to their country of origin. In former assimilation research the underlying assumption has often been that migrants carry their culture as a kind of luggage from their home country to their country of immigration. Nowadays the underlying assumption is usually that migrants resist assimilation and that one reason for this resistance is that they stay in close contact with their country of origin, that they have ongoing relationships of different kinds. More or less strong bonds keep them in a space in between.

In these assumptions, the country of origin is seen as a locality that offers migrants a cultural identity as well as a socially determined identity. But ongoing contacts, such as regular visits, do not per se imply that migrants still feel at home in their country of origin. Such assumptions are often based on a notion of primordial bonds. Without such about primordial bonds we cannot assume that social and emotional relationships when the migrant can only partake in social life from a distance or during more or less extended, more or less regular visits. Thus, if we assume that migrants live in a transnational space, we would have to show that their relations are able to change, rather than that they stay the same. For the country of origin changes over time and – of course – migrants change themselves, at least most of them do.

However, it is still an open question whether and how migrants localize themselves in relation to their country of origin. And it is an open question, whether migrants see their fellow countrymen at home as their group of reference. Do Turks in Germany include Turks in Turkey when they speak about what is means to be a Turk? And in which way? In the following we will show that the self-localization with regard to a group or a category named 'Turks' does not necessarily imply that one sees Turks in Turkey as part of this group.

Our definition of collective identity given above does not include reference to *space* as an identity factor. The notion of self-localization implies reference to a group as well as reference to a space or place. The question is here: How far are these different ways of localization connected?

Let us first examine group affiliation. If someone sees him or herself as member of a group, we might expect that this group has a name. The name enables the group to be recognizeable and be addressed as such in social communications.

How do the Migrants Refer to Themselves?

In the interviews the migrants were asked: What would you call yourself? Would you call yourself a Turk, a German Turk, a German, or what else would you call yourself? Table 9.1 gives an overview of the answers to our question.

Table 10.1 Self-localization, group dimension

	Turk	German Turk	Muslim	German	Other categories or none at all	Total
Total	51	32	8	2	19	112
	(46 %)	(29 %)	(7 %)	(2 %)	(16 %)	(100 %)
Second generation	18	29	2	2	8	59

Nearly half of the respondents, 51 out of 112, call themselves 'Turks', 18 of them second-generation, 32 have chosen the label 'German Turk'; here 29 were second-generation.[2] Eight call themselves 'Muslims' (two of them second-generation).[3] Finally, 2 said they are 'Germans' (both second-generation), and 19 respondents either mentioned other labels, like foreigner (*Ausländer*), or human being (*Mensch*), or refused any kind of category. Clearly, self-localization as a 'Turk' was most frequent. It is relevant for most first-generation, but also for second-generation migrants. A quarter of the interviewees call themselves 'German Turk', a label chosen mostly by the second-generation. And self-localization as 'German' is rare among our interviewees.

To know, how people refer to themselves with regard to group-labels is clearly not enough. We need to know what meaning they attach to the chosen label. We will have a closer look here at the label 'Turk'. The most frequently chosen label, 'Turk', is the one with the most diverse meanings.

At one end of the spectrum there are those for whom the label 'Turk' has a deep meaning and great importance. For them, a Turk is someone who is loyal to the Turkish nation, someone who defends its honour, who stands 'under the Turkish flag'. In these cases membership is defined from

[2] We counted six persons within the category 'German-Turk' who have chosen no label but describe themselves as mixture of Turkish and German cultural elements and identifications.

[3] Note that for many interviewees religion is important for their lives. However only few have called themselves 'Muslim' as the primary way to describe themselves in the group dimension. It is possible that this is partly due to the form of our question. But if we look at the interviews we do not have much reason to expect, that many of the respondents would call themselves primarily 'Muslim'.

a group perspective and by the group or in the name of the group. However, only few of the interviewees attach this typical 'national' meaning to the label 'Turk' when they use it to describe themselves. Especially among second generation respondents this meaning of the label is rare.

Some respondents used a special kind of imaginary collective identity: 'true Turks' were those of former times. In these cases the reference group was the same for Turks everywhere in the world, but in reality it does exist nowhere today.

Especially among second generation respondents, to choose the label 'Turk' implies personal identification. Some of them think that identification is enough. Others insist that the person should also hold on to some Turkish traditions. However, usually these respondents did not or could not specify this implication further. Thus, to be a member of the group means foremost to have a sense of belonging. In this construction it is the individual person who decides if she is a Turk and what this implies.

At the other end of the spectrum there are those who think that the label means descent and nothing more. They or their parents came from Turkey, they have a Turkish passport – that is all, there is no further meaning attached to these facts.

Place of Belonging

Our next step will be to see whether the chosen group labels correspond to references along spatial lines. In the questionnaire the migrants were asked: Which is the location where you feel that you belong to first? We have given the following possible answers: the city where you live, Germany, Turkey, Europe, the whole world. The question was half-open, the respondents could also name a different place of their own choice, which only a few did. In a follow-up question, we asked for another location that the migrants feel they belong to in the second place.

Compared to the dominance of 'Turk' as a group label, strong feelings of belonging to Turkey are not as important: less than a quarter of our interviewees see Turkey as the place were they belong to first (see table 9.2). However, Germany was not mentioned most frequently either, but rather the city where the migrants live their daily lives. While the city was mentioned most frequently by second-generation migrants, within the first generation no place stands out: Turkey, the whole world, Germany and the city have been mentioned each by roughly a quarter of the interviewees.

Table 10.2 First place of belonging

	City/ city district	Germany	Turkey	Europe	Whole world	Other answers and no answer	Total
Total	41 (34 %)	18 (15 %)	24 (20 %)	4 (3 %)	24 (20 %)	11 (3 %)	122 (100 %)
1. gen.	12	13	15	1	15	4	60
2. gen.	29	5	9	3	9	7	62

When we combine affiliations to groups and locations we see that those who categorize themselves as Turks do not necessarily say that Turkey is the place where they feel that they belong to first. In fact, only in 16 interviews a self-localization as Turk appears together with Turkey as first place of belonging (table 9.3).

Table 10.3 Self-localization and first place of belonging

	City/ city district	Germany	Turkey	Europe	Whole world	Other answers	Total
Turk	10	8	16	1	11	5	51
German Turk	15	4	3	3	4	3	32
Muslim	1	2	1	-	3	1	8
German	1	-	-	-	1	-	2
Other answers	10	2	1	-	4	2	19
Total	37	16	21	4	23	11	112

As the table suggests, there is a correlation between seeing oneself as 'German Turk' and feeling that one belongs to the city in the first place. Yet there is no clear relationship between self-localization as a Turk and feelings of belonging to one location. Here, three locations were mentioned by a considerable portion of these interviewees: Turkey, the city and the whole world. Moreover: Among those who call themselves 'Turks', one third neither names Turkey as first nor as second place of belonging.

What meaning do the spatial affiliations have and how do the two forms of self-localization relate to one another? Feelings of belonging to the whole world correspond to categorizing oneself as cosmopolitan or simply as a human being. But these categories were rarely chosen by our interviewees.[4] What we may have found instead is a relationship between belonging to the whole world and categorizing oneself as a Turk. One can assume that expressing a feeling of belonging to the whole world is a way of solving the problem of self-localization when faced with the experience of migration. One refers to a spatial frame which is so broad that one cannot be excluded.

Feelings of belonging to the city where one lives have no correspondence on the part of group affiliations. Self-localization as a 'citizen of Bremen' would imply too much emphasis and can be expected only in some instances, if at all. This may be different in metropolitan cities like London, Paris or maybe Berlin. The significance of the city as a location – where migrants feel that they belong to – rather seems to hint at the general importance of the immediate local level, that is: the place where concrete daily lives are lived, the place of intersection of various social relationships (compare Sauter, this volume). In that respect it comes as no surprise that feelings of belonging to the city are especially common among those who call themselves 'German Turk'.

Summing up, it may be fair to say that Turkey does not stand out when it comes to interviewees' feelings of belonging. However, half of our interviewees mention Turkey either as first or as second place. But another half do not mention Turkey at all.

What is more interesting, when the migrants refer to themselves as Turks or as part of a Turkish group, usually Turks who live in Turkey are not included. Despite maintained relationships to Turkey – most of our respondents visit Turkey on a regular basis – despite these ongoing connections, various feelings of alienation keep the migrants from constructing a group image that includes Turks in Turkey. This became obvious on many occasions during the interviews.

In one question the migrants were asked whether they find that there are differences between Turks in Turkey and in Germany. Many, both first-

---

[4] For some interviewees a feeling of belonging to the whole world mirrors their migrant experience. They emphasize during the interview to live at several places in the world has altered their attitudes. They have now a different understanding of nations, membership and questions of belonging.

and second-generation, indeed saw considerable differences and reported experiences expressing a certain degree of estrangement.

> There will be no differences? Definitely there are differences between Turks who live in Turkey and Turks who live here. Differences exist. We go on holiday, to give a simple example, we can't adapt ourselves in Turkey, we do not match, we can't create harmony. In all areas. Starts with shopping, whatever. Because we have settled down here, already for years now. Differences do exist [1. Generation (mother); self-naming 'Turk'; 1. place of belonging: Germany, 2. place: city].

When talking about feelings of estrangement many hold the opinion that Turks in Turkey have changed, while the migrants in Germany have stayed the same:

> Unfortunately, there is a difference between Turks in Turkey and Turks who live here. Turks who live here have stayed honest and honourable to a degree of 60 percent. Every year I go on a trip to Turkey, and every time I miss our home here. Why do I miss it? Because we have our good friends and neighbours here. The atmosphere is totally different – friendlier. Turks in Turkey are not that way anymore. Yes, our friends are here. Even though they are integrated in many ways, they have remained true to themselves and kept their pure, good heart [1. Generation (father); self-naming 'Turk'; 1. place of belonging: whole world; 2. place: city].

It has to be emphasized that feelings of estrangement and adaptation or assimilation to the German context are not restricted to those who do not name Turkey as the location where they feel that they belong to first. The same phenomenon was found in interviews with migrants who call themselves Turks and who feel that they belong to Turkey first.

> I believe there is a difference. Turks abroad are somewhat more developed with respect to material things as well as with respect to their behaviour. When you go to Turkey they appear to be strangers. Or they look at us as if we were strangers. This would not be the case if one could get together. The problem is caused by us. We have been here for too long. And when we go there, they are like strangers. We can't form a bond [1. Generation (father); self-naming 'Turk', 1. place of belonging: Turkey; 2. place: city].

Usually asymmetric changes are noted: Turks in Turkey have changed somehow, or Turks in Germany have changed. But in any event: the migrants feel that they do not share the same life-world and the same views with Turks in Turkey. They have become strangers to one another. At the same time there are strong personal relationships that bind our interviewees to Germany. And, we can add some other information from the interviews here: some aspects of the German society are valued highly by our interviewees, for example the welfare state or the fact that labour relations are regulated and labour contracts are binding, or that civil servants do not await bribe money. What might be more interesting: freedom of opinion and religion are often mentioned. These evaluations show that – even for those interviewees who see themselves as Turks in Germany and not as Turks of Germany – some positive relation to the German context does exist.

Of course, our interviewees came from Turkey or they have parents that came from Turkey. And of course, Turkey is the place where Turks live. But as migrants or children of migrants our interviewees usually made additions to these lines of origin, when they define membership in a group called 'Turks', or when they explain, what it means to be a Turk, a German Turk, a Muslim or a foreigner with a Turkish background. Most of them feel a need to interpret their situation and, by doing this, to define their own position within a field of possible localizations. These definitions are especially important for the second generation, but many of the first generation are also engaged in these processes.

To sum up the findings: Our findings open the perspective on two ways to sidestep the question of national belonging of which our respondents make use. The first and most important is the localization within the narrower space of the locality, the place of living. The second is reference to the whole world as place of belonging. Our data show that for some migrants, Turkey still plays a role as a location they feel that they belong to. But, in general, reference to the German context is common and especially the city is important as first place of belonging.

Examining feelings of belonging to a social group, our study suggests that only few migrants include Turks who live in Turkey when they refer to 'Turks' as a group. Most of our interviewees believe that Turks in Germany are quite different from Turks in Turkey. As one of them remarked: they have become two peoples.

PART III
WHERE IS 'HOME'? THE PERSPECTIVE OF TRANSNATIONAL THEORIES

Chapter 11

Adolescent Positioning in Urban Space – Locality and Transnationality

Sven Sauter

Introduction: Two Spaces of Transition

Today, certain shifts of the conception of culture and society can be observed in big cities. These changes are related to worldwide movements of migration and cultural globalisation:

> The co-presence of migrants and longer resident population groups and the emergence of new, culturally determined forms of social inequality as well as new connections of hitherto separate societal spheres – culture, politics, economy – are transformations that first of all become visible and effective in cities. New forms of social arrangement with these processes of change, too, in particular the increase in attempts to culturally umpire society, are of particular significance in large cities (Welz, 1996, p. 131).

In her study 'Inszenierung kultureller Vielfalt' (1996), Gisela Welz describes her field of research in cosmopolitan cities from the angle of a cultural-anthropological viewpoint. She tries to develop a cultural-analytic model which implies a theory of metropolitan culture on one hand, and the consideration of cultural aspects typical of a cosmopolitan city, on the other hand. One point of interest is 'cultural brokerage', which in the process of development of cities into (global) capitals appears as a strategy for producing and presenting cultural varieties.

In the following I want to describe how young people coming from immigrant families in urban environments appropriate important spaces in the urban context and thereby create a field of acceptance on two levels. As a result of this process, a certain kind of transnationality is visible. Frankfurt is taken as an example of a metropolitan city.

The first level is the reconstruction of a social space, the ways of dealing with assimilation and the conditions of developing. The second is the research of enlargement of viewpoints that on a theoretical line helps to win an additional vocabulary and a new way of access. The problem, cultural variety versus cultural difference is of great importance.

Two spaces of transition, the one of adolescence on one hand and the one of experience of migration on the other hand, are in the focus of attention. In the following text I want to describe in detail these deeply connected spaces of transition, falling back on results of research obtained while observing the adolescent process of detachment in immigrant families. For two years I talked to young men and women who belonged to a Turkish folklore group, part of a Frankfurt migration organisation. We had individual interviews and group discussions about subjects such as family, parents, racial discrimination and hostility towards foreigners, that means problems of their everyday lives (cf. Sauter, 2000).

I chose one scene referring to transition and local – that means urban – positioning. After explaining the results of research I will start a theoretical reflection on enlargement of the dominating view of foreignness. At first I want to draw your attention to my empirical research and start a small case study.

Tülay – a Portrait

Tülay is German. She was born in Frankfurt, went to school and is a saleswoman. She is an average female adolescent. Her parents were immigrants from Turkey who, after thirty years of working in Germany, could perceive no further prospects and went back to Turkey. Tülay stayed in Frankfurt. It is strange that Tülay has no German passport; her residence permit can be withdrawn at any time in this country that is hers. But Turkey, the other country, is also hers. When you ask her what her nationality is she answers: 'I am a Frankfurt human being'. She lives – as she explains – in two cultures.

Problems appear only when the ethnic community is too strictly delimited. 'Sometimes I feel like a foreigner when I see how foreigners are treated. But sometimes I don't feel like a foreigner, I feel at home.' The expression 'Frankfurt human being' does not fit exactly into any technical or ethnic category of local communities.

How does Tülay describe her situation? How do young people of the so-called second or third generation feel? What value do they put on their coexistence with Germans, with others in the multiethnic situation of the city? What conditions are usual in this area? What are the aims of observation? Is it possible to discuss multiculture, ethnic differences or similar problems, without referring to the individual strategies for dealing with these abstract categories?

Can we find clear conditions for these various life plans and their realization as members of the folklore group described them? Or is it true – as Tülay mentions – that all the young people are Frankfurt human beings? This general hint to a not self-chosen environment refers to obvious problems which become apparent when someone tries to describe in a mere macroscopic way the coexistence in urban, heterogeneous and multiracial surroundings.

In the following I want to show how in this situation young people mark off their place in society. Their definition of their situation becomes obvious as a result in the discussions with the young people. It is important to pay attention to their own definition of position/localization in society and how they give rise to different kinds of interpretation of the situation.

A New Description of the Foreigner

Referring to the self-presentation of German-Turkish young people, one can find a very reflected definition of their situation. In this context I intentionally avoid the term 'identity'. I started my interview of the group by questioning where they feel at home. They answered: 'Nowhere are we at home!' a surprising reply at first. This symbolic homelessness is counterbalanced by the term 'home' composed by different non-local elements, of more psychosocial ones. Home is the place where you feel happy and this can be in a circle of friends, the folklore group where you spend your leisure time, but it can be in the family as well. 'Nowhere are we at home!' is a description of a non-existing place that allows no clear classification. It is a utopian dream and means lack of an absolute integration. They do not complain about this situation but constantly understand is as a personal quest. Questions appear which cannot be answered definitely.

'But sometimes it is quite different. I ask myself where my home is' – as Tülay says. The first reference is Turkey, the second is Germany and the third and important one is *foreignness*. The traditional classification as German, Turkish or Turkish-German is enlarged by the hyphen. This hyphen symbolises the place where young people are represented in the society, it is a place 'in between'. The feeling of affiliation is not created by a culture of a minority, nor by a culture of a majority, but by this definition 'to be at home nowhere'. This place within different cultures is 'to be abroad'. To be abroad does not mean to be foreign in this or that culture, it means not to define a concrete place. It is a new definition of foreignness.

This definition is linked to a concrete place, it can appear in personal discussions, in society and in the family, as well as in the folklore group – an important place where young people meet, discuss and feel understood. It is a personal question of mine whether this idea of foreignness is really taken into consideration in social-cultural and educational discussions. The answer must be negative, because the mainstream intercultural discussions in Germany are mostly still focused on life *between* different cultures. (cf. Gemende et al., 1999)

The sociologist Albert Scherr proposed tackling the problem of foreignness in a consistent social-constructive way and not to consider it as a quasi natural fact of social life (cf. Scherr, 1999, p. 49) In his examining reports and recommendations for development of sociological and educational discourse of foreignness focusing on intercultural social activity, or rather intercultural educational theory he adds:

> Thus, with regard to the immigrants the task of social-scientific enlightenment ought not be seen first and foremost in conducting empirical research into how they differ from us, based on the postulate that migrants are something foreign. More to the point is to perceive an awareness that migrants as strangers, their conditions, forms and consequences themselves are result of a social practice (Scherr, 1999, p. 53).

Two social facts are confronted: The first is the social experience of young people in immigration families as they are presented in conversation and as they are in opposition to the social scientific experience.

> Tülay: Sometimes they don't like me. You go to Turkey, to your country and you are a foreigner.
> Sven: Yes.
> Tülay: You don't feel happy there, either. Most of them think you are born in Germany, you stay there and you are in Turkey only once a year and then you pretend to be a Turkish girl. I often heard this, very often. My Grandma told me: You behave like a German girl and you get involved??? with the Germans. This happens sometimes.
> Sven: Is this frustrating?
> Tülay: It is. I think you cannot change anything. I try to do so, but it doesn't work.
> Sven: Yes.
> Tülay: It is because you grow up in two cultures and not between two.

This notion 'growing up *in* two cultures' refers to another set of criteria. Adolescents of immigrant families are of a different opinion to the mainstream description of their situation. In this area of conflict, in the extremely large space in two cultures, it is a tightrope walk between a positive or negative life-plan.

> In so doing, one's own roots are gazed upon as being foreign, and the foreign is perceived as the own. Not a mummification of traditional identities, rather a masterful coping with standpoints and perspectives (Senocak 1993, p. 15).

The essayist and poet Zafer Senocak himself is an example of an ambiguous existence between all categories (he is German, Turk, intellectual and poet). He comprises an attractive mixture of all of them and has the function of a translator (cf. Waldhoff, 1997). Translation does not mean the translation of one language into another in the strict sense of the term; it is used in a more metaphorical sense. The notion of translation used here is based on the theoretical concepts of Stuart Hall (1994; 1997) and Homi Bhabha (1990; 1994). They gave a rich theoretical framework for the analysis of immigrant life in the scale of Diaspora experience and describe 'home' for the immigrants as a permanent transition and translation between home and abroad. The notion 'translation' describes a creative and open space of hybrid identities and a consciousness of ambiguity. I will refer to this point later.

Whilst exploring the socio-biographic genesis of a transnational paradigm, Waldhoff uses the biography of the German-Turkish intellectual Senocak as a case study to show the *inner landscape* of social, affective and cognitive references. Senocak describes best the capacity of a self-reflective ethnic group-identity by creating a transnational social space (Waldhoff, 1997, p. 351). He shows the different personal concepts in social-cultural life in opposition to the stereotype and homogeneous prejudices by his confession to be unequivocal.

The notion 'between' can be found in another metaphor: As Salman Rushdie in his essays *East, West* (1995) puts it; the comma in the title is the most important part. He himself is the comma. In his story 'The Courter' combining a Western and an Eastern narrative point of view as a synthesis of the two different angles, he explains this metaphor:

> But I, too, have ropes around my neck. I have them to this day, pulling me this way and that, East and West, the nooses tightening, commanding, *choose, choose.*
>
> I buck, I snort, I whinny, I rear, I kick. Ropes, I do not choose between you. Lassoes, lariats, I choose neither of you, and both. Do you hear? I refuse to choose (Rushdie, 1994, p. 211).

This lucid metaphor reflects the situation of the young people of the folklore group as they explain in their talks. They are Turkish and they are Frankfurt citizens at the same time and permanently ambiguous. This appears of course not in an intellectual habit model as in the case of the poet Senocak but it is transformed in an everyday social practice.

As Frankfurt Turks they are living exactly at the interface between all standards, which influence them from at least two directions. Their parents often want them to be obedient to tradition and origin. But even for the parents, their tradition is not identical with the culture in their home country. The significance of expressions like 'national identity' or 'nation' – understood as foreignness until now – is defined by the dicourse of the hegemonial society. National identity is not a stigma which separates members of society. It is considered as an essential part of society. Turks belong to Germans.

'We live here! We were born here and grew up here!' The young people claim their place in society and they hold on to their share of this ambiguous space. The situation of young people is multi-dimensional, not fixed, not damaged or fixed to a certain place. But it is formed in an area of permanent negotiation. They are called 'Germans' (almanci) in Turkey in the pejorative meaning that they are no real Turks.

In Germany they are foreigners, outlaws at least in the democratic aspect. Many of them feel foreigners in both countries. 'When I am in my home country in a way I am a stranger', Tülay explains. The exclusion from society produces a new awareness of 'we' as a group. Turkey is regarded as her home country, not the place where she lives.

As I mentioned above, the local fixation is a sign of feeling homeless in a society with strict ethnic conceptions and rigid limitations in citizenship. Home can be a certain district, a social space that means the direct environment and is taken out of this context. The young people – as in the example – are Frankfurters and not Germans, because they are not allowed to be. They grow up as foreigners in two cultures and are able to find their way around – not as chameleons that do not but change the colour. They are more travellers with their shadows: 'You take all these cultures along when you are on holidays and then you raise the question: Which is the right one?' – as Tülay tells us.

As Zygmunt Bauman pointed out in his case study in the sociology of assimilation that the horror of indetermination is closely related to the phenomena of strangerhood. He writes:

Some strangers are not, however, the *as-yet-undecided*; they are, in principle, *undecidables*. They are the premonition of that 'third element' which should not be. These are the true hybrids, the monsters – not just *unclassified*, but *unclassifiable*. They do not question just this one opposition here and now; they question oppositions as such, the very principle of the opposition, the plausibility of dichotomy it suggests and feasibility of separation it demands (Bauman, 1991, p. 58).

By their reports and reflections the young people demonstrate that the different cultures they belong to complete one another, that they are combined and there is a certain change of ethnic conception. They are the unclassifiables. But the social or local identification, the urban positioning is most important. It is the special faculty of these young people to live in the space of two languages and two cultures. They learn to appreciate the advantage of the coexistence in a pluralistic democracy. The ethnic conception is diametrically opposed to this conception of coexistence in democracy. Its starting point is the uniformity of a cultural development of a majority trying to maintain their influence against foreign influence. This is a naive enthusiasm. The stressing of variety turns out into a problem (cf. Welz, 1996, p. 107; Radtke, 1991). Local identification and self-assessment and the observers point of view cannot be combined in the large part of ethnic studies.

Theoretical Implications

Theoretical reflections and an interpretation of a practical conception of culture seem to be necessary against the background of the dominating studies in the field of intercultural research. We should be aware of our point of view and test carefully whether our instruments of investigation are appropriate. To be foreign within society does not correspond with the level of expectation. They are most perceived on the fringe of society. You find them – according to the conception – only on the periphery of society. That means: There is a homogeneous centre with a homogeneous periphery. The reason of this point of view is a very narrowly defined conception of culture. Zafer Senocak explains his 'Discontent with culture':

> The concept of culture is tied to a particular perception of the world, of man and man's history. When we talk of 'cultural conflict', it means we have reached the boundary of our *own* concept of culture. Our gaze on others falls back on ourselves. On the basis of our own culture we perceive differences which must be remedied in order to resolve the conflict. Otherwise we perceive the threat of relinquishing our own identity, or are at least we are threatened with an identity crisis (Senocak, 1994, p. 59).

How can we understand the facts? Senocak proposes the following
principle as it is already explained and practised by the young people of the
folklore group:

> The concept of culture is abandoned and language is no longer comprehended
> as an instrument in the investigation of other cultures. Once we have realized
> that our languages are unusable we are freed from the necessity of defining
> what is foreign in order to define ourselves. We do not have to tie down the
> concept in order to free ourselves (ibid., p. 62).

Tülay refused to be obliged to define herself. This is done by others and
abused. The formal frame of the national law defines Tülay and her friends
born in Germany as foreigners. They do not think they are foreigners, but
they are treated as such. The emphatically used term of multiculturalism
begins to be indistinct here. I want to make a statement: I plead for an
enlargement of conceptions. I want to confront the common term of
diversity to the term of difference. In that way we find a methodical and
theoretical access to the above-mentioned conception of foreignness. I want
to define this enlargement more precisely. The most convincing theory of
migration, globalisation, new ethnology (cf. Hall, 1994, 1997b) – as to my
opinion – is presented in a far-reaching outline:

> In various fields of *Cultural Studies*, the sensitisation for differences and the
> simultaneous growing scepticism vis à vis binary oppositions has led to the
> development of new concepts and models for describing complex social
> realities (Lutter and Reisenleitner, 1998, p. 127).

In this context we should quote Homi K. Bhabha. He breaks in a radical
way with the point of the hitherto dominating view of ethnic minority,
foreignness and cultural representation by redefining western modernity in
the context of the postcolonial perspective. The cultural studies of our days
need – as Bhabha demands – a new, 'critical' theory when they keep
cultural differences in focus.

> Post-colonial theory forces us to rethink the fundamental constraints of a
> consensus-oriented and mutually-subscribed to liberal understanding of cultural
> communities. It emphatically postulates that cultural and political identity are
> construed by means of a process of alterity. [...] The era in which it was
> possible to assimilate minorities by means of holistic and organic values is
> definitively past. Even the way we speak of cultural communities must be
> rethought in the light of a post-colonial perspective (Bhabha, 1996, p. 347).

Bhabha in his very fruitful theoretical concept does not assert that the time of colonialism is still prevalent today; on the contrary his suggestion is to find new ways of instruction and understanding and not to reproduce colonial prejudices, awareness and strategies. We should think about colonialism and its consequences. 'The term "post-colonialism" means becoming aware of the consequences of hundreds of years of colonisation of the greater part of the world by the smaller part', as Peter Weibel defines (1997, p. 14).

It is the goal of this essay to obtain a change of viewpoints. The crucial question is: 'Can we discuss culture, identity, ethnics and minorities without prejudices?'. All these terms are not clear at all. The essential goal of the postcolonial theory is to regain/redefine terms as culture, tradition, identity etc. that can be found nearly all in the dictionary of essentialistic knowledge. The postcolonial theory offers a sharp instrument to uncover the classical, Eurocentric discourse about foreigners, to change the homogeneous, uniform concept of the foreigner. In another passage Bhabha refers to the pushing power of modern times. Worldwide migration movements characterize this century of Diaspora on one hand and of dislocation of information – and communication systems:

> In view of post-modern media, nowadays we must take into account *Dis-Locations* of historical culture or ethnic affiliation via a problematical break with indigenous – yet endogenous – connection of the ontological value[s] of otherness – of the political subject or cultural citizen – at his situation ... the stable and presentable definition of locality (the *topos* of a territory, the earth, the city ...) (Bhabha, 1997, p. 24).

The postcolonial position is intensified by the feelings 'out of place' and 'out of time'. (cf. ibid., p. 25; see also: Said, 1999) in this area of conflict. In this essay I hope I explained the problem of space – time connection in their inextricable relations. But it is the main goal in these postcolonial studies to reconstruct scopes of action and outlines not linked by a fateful conception of culture, identity and ethnology. Difference should be understood beyond the usual terms of polarisation, dichotomies and stereotypes of foreign-familiar, East-West, North-South, near-abroad etc. They should be understood as binary characteristics of the colonial view of knowledge. It is obvious and intended that this study does not offer a complete and logical concept. I do not only deal with the opposite terms 'theory' versus 'experience' but also with the term 'home' and 'abroad' which puts experience, language, politics in a productive, completing system (cf. Bhabha, 1996, p. 350).

A relation – as Bhabha described – should be between theory and experience. Fragments of a new conception of society are put together here (cf. Hall, 1997; summarizing Lutter and Reisenleitner, 1998). The different accesses and reflections have in common the view of culture and its representations. Hall (cf. Hall, 1997) calls them 'signifying practices'. The central premise of Cultural Studies is,

> ... that all the different forms of reality, all the different practices via which man is shaped, are in need of explanation. They cannot be reduced to themselves (Grossberg, 1994, p. 23).

Difference vs. Diversity

Here the inclusive and exclusive strategies of modern societies are analysed, the outlook is focused on construction and definition of foreignness. Bhabha presented his concept of hybridism in an interview with Jonathan Rutherford. He did so with regard to a relativistic and universal viewpoint starting at the term 'difference' as well. He could stress on diversity instead of difference meaning cultural representation in accordance with the conservative, dominant standards and cultural concepts. Diversity explains the so-called urban, multicultural life. In the context of life in big cities, the influence of urban diversity is described again and again:

> Multiplicity of uses, on the one hand, and users on the other – different social groups, cultural forms and patterns of behaviour, norms and values (Dangschat, 1995, p. 179).

> Social heterogeneity includes cultural diversity. Cultural variety is thus twofold: First, it is a confrontation in neutral public space, whereby common ground and foreignness must be quickly weighed up, resulting in corresponding behaviours of rapprochement or rejection. Secondly, there must be homogenous rooms to ensure that one can mix with one's own kind; this compensates on the one hand for the irritations of hyper-urban inner cities and on the other it provides confrontation with the mirror of one's self in order to be able to cope with a world of different requirements and to find one's place in all this (ibid., p. 183).

When mentioning the reference of growing socio-economic polarization and socio-cultural heterogeneity in cities, the urban sociologist Jens Dangschat pleads for looking at the occupation of rooms under the aspect of power. The term 'forgotten rooms' should be taken into consideration. In this aspect Bhabha takes a step forward. His theory is not based on the notion of diversity. He goes on using the notion of difference, but he does so in an ideology-critical manner, best fitting to analyse power strategies. He examines the different forms and the interplay of intern symbols and extern significance. The widespread habit of exclusion and racism in modern multicultural societies helps Bhabha to understand that universalism can be useful here.

> My purpose in talking about cultural difference rather than cultural diversity is to acknowledge that this kind of liberal relativist perspective is inadequate in itself and doesn't generally recognise the universalist and normative stance from which it constructs its cultural and political judgements (Bhabha, 1990b, p. 209).

Here begins Bhabha's conception of translation. Translation means the connection of all cultures because they – as different as they might be – are forms of symbols and meanings, they are systems of representation. 'By translation I first of all mean a process by which, in order to objectify cultural meaning, there always has to be a process of alienation and of secondariness *in relation to itself*. In that sense there is no 'in itself' and 'for itself' within cultures because they are always subject to intrinsic forms of translation.' (ibid., p. 210).

This process of distant self-observation reveals the outstanding advantage of contextual and reconstructive reflection of special adolescent culture. As to my opinion, there is exactly the exclusive strength of a methodical and theoretic research of a postcolonial, individual reconstructive experience. Ethnic categories are deconstructed and focused on individual and social strategies and forms of activity and appropriation. This strategy is accompanied by a subversive element. Hybridity is a confession of uncertainty. Bhabha explains uncertainty as an important metaphor:

> The notion of hybridity comes from the two prior descriptions I've given of the genealogy of difference and the idea of translation, because if, as I was saying, the act of cultural translation (both as representation and as reproduction) denies the essentialism of a prior given original or originary culture, then we see that all forms of culture are continually in a process of hybridity. But for me the importance of hybridity is not to be able to trace two original movements from which the third emerges, rather hybridity to me is the 'third space' which enables new positions to emerge (ibid., p. 211).

It is important for the interpretation of hybridity that Bhabha considers the actual constitution of modern national states to be ambivalent and hybrid (cf. Bhabha, 1990a, 1994). Colonial and modern strategies, phenomena and stories get mixed, because there is no linear historical development. Bhabha understands by third space more a metaphor than a statement of identity. He associates hybridity with a process of identification with or by another object. This indicates his ambivalent position. Important for the comprehension of hybridity is that Bhabha uses this notion as an *analytic* category – not as a descriptive one. The metaphor of the third space picks out life in spaces of transition as a central theme. Ambivalence is not translated as a deficit but as a competence of action and a possibility of maintaining the suspense between desire and reality in a creative way and of discovering cultural translations as an act of creativity.

I assert that this metaphor of the third space is a typical space of transition of the folklore group. It is too a real and a virtual room, a meeting place of young people, a social room where discussions about self-perceptions and self-localization take place. And furthermore a room of reflection was realised here where you can find a certain area of agency and of special experience. Adolescence and the room of conversation turn out as a sort of 'training centre' for the folklore group. The environment of a self-invented language enables all to reflect on self-localization, life-plan and questions of ethnic and gender identity. This is manifested in a third space created and maintained by the folklore group. The recently developed concept of foreignness to my opinion influences the competence of action and location.

This process becomes obvious in individual stories and biographies as well as in discussions about 'difference' and 'diversity'. The appropriation takes place without any educational influence in a room given to the young people to have use of. The folklore group as a part of self-organized work with immigrants reveals another aspect if you do not stick to a one-dimensional view of cultural way of looking at things: you should try to reconstruct the individually different valuation and to examine the case studies. I do not want to give rise to misconception: This analysis deals with the area of self-affirmation and representation in the surroundings; it is a remarkable political act.

> The crucial political issue remains, though; whom is one to be in the midst of this ambiguity in order to be able to claim legal and political recognition and cultural representation. Who is, or rather, what does it mean to be 'one of us'? (Lutter and Reisenleitner, 1998, p. 129).

I would like to emphasize again the goal of these efforts to maintain subjective contradictions and interpretations or conflicts against the pressure of homogeneity and clearness.

The process of cultural hybridity gives rise to something different, something new and unrecognisable, a new area of negotiation of meaning and representation (Bhabha, 1990b, p. 211).

Understanding of foreigners means understanding of the unknown parts in ourselves. We found out up to this moment that a new definition of the term is necessary to find new ways of description. Bhabha's outline associated with the new theoretical concepts of the 'Cultural Studies' is basically an abstract varietization. But it is pathbreaking as well.

Shared Cultures?

Another new definition of culture appears in the background of modern theoretical analysis concepts of local communities referring to global transformation. This definition will help us to find a practical method for theory and experience. Ulf Hannerz' revision of the term 'culture' from a social-anthropological view can be an important starting point. Hannerz in his study *Cultural Complexity* investigated forms of urban heterogeneity (1992) and raised the question: What conditions must be set to change the urban variety into a productive heterogeneity? An important aspect is the 'open inside'. It can be achieved by the fact that individual population groups and culture forms are not hermetically sealed against each other, but rather that the different population groups and culture forms remain continually in spontaneous contact and that coincidental interchange and mutual awareness is possible (Hannerz, quoted in Welz, 1996, p. 142).

'Modes of managing meaning' (quote ibid.) means dealing with, creating and distributing cultural meanings. This concept breaks with the ethnological stance of 'shared cultures' of a group and analyses the interrelations between difference and social inequality. So this is a more relational and not a essentialistic definition of culture. Therefore this theoretical framework can be developed basing on mutual negotiation of different interpretation of meaning. These 'modes', these specific forms of production and transferring of cultural meanings are called the core of a social-anthropologic conception of urban culture by G. Welz.

In this aspect the concept of Martin Albrow, Research Professor in the Social Sciences at the University of Surrey, should be emphasized. As in the beginning of the cultural studies, Albrow constantly tries hard to examine terms and instruments. He explains globalisation as a local process. After examining case studies from the London suburb Tooting he assumes that the instruments of an urban description influenced by globalisation need a fundamental revision. The concept of 'nation-state sociology' (Albrow, 1997, p. 37) is no longer appropriate for investigating the complex, social reality.

At first sight his starting point seems to be a far-reaching addition to postcolonial studies. But different to the primarily analytical and critical view on cultural studies in his field of research – urban district – he proceeds in a concrete and primarily empirical way. Looking for a new concept of description apart from classical paradigms Albrow proposes the following:

> The missing term here surely has to be 'socioscape', the vision of social formations which are more than the people who occupy them at any one time. Under globalized conditions people are increasingly uncomfortable when referring to them in old structural terms like 'community' or 'neighbourhood' (Albrow, 1997, p. 38).

In his case studies Albrow shows an absolutely different affiliation and valuation of the urban space. The 'user' can only reconstruct it individually, but it refers as well to structural experience and social situation in general as the studies prove. Albrow covers this wide range of themes, he points out the cases of study aiming at

> not to confirm a general picture, nor to find a common thread. Indeed it would be possible to construct a different general type of orientation to living the global city to each of our respondents (Albrow, 1997, p. 50).

We must understand this information, its different conditions of genesis and common references to gain a new understanding of the urban local concept. Here we see that a local culture is indicated by the 'possibility that individuals with very different lifestyles and social networks can live in close proximity without untoward interference with each other' (Albrow 1997, p. 51).

Albrow calls these creative forms 'sociospheres', 'evoking a common use of the term 'sphere' to mean a field of concern or relevance which does not have in any geometrical sense to be spherical. It leaves open whether older categories like family, community, friendship or newer ones like partnership, enclave and lifestyle group apply to these formations, recognizing that along with delocalization there is also a growing indeterminacy in applying such classifications' (ibid., p. 52).

As an outlook on a wide field of research, which waits to be disclosed, Albrow put it 'we know precious little about the ways in which the different sociospheres relate to each other except in stereotypes formed in the stage of nation-state sociologies' (ibid.).

Both starting points as presented refer to the concept of *difference* instead to a one-dimensional concept of *diversity*. As we discovered, new spaces of foreignness can be found by this form of investigation. Foreignness is not located in a binary and polarized difference between two cultures. Foreignness, that is the conception of foreignness, is a social and cultural factor of division with a local influence. Here we should go on investigating this factor as a sign of differentiation accompanied by a social exclusion. I would assert that this illustrated new type of foreignness covers the description of Albrows' concept. The socioscapes of the members of the folklore group are related and located in the urban space of their suburb. They call themselves 'Frankfurt Human Beings' but differentiate by the suburbs they stem from. A well-balanced form of cultural appropriation mixes the ethnic resources of their life history, the suburb they actually live in, with own (youth-) subculture orientations and the traditional authochtone feeling of belonging to a smaller part of the city. Important social categories like family, friendship and community are spread out over the narrow boundaries of nation states.

A paradox example for this transnational form of local cultural appropriation may be the fact that the type of folklore dancing the group practised was strictly forbidden (because men and women danced together) in the villages in the east of Turkey from where most of the members of the group originate. This was due to the influence of the Mullah-Regime of Iran; the village of origin of most of the members of the group was very near the border. Since the emigration of the villagers to Frankfurt, Germany made the *authentic* form of folklore dancing possible.

The described differentiation and the subversive strategies in these differentiations and agencies can also be established in hybrid cultures. The theory outlined above as presented by E. Bronfen and B. Marius (1997, p. 7), shows that the change of view from identity to diversity produces a new interest in moments of transition and discontinuity in opposition to concepts of origin and unity. It was my intention to direct your attention to discontinuity, transition and periphery because I want to give a new impetus to the discussion of foreignness in the context of urban and social groups. We understand more when it is possible to analyse the combination of social and symbolic topography (cf. Carter et al. 1993). The still dominant interest of migration research on children of immigrant families prevents further insight into the process of transcultural appropriation of urban space in adolescent subcultures. The narrow view of cultures, identity and ethnics is not helpful, but efforts of discussion and self-construction are useful for self-position in space and time. I take it very seriously while criticising the research of migration to point out that 'foreignness' is not the result of a however objectified original culture, but it can be developed as an individual valuation at a relevant place.

References

Albrow, M. (1997), 'Travelling beyond local cultures. Socioscapes in a global city', in J. Eade (ed.), *Living the global city. Globalization as a local Process*, London; New York.
Bauman, Z. (1991), *Modernity and Ambivalence*, Cambridge.
Bhabha, H.K. (1990), 'The Third Space', in J. Rutherford (ed.), *Identity, Community, Culture, Difference*, London.
Bhabha, H.K. (1994), *The Location of Culture*, London; New York.
Bhabha, H.K. (1996), 'Postkoloniale Kritik. Vom Überleben der Kultur', *Das Argument*, vol. 215.
Bhabhba, H.K. (1997), 'Globale Ängste', in P. Weibel, S. Zizek (ed.), *Inklusion : Exklusion. Probleme des Postkolonialismus und der globalen Migration*, Wien.
Bronfen, E., Marius, B., Steffen, Th. (1997), *Hybride Kulturen. Beiträge zur anglo-amerikanischen Multikulturalismusdebatte*, Tübingen.
Carter, E., Donald, J., Squires, J. (1993), *Space and Place. Theories of identity and location*, London.
Dangschat, J.S. (1995), 'Multikulturelle Gesellschaft und sozialräumliche Polarisierung', in U. Schwarz (ed.), *Risiko Stadt? Perspektiven der Urbanität*, Hamburg.
Gemende, M., Schroer, W., Sting, S. (1999), *Zwischen den Kulturen. Pädagogische und sozialpädagogische Zugänge zur Interkulturalität*, München; Weinheim.
Grossberg, L. (1994), 'Cultural Studies. Was besagt ein Name?', *IKUS-Lectures*, no. 17+18.
Hall, S. (1994), *Rassismus und kulturelle Identität*. Ausgewählte Schriften 2, Hamburg.
Hall, S. (1997a), *Representation. Cultural Representations and Signifying Practices*, London.
Hall, S. (1997b), 'New Ethnicities', in J. Donald and A. Rattansi (eds), *Race, Culture and Difference*, London.
Hannerz, U. (1992), *Cultural Complexity. Studies in the social organization of meaning*, New York.
Lutter, C. and Reisenleitner, M. (1998), *Cultural Studies. Eine Einführung*, Wien.
Radtke, F.-O. (1991), 'Lob der Gleichgültigkeit. Die Konstruktion des Fremden im Diskurs des Multikulturalismus', in U. Bielefeld (ed.), *Das Eigene und das Fremde. Neuer Rassismus in der alten Welt?*, Hamburg.
Rushdie, S. (1995), *Osten, Westen*, München.
Said, E.W. (1999), *Out of Place. A memoir*, New York.
Sauter, S. (2000), *Wir sind Frankfurter Türken. Adoleszente Ablösungsprozesse in der deutschen Einwanderungsgesellschaft*, Frankfurt/M.
Scherr, A. (1999), 'Die Konstruktion von Fremdheit in sozialen Prozessen. Zur Kritik und Weiterentwicklung soziologischer und erziehungswissenschaftlicher Fremdheitsdiskurse', in D. Kiesel et al. (ed.), *Die Erfindung der Fremdheit. Zur Kontroverse um Gleichheit und Differenz im Sozialstaat*, Frankfurt/M.
Senocak, Z. (1993), *Atlas des Tropischen Deutschland*, Berlin.
Senocak, Z. (1994), *War Hitler Araber? IrreFührungen an den Rand Europas*, Berlin.

Waldhoff, H.-P. (1997), 'Ein Übersetzer. Über die sozio-biographische Genese eines transnationalen Denkstils', in H.-P. Waldhoff, D. Tan, E. Kürsat-Ahlers (ed.), *Brücke zwischen den Zivilisationen. Zur Zivilisierung ethnisch-kultureller Differenzen und Machtungleichheiten. Das türkisch-deutsche Beispiel*, Frankfurt/M.

Weibel, P. (1997), 'Die koloniale Kondition', in P. Weibel and S. Zizek (ed.), *Inklusion:Exklusion. Probleme des Postkolonialismus und der globalen Migration*, Wien.

Welz, G. (1996), *Inszenierung kultureller Vielfalt. Frankfurt am Main und New York City*, Berlin.

Chapter 12

Between Europe and Nation-States: The Turkish Transnational Community

Riva Kastoryano

Introduction

Over four million people from Turkey live in Europe today. They mainly immigrated for economic reasons, arriving *en masse* from the beginning of the 1960s, generally following bilateral agreements between Turkey and European countries, primarily Germany. Their dispersion throughout the various western European countries sets them apart from other post-colonial immigration movements. In fact, unlike North Africans and people of the Indian peninsula whose routes, drawn by the history of decolonization, led to France and Great Britain respectively, migrants from Turkey represent the European space as 'undifferentiated', even if a very large majority of them live in Germany, a country which remains the prime reference for Turkish immigration and that refers to its Turkish immigration as the *Türkenproblem*. For Turkey, they are a new social category: the *Turks abroad*. Navigating along various family, business and associational networks, they establish a link between the private and public space, as well as between economic and political space within Europe and between Turkey and Europe. They are hence invested with new roles.

The presence of populations having the same geographic, national, and religious references in various national spaces has given rise to the elaboration of the concept of *diaspora*, derived from the Greek and meaning *dispersion*. Often used at first for the Jews, then for the Armenians and Palestinians, the term has a territorial reference as well as identity-based features founded on a common religion or language.[1] With regard to the Turks, Stéphane de Tapia develops the idea of migratory circulation to describe the migratory flows and demonstrate the 'multitudes of individual

---

[1] For an analysis of the definitions and the application of the terms diaspora, see M. Bruneau, 'Espaces et territoires de diasporas', in *L'Espace Géographique*, vol. XXIII, no. 1, 1994, pp. 5-19.

or family movements and the thousands of relocations that support or contradict the presence of a "workers' diaspora" having commercial, associational, political and religious information networks as well as firm state support' (Tapia, 1994).

The 'Turks of Europe', despite the heterogeneity of their makeup, make reference to a territorially defined Turkish state, even the Turkish nation-state. Their modes of organization, mobilization and participation reflect multiple memberships both in the European space, the space of immigration – their place of residence and political participation – and in the space of the national territory, source of identity. The development of commercial, family and associational networks (depending on regional identities and/or political identities) that *de facto* make Turkey part of Europe more calls to mind the emergence of a *transnational community*.

Like the concept of diaspora, this fashionable concept also echoes the idea of dispersion. But *diasporas* must nevertheless be distinguished from *transnational communities*. The former correspond to a group dispersed before the era of nationalism and nation-states; the latter designates a group dispersed after that era. The classic cases of diasporas refer to individuals or groups sharing the same history (or dispersion), united by a common identification and similar ideas about the myth of a territorialized state. *Transnational communities*, as they appear today, are on the other hand composed of migrants coming from territorially-defined states, even if some of them claim autonomous political frontiers within these states, such as the Kurds for instance. Diasporas are composed of people belonging to the same 'imagined community' with the same territorial reference, whereas transnational communities are characterized by diverse national and linguistic identities as well as by different relationships with the country of origin, which can constitute an obstacle to the reconstitution of this sort of community. But at the same time, this diversity ends up being 'focused' in the process by which supranational institutions recognize these identities by granting them legitimacy on the international scene.

In Europe, the reclaiming of identities and the consequential reconstruction of real or imagined transnational community ties among Kurds, Turks and Islamists transcend the territorial borders between Turkey and Europe. These 'imagined transnational communities' organized on the basis of a common language (or family of languages) and religion (Sunnite or Alevite branches of Turkish Islam) as well as a sense of belonging (or non-belonging in the case of the Kurds) make the European space a space of deterritorialized political participation. This evolution is due both to the integration policies of the countries of residence that have a direct effect on the modes of Turkish integration and to the emergence of a transnational

European space which, through the complex and multifaceted interaction between nation-states and supranational European institutions, include Turkey in Europe – the entire web of interactions giving rise to a 'transnational actor' whose attributed or assumed role is to link Turkey to Europe.

Europe: Space of Participation and Mobilization

Even if Europe is perceived as an 'undifferentiated' space for immigrants from Turkey, this is not true when it comes to the forms of organization, the terms of mobilization, the means of participation and lastly, the demands of Turkish immigrant populations in Europe. Despite a certain convergence among European countries in terms of immigration and integration, each state defines the modalities by which the immigrant population should be included both in the institutional framework and in the civil society of the host country. In fact, since the 1980s Germany and France as well as Belgium and the Netherlands – where over 2 million, 300,000, 85,000 and 250,000 Turkish citizens reside respectively (SOPEMI, 1997) – have supported projects for the creation of associations either to help them form a united and representative community as in Germany, or to designate an intermediary between the public authorities and the community as in France, depending on the political traditions and institutional practices of each state. As for the associations, they are integrated into institutional structures, and their leaders have adopted the political 'rules of the game' in each country in order to deal with the state and negotiate on an equal footing.

Differences between European countries in turn affect the migrants' mode of political participation. The absence of legal citizenship in Germany, for instance, has led the Turks to develop compensatory strategies to take part in German local and national political life. This translates to a higher visibility in civil society through association activities with an aim to influence public opinion and government decisions. Their demand has to do with equal political rights by requesting a revision of the law on nationality founded on common ancestry and by the adoption of dual citizenship. In France on the other hand, their lesser numbers translates into political invisibility on the national level. The same is true as regards their demands, which basically combine with those of the Muslim population seeking institutional recognition.

In sum, these examples highlight the 'nationalization' of the organization and mobilization of Turkish immigrant populations and confirm their adaptation to the rules of the game established by the states. In other words, groups gathered together in associations use the same tools as the public authorities and national institutions in negotiating their collective interests and the recognition of specific features of their identity with the various states.

But at the same time, numerous studies on Turkish immigration in France, as in other European countries, underline the communitarian aspect of family organization, particularly in areas with high concentrations of inhabitants from Turkey. The various competing associations reflect different aspects of immigration as well as those of Turkish political life. Such a similarity in organization also tests the limits of state immigration and integration policies, as do associational networks which cross European borders and contribute to the formation of new transnational solidarities that act directly on the supranational European institutions and constitute a challenge to nation-states.

Indeed, with the construction of Europe, the quest for an identity-based representativity goes beyond the state framework, now extending to the European scale, in that Europe is perceived as a new political space open for interest and identity claims. Immigrant populations address Europe by the same token as other organizations – professional groups or interest groups – that seek to influence national policies through their action at the European level. This would allow them to strengthen their representativity both at the national and the European level, wherefore the development of new forms of solidarity situated above and beyond the 'nationalization' of immigrant populations' action. This is how transnational networks are woven and new structures of solidarity are outlined crossing European borders, which include Turkish immigrant populations in the various European countries and Turkey, too.

Studies on the emergence of so-called transnational communities highlight a post-colonial type of immigration and economic relations that individuals maintain with their country of origin. They perforce operate in two political spaces (cf. Basch, Schiller and Blanc 1997; Cohen, 1997; Hannertz, 1996; Portes, 1997; Levitt, 1998). In the context of the European Union, a transnational community transcends the border of the member-states. Some networks emanate from local initiatives of the host countries, others from the country of origin, others are encouraged by supranational institutions such as the European Parliament or the European Commission. In fact, the involvement of supranational institutions puts transnational communities on a par with lobbies that act directly on the European level and define their action as transnational (Smith et al., 1997). But while seeking to circumvent state policies, these communities must deal with the host state in matters of equal rights and treatment and with Turkey for recognition of cultural specificities that have legitimacy in the associational framework in Europe and respect for human rights. This, in fact, is one of the paradoxes of supranationality and transnationality: while challenging the relevance of nation-states as a political, cultural and territorial unit, transnationality reinforces the role of nation-states, considered by the actors as the sole adversaries with which they must negotiate in the final instance (Kastoryano, 2002).

Apart from informal networks based on family or commercial ties, Turkish associational networks are thus part of this 'web' that covers the European space. Their aspirations and their activities find an echo in the project of the European Parliament which, since 1986, has made funds available to immigrant associations to help coordinate their activities. A new transnational structure grew out of this initiative, known as the 'Migrants' Forum'. Although it is the result of the Union's budgetary policy. The Forum nevertheless aims to become 'a locus of expression for non-Community populations established in Europe through which they can make their claims known, but also disseminate information emanating from European authorities' (Neveu, 1994). According to the official in charge of overseeing the Migrants' Forum at the Commission of the European Communities, the aim is to obtain for nationals of third countries 'the same opportunities and the same rights as natives, and thus to compensate the democratic deficit'. Explicitly, the objective is therefore to provide a legal framework for combating the rise of racism in various European countries. Consequently, it is especially associations whose activities receive the most support from the welfare states of the various member countries and whose leaders develop a rhetoric on equal rights, human rights and their universal nature that view transnational mobilization as an effective means of fighting racism and xenophobia.[2]

The Migrants' Forum theoretically brings together *immigrant* associations formed principally by the criterion of nationality. But at the same time, the organizational capacity measured in terms of multiplicity of nationalities represented, the number of branches, the extent of the networks, the plurality of sectors they cover (economic, social, cultural) and of course their representativity in the countries they are located, constitute selection criteria for the member associations of the Forum,

---

[2] In 1990, 29 percent of the people interviewed wanted to see immigrants' rights curbed. In 1992, this percentage rose to 34 percent. By the same token, in 1991, 60 percent of the respondents would have accepted the arrival of immigrants from Mediterranean countries with restrictions, and in 1993, only 46 percent did. *Eurobarometer*, December 1992.

which therefore encourages immigrant actors to place themselves above the nation-state through a transnational action.

As soon as it was created, Turkish associations made up a significant portion of the Forum. They have become part of the network through their capacity to represent Turkish immigration at the national level or by the scope of their activities recognized by the public authorities without paying heed to representativity. Or they enter the network through the forms of organization in federations of associations as they exist in Germany in particular, encompassing all ethnic, regional, religious and linguistic divisions as well as ideological divisions that are reproduced in immigration.[3] More important still are the associations that define themselves as Kurdish, active both in the context of immigration and in their political aspirations in the framework of Turkey, which thus has to do with recognition both by European institutions and Turkey.[4]

Alongside so-called 'immigrant' associations, the Forum encourages the formation of groups known as 'national support groups' and 'regional support groups',[5] the former in reference to member-states, the latter to third countries to which are added the 'stateless' populations.[6] This procedure, the result of a co-development policy in effect in the host countries, actually boils down to including the country of origin in the representation of migrants in Europe and consequently lends a certain legitimacy to their action, even the demands of immigrant populations, depending on their national, regional and ethnic affiliation as well as according to identity-based divisions in the country of origin. Thus a new transnational European political space including Turkey has developed, making the latter a source of ethnicity and making of Europe a source of legitimacy for any mobilization and claim.

Turkey: Source of Identity and Mobilization

For the Turkish migrant, the territory of residence is actually becoming more and more European. For populations of Turkish immigrant origin, the

---

[3] There are currently 16 Turkish associations represented in the Forum including 10 organized as federations of associations.

[4] The Kurds (identifiable only by self-definition as such) represent approximately 30 percent of Turkish immigration divided proportionally in the various European countries.

[5] Defined as regions are: North Africa, Sub-Saharan Africa, Latin America, the Caribbean and Turkey. Thus whereas regions are defined as a grouping of countries according to their geographic and cultural proximity, Turkey as a whole and in itself is defined as a region.

[6] The Forum defines Kurds, Caldean and the Armenians as making up 'stateless groups'.

European Union now constitutes a new step in their political socialization, the prior ones being, for some of them, those taken in Turkey before their immigration, and for others in the context of national societies of immigration. It is in this realm that since the 1980s, due to the proliferation of so-called immigrant associations created and sponsored by the public authorities, religious, national and ethnic identities have been expressed and politicized to take a stand with respect to the host countries with a view to their recognition (Kastoryano, 2002). In France this fits within the framework of the 'right to be different'. The idea was launched in 1981 by the Socialist Party in power; as for the right, it found support in associations of foreigners through the liberal measures introduced in the law (October 1981). In Germany, these associations are an answer to the policy toward foreigners (*Ausländerpolitik*) and its aims to integrate the population through community organizations. This new approach thus transforms neighborhood 'de facto communities' by formalizing, even institutionalizing them via these associations. An identity with a collective outlook remains to be defined, its contours outlined, and new solidarities created to give rise to new forms of organization.[7]

The creation of these associations is largely responsible for the fragmenting of identities and new allegiances. It is around associations that immigrant political actors have reorganized their interests and their identities, be they social, cultural, ethnic or political. Some associations have replaced the militant and revolutionary actions on the left or right, religious or ethnic, represented in Turkey and transposed in 'exile' that were mainly directed at the country of origin and whose adversary was the Turkish state;[8] others were created, often with the aid of the political authorities of the host country to ensure 'integration' of the Turks (as of immigrants in general) in their country of residence. Still others have sought to combine both aspects to be more convincing among the Turkish immigrant population in general, and developed as a political force both in Turkey and abroad in Europe. This is true of the successive religious parties

---

[7] According to Charles Tilly, associations, viewed as new forms of organization of a collective identity, are a link between a specific action based on the common characteristics of a group and the structural changes that can, in the long run, restructure bonds of solidarity.

[8] Mobilization, which rose with the arrival of political refugees and organized around associations financed by individual, Turkish political parties or by private international bodies appeared as the transposition of Turkish political life with its ideological divisions. These movements of various tendencies were based in protest against policies conducted in Turkey, its conception of the nation and or religion. It even occurred that the Imams representing Religious Affairs, once settled in a European country, joined religious sects or other Turkish Muslim associations of various tendencies independent of the Turkish state.

(*Refah*, then *Fazilet*, and lately *Saadet*) and its supporting body, the association known as *Milli Görüs* (the National Vision).[9]

But on the whole, whether they are derived from political groups already active in Turkey, or they are the result of a conversion of worker movements in Turkey or other European countries, or again if they have grown out of local initiatives in France or Germany, since the 1980s, the rhetoric of their leaders has devoted considerable importance to culture and identity, the definition of which varies according to their ideology: national identity, religious identity or political identity.

The demand for recognition also brings out all the differences in the public space. But these differences are not only expressed with regard to France or Germany, they also and especially emerge, particularly in the case of Turks, within representations of Turkey. Each specific trait thus constitutes a distinctive feature and is found at the origin of new internal cleavages among the population of Turkish origin. To this are added ideological divisions, stands taken for or against the incumbent authorities in Turkey and also those that touch on policies in France, Germany and other European countries. It is within this division that *ethnicity* is invented and redefined, a means of asserting oneself as Turkish or Kurd, as a Sunni or Alevite, as being from the East or the West of Turkey, and organizing according to identity-based elements however diverse and multiple they may be.

Paradoxically, all these divisions contribute to forming a community that can be qualified as 'segmented', even 'conflictual', but transnational all the same. In fact, the conflictual relations or internal rivalries which actually lead people to take part in the game paradoxically reinforce interwoven bonds of solidarity and encourage identification with the 'transnational community' thus created. The attachment of these associations and their representatives to political life in Turkey, despite their striving to maintain a distance, despite the actions they conduct among Turkish families to better 'integrate' them in French or German society, situates politically active migrants with respect to one another according to the association patronized and its overt political tendency, and this without distinction of political space or participation or action. The demarcation line between the various 'identities' expressed is not very clear and the manifestation of this diversity does not present a challenge to the community structure. On the contrary, internal conflicts within crisscrossing networks are rather the sign of the transnational community's isolation rather than its fragmentation. They attest to a mode of individual

---

[9] Party banned in Turkey and replaced by the *Fazilet*, banned also and replaced lately by *Saadet* which however, maintains the same associational network.

participation and consequently their identification with a community whose frontiers are defined by the interplay of rivalry, solidarity and clientelism, but above all a common reference point: Turkey, whether it is defined in geographic, social, political or cultural terms. It is this common denominator that gives rise to the invention of an ethnicity that embellishes the past on the basis of current concerns so as to increase the influence of these components in immigration and act in a more efficient manner on Turkish political life by creating awareness in international public opinion and supranational institutions.

The Turkish state has an effect on Turkish immigration through the teaching of the 'native language and culture'. Its action usually takes place within the context of bilateral agreements between the various host countries. This necessarily has an influence on the diplomatic relations between Turkey and the various European countries. But the ongoing role of the Turkish state in immigration helps to maintain immigrant Turkish people's attachment to their country. In this way, even the national ideology expressed in the Kemalist rhetoric is subject to control by the Turkish government. It thereby exerts its control abroad as if to maintain the idea of a Turkish citizenship, but an extraterritorial citizenship, in other words a citizenship that is practiced beyond the national territory.

The Turkish state's control extends indirectly through the associational movement and the claims of being 'different' that fit into the framework of the legitimacy of the respective states. In fact, the politicization of identities newly informs the relations between migrants from Turkey and the host countries. It sometimes even complicates diplomatic relations between the two countries. Spurred by a concern for democracy and human rights, France, Germany and other European countries recognize fragmentations within the legally acknowledged associational framework. But Turkey's blindness with regard to the social, cultural and political realities of the country prompts migrants to amplify their movement and reinforce their demand for recognition of 'differences' in immigration situations.

This does not prevent the Turkish government from cooperating with certain associations or competing with others. It established the *Diyanet* (official religious body of the Turkish state) for instance to combat the growth of Islam as a political force embarked on by the successive religious parties both in Turkey and among the immigrant population. As for its relations with social and cultural associations, it works with family organizations that have a local and national impact and that claim to be 'multicultural' and are recognized as such by the respective states. All of its action is based on the 'ethnic' definition of the group, a definition that is founded on a common nationality. This does not contradict the Kurdish demand whose nationalist movements developed in Europe, where they represent about 30 percent of the immigration from Turkey, who highlight demands not only developed in a situation of immigration but on the basis of a 'dual minority' in the country of origin and in the host country, thus positioning itself with respect both to Turkey and the host countries.

The Kurds, moreover, are an interesting case combining transnational community and diaspora. In fact, in their case the notion of ethnicity refers to a 'national' definition within the Turkish territory, defined by a language, a history and a territory. Their immigration organization is part of the *transnational community* as we previously defined, through their reference to the Turkish state, but their mobilization is closer to classical *diaspora* movements through their aspiration to create a territorialized state. In other words, this fragmentation of identities specific to immigration has led them to demand the same treatment as Turks whom they consider, however, to be another ethnic community, with their own cultural association, access to the radio, television, language classes and religious teaching. Through the voice of their militants, the Kurds seek recognition as a 'Kurdish community' with its own culture and history, distinct from the 'Turkish community'. This differentiation exists in Turkey today and takes the form of a conflict between 'nationalisms'. But in the European context, this manifestation of distinct identities puts the Kurds in a minority situation within a transnational community, whereas they are not recognized as a minority in Turkey.

Europe-Turkey: Back and Forth

Migrations obviously involve not only flows of individuals, but also of capital, at least at the beginning. The new measures to curb immigration in the various European countries seek to reactivate this characteristic of migrations with co-development and cooperation policies to dry up the flow of populations at the source. Unlike bilateral policies, the main actors of which are states, the new policies in question are based on the individual, the migrant himself, who becomes a de facto transnational actor due to the economic ties he establishes between the country of origin and the host country.

But transnationality is also defined by cultural and political flows generated by these actors. These flows end up being amplified by new means of communication and the development of the media, particularly satellite broadcasts, which erupt into the homes of Kurds and Turks, of Alevites and Sunnis from Turkey. In fact, families experience Turkey on a daily basis through images broadcast by the twelve or fourteen private and public stations that exist. Apart from the obvious effects on their integration in the host societies, the programs watched at the same time as the inhabitants of Turkey blur the link between territory and identity. The territory to which one belongs remains regional, the region, town or even village of origin determining family relations. The territory to which one refers becomes national/religious between Kurds and Turks, Alevites and Sunnis. The territory of residence is nevertheless French, German, Dutch, and so on.

As for political flows, transnationality refers to a reciprocal influence and interdependence between the identity policies developed in the space of the 'diaspora' and that of the original country. In Europe and in Turkey, just as claims for rights of residence and/or citizenship as well as protection against expulsion that are henceforth addressed to European institutions, interests expressed in terms of identities – of the immigrant populations as well as the states – find a field of action in a Europe under construction, leading to new forms and structures of representation and new negotiations.

Migrants from Turkey perceive Europe as a new democratic space above and beyond the territorial nation-state, which will allow them to act for the recognition of their rights in the various countries of immigration. As for the Kurds, there is a European move to recognize their identity both in the host country and their country of origin. With more political resources abroad, they seek to legitimate their claims in the European Court of Human Rights, the Council of Europe, the European Court of Justice and the European Parliament. It is now through European institutions that populations defined as minorities or communities in a national (and European) context obtain both recognition and the capacity to negotiate with the country of residence as well as the country of origin. In fact, 'decentralized' identities with respect to the nation-state give rise to a new ethnic 'centralization' that is no longer territorially defined (Létourneau, 1977).

We are witnessing here a reversal of the immigrant situation that implies a redefinition of relations between political spaces and actions. In fact, at the outset of their immigration, the populations arriving from Turkey had transposed the political and ideological cleavages and conflicts expressed by social classes in European countries, making Europe the extension of Turkish political life. Today, organizations that enjoy official recognition and legitimacy in European countries of residence, according to identity fragments in the Turkish national context, act on the political life of their country of origin. This translates as political know-how and values acquired in the associational network in Europe and which, in turn, gives another form and content to militant action and speech in Turkey.

As for the Turkish state, it seeks to create an image of 'unified community' that represents Turkey's interests. It redefines the various aspects of Turkish national/religious and political identity. These attempts aim to influence the European public opinion regarding Turkey's image and result in a 'community representation' of *Turks abroad*. The political actors of Turkish immigrant stock in Europe meet the state's expectations through their efforts to form lobbies recognized in both countries, based not only on community institutions determined by Turkish political life but incorporated in the German political system or opposed to it, and reacting similarly to any declaration from the government in Berlin with regard to Turkey and vice versa. Their power is founded on financial success. A report published in Brussels in 1991 estimates direct or indirect Turkish economic input to be about 57 billion DM, an amount that by far exceeds expenditures of the welfare state, which only reached 16 billion DM. Out of the 1.8 million Turks residing in Germany, in 1992 there were 35,000 business people ranging from restaurant proprietor to industrialist, employing a total of 150,000 Turks and 75,000 Germans, with an annual turnover of 25 billion DM. In 1991, these businessmen paid 1 billion DM in taxes.[10] Organized into Turkish business associations in several regions, particularly in Germany, they seek to weigh both in the national political life of their country of residence and in Turkey by posing as intermediary between the two countries as 'informal ambassadors' negotiating the economic interests of the country of origin. Furthermore, by collaborating with Turkish businessmen in Turkey, they seek to influence decisions in Brussels regarding Turkey.

The Turkish government is also involved in mobilizing nationalist forces outside national territories to counteract the development of movements against its national interests and principles of a nation-state. By helping official organizations in Turkey reform as associations in Europe, the Turkish government contributes to developing a nationalism that in fact becomes transnational, as do the nationalists movements that oppose it, such as the Kurdish movement or Turkish Islamic associations and their transnational European mobilization. Many Kemalist associations are

---

[10] In Migration News Sheet, Bruxelles, December 1991, cited by the Economic and Political Impact of Turkish Migration in Germany, *Zentrum für Türkeistuden, Konsumgewohnheiten und wirtschaftliche Situation der türkischen Bevölkerung in der Bundesrepublik Deutschland*, Essen, September 1992. Since then the Centre publishes on a regular basis reports on firms created by Turkish nationals as well as the taxes they are paying every year. See also the statistics of the Association of Turkish Businessmen of Berlin.

active in Turkey, such as the Association of Ataturk Thought (*Atatürkçü Düsünce Dernegi*), which amplifies their mobilization and diversifies their activities in Germany as if to assert their presence among other associations or in opposition to them.

Thus the 'imagined transnational communities' forged on the basis of a common language and religion and a sense of belonging to a 'deterritorialized nation', give current nationalism a shape that is different from the highly territorialized nationalisms of the 19th and even mid-20th centuries. Such a 'transnationalisation of nationalism' does not imply going beyond centrifugal rationales (regionalism, separatism), it instead breathes new life into them. Identity claims that are strongly based in a transnational community organization fuel new expressions of nationalism.

The emergence of a transnational community of Turks of Europe draws its basis on several intersecting conditions:

1) the dispersion and settlement of populations of Turkish stock in several European countries as well as their political mobilization in several national spaces,
2) the emergence of a European transnational public space that fosters the structuring of networks on the basis of identities and common interests,
3) denser interactions between Turkey and Europe and the role given to migrants or taken by them in these exchanges.

The emergence of transnational communities implies a redefinition of territory, nation and polity, all of these challenging the nation-state as a culturally and territorially unified political structure. In fact, transnational communities enable political actors involved in structuring networks to circumvent national policies. Even more, their organization, based on mobilization around the recognition of identities that characterize their organization, are akin to 'deterritorialized' national movements. From this standpoint, transnationality is part of a broader process of globalization.

But transnationality as globalization presents a certain paradox. Transnational communities, while challenging the nation-state, appear more and more as indispensable structures to negotiate with public authorities the recognition of collective identities forged in contexts which remain national, those of the country of origin and the host country. They aim in sum to influence states from the outside (cf. Kastoryano 2000). Their objective is to strengthen their representativity at the European level, but their practical aim is to achieve 'recognition' at the national level. Is it worth specifying that activists, even the most active at the European level, see states as the only 'adversaries' with which they have to deal in the final analysis.

In the case of the Turks of Europe, the modes of mobilization and claims reflect the institutional specificities of the host country. For Turkey, do these transnational communities imagined on the basis of a common language (or family of Turkic languages) and religion (Sunni branch of Islam), as well as a sense of belonging (or non-belonging in the case of the Kurds) to a deterritorialized nation not further weaken the state at a time when the state is negotiating its role on the international scene and more specifically in Europe? But at the same time, the Turkish transnational community must be seen as a mainspring for political and social change in Turkey due to the introduction of a democratic 'know-how' acquired in the struggle for equal rights in a situation of immigration in Europe.

Europe has always served and will continue to serve as a mirror to Turkey. It is currently behind a questioning of its political culture, its constitution, its respect for human rights, its democratic sense, particularly through the Kurdish question, but above all through its identity. The desire to be part of a unified Europe may be perceived as confirmation of a western-style nation-state. But is this the image that United Europe reflects, especially when the Kurdish nationalist movement finds support among European authorities that directly negotiate the conditions for recognition of ethnic minorities in the framework of the Turkish nation-state?

Given the increased interdependence of internal and external questions of nation-states and the interactions among them, the Turks of Europe constitute both a challenge and a chance for Turkey, a challenge regarding its capacity to negotiate its identity, and a chance regarding its affirmation as a nation-state.

References

Basch L., Schiller, N.G., Blanc C.S. (1997), Nations Unbound. Transnational Projects, Postcolonial Predicaments and Deterritorialized Nation-States, Gordon Breach Publishers, (4ème édition).

Bruneau, M. (1994), 'Espaces et territories de diasporas', in *L'Espace Géographique*, vol. XXIII, no. 1, pp. 5-19.

Cohen R. (1997), *Global Diasporas. An Introduction*, University of Washington Press, Seattle.

Gupta A., Ferguson J. (eds) (1997), *Culture, Power, Place*, Durham, Duke Unversity Press.

Hannertz U. (1996), *Transnational Connections. Culture, People, Places*, London, Routledge.

Kastoryano, R. (2000), 'Settlement, Transnational Communities and Citizenship', in *International Social Sciences Journal*, 165 (September 2000), pp. 307-12.

Kastoryano, R. (2002), *Negotiating Identities. States and Immigrants in France and Germany*, Princeton, Princeton University Press.

Kastoryano, R., (forthcoming), 'Transnational Participation and Citizenship. Immigrants in Europe' in M. Berezin and M. Schain (eds) *Remapping Europe*, Cornell U. Press.

Létourneau, J. (1977), 'Le lieu (dit) de la nation: essai d'argumentation à partir d'exemples puisés au cas québécois', in *Revue Canadienne de Science Politique*, XXX: 1, (March 1977), pp. 55-87.

Levitt, P. (1998), 'Local-level Global religion: The Case of U.S.-Dominican Migration', in *Journal for the Scientific Study of Religion*, (37) 1, pp. 74-89.

Neveu, C. (1994), 'Citoyenneté ou racisme en Europe: exception et complémentarité britanniques', in *Revue Européenne des Migrations Internationales*, vol. 10, no. 1, pp. 95-109.

Portes, A., (1997), 'Transnational Communities: Their Emergence and Significance in the Contemporary World System', in R.P. Korzeniewicz and W.C. Smith (eds.), *Latin America in the World Economy*, Greenwood Press.

Smith, J., Chatfield, C., Pagnucco, R., (eds) (1997), *Transnational Social Movements and Global Politics. Solidarity Beyond the State*, Syracuse University Press.

Tapia, S. de (1994), 'L'émigration turque: circulation migratoire et diaspora', in *L'Espace Géographique*, vol. XXIII, no. 1, pp. 19-28.

Chapter 13

Amalgamating Newcomers, National Minority and Diaspora – Integration(s) of Immigrants From Poland in Germany

Thomas Faist

Things are only ever seen in perspective, and only understood in perspective: and the more effects we can muster about a subject, the more ways of seeing, different ways of seeing, we are capable of, *the more complete our "concept" of it and our "objectivity" will be.*

Friedrich Nietzsche (1877), *Genealogy of Morals* 3, 12 (own translation).

1 Three Puzzles of Immigrant Integration – Theory vs. Observations: Assimilation, Cultural Pluralism, Transborder Spaces

In public discourse and political debates, the goal of *assimilation* – referring to the amalgamation of immigrants with the core of an immigrant society – is in ill repute. Since the 1960s it has been a debated and, according to some views, even politically and normatively incorrect term. In an age of multiculturalism and global diasporas, it is especially the normative prescriptions of amalgamation and the ideology of assimilation – assimilationism – that have been the constant target of criticism (Bauman, 1991, p.102). In addition to social and civic integration, assimilation seems to demand the almost complete cultural adaptation of newcomers to the new country of immigration. There is also a rich literature on subcultures which suggests that such a concept depicting the core of a society to which immigrants can eventually amalgamate would be questionable. Even French policy-makers, who have been known to constitute the vanguard of upholding the idea of assimilation, have replaced this term with diffuse words such as *insértion* or *intégration*

(Vermeulen, 1997). One may contend that the underlying French policies have not changed much. Nevertheless, even among hard-nosed representatives of assimilation in public debates, there has been a rhetorical sea change. However, a look at empirical, real world developments of immigrant integration raises doubts as to whether assimilation is really a phenomenon of the past. After all, empirical studies of the integration processes of labor migrants who have arrived since the 1960s in the USA and Europe do not contradict the projections of the assimilation model: One of the tenets of the assimilation model developed by the Chicago School of Sociology is that the first generation partly acculturates to the country of immigration, and that the second generation experiences full acculturation and social integration. Despite manifold exclusionary processes in the socio-economic and political spheres, empirical studies have usually confirmed some sort of assimilatory process (DeWind et al.; 1997, Esser and Friedrich, 1990; Brubaker, 2001). And even novel processes, such as the adaptation of recent immigrants to sub-cultural groups and not to the core of society – 'segmented assimilation' (Portes and Zhou, 1994) – do not contradict this general finding. How do we make sense of this puzzling situation? On the one hand, assimilation seems to be outdated as a practical concept guiding policies, but, on the other hand, analysts who study integration processes cannot do without some sort of assimilation model.

The situation is very similar when taking a closer look at the concept of *cultural pluralism*. Often called *multiculturalism* in the European context and connected to older understandings of cultural pluralism in the American scene, it reappeared as a serious competitor to assimilation in the 1980s and 1990s. In various incarnations, cultural pluralism is concerned with cultural resistance on the part of immigrant newcomers or even cultural difference between migrant and autochthonous people. Ironically, cultural pluralism has been attacked from a cosmopolitan view on grounds of weak conceptualization and cultural essentialism (Waldron, 1995) at just about the time academic analysts have conceded that 'We are all multiculturalists now' (Glazer, 1997). Yet, the public debates and policies concerning the accommodation of new categories of religious organizations into state-religion and state-church relations indicates how crucial cultural pluralism actually is. In Europe, the issues range from Islam as a subject of instruction in public schools to conflicts around the integration of Muslim organizations as 'corporate bodies of public law' in Germany.

Not surprisingly, we encounter yet another puzzle when looking at the third concept – *transborder social spaces* or *diaspora*. Essentially, models in this vein assume that immigrants entertain dense and continuous transborder transactions in networks, organizations and communities reaching across immigration and emigration states (see the overview in Kivisto, 2001). It is not clear, however, which categories of immigrants and refugees and for how long certain groups live in such interstitial spaces. Also, we know very little concerning the conditions under which transnationalism is mainly of a transient kind – for example, remittances of first-generation immigrants – or of a more reactive kind as a response to discrimination or multicultural opportunities encountered in the new countries of settlement; or even a combination of both. Nevertheless, official recognition of cross-border ties has been on the increase in recent decades – public policies have come a long way from nationalist naturalization policies about a hundred years ago. Almost half of all sovereign states on earth nowadays tolerate or even accept multiple citizenship. And even in countries characterized by restrictive policies towards dual citizenship, de facto rates of multiple membership are increasing.

The specific *question* is: What aspects of immigrant integration in contemporary liberal democracies are best described and explained by which model? It is my contention that we need to employ various concepts to make sense of the integration processes contemporary immigrant groups have experienced in modern immigration societies – not only the assimilation model, but also competing explanations such as cultural pluralism and the expansion of transborder social spaces. Only then will we be able to gauge and evaluate the relative merits of these three conceptual approaches. The *proposition* is that the utility of each conceptual approach mainly depends on the category of immigrants and the specific conditions of integration we look at. Of course, it makes a difference whether we look at ethnic Germans from Russia in Germany who usually cut all ties to the country of origin, moving with their whole family – or whether we analyze Russian Jews in Germany, who often engage in projects of onward migration to Israel or the USA and are thus likely to maintain dense transstate ties. Also, subdivisions of immigrant categories from the same country, such as Poles in Germany, often experience very different integration trajectories.

2 A Crucial Case: Immigrants from Poland in Germany

This analysis looks at immigrants from Poland in Germany to exemplify and illustrate this claim. These immigrant categories from Poland present a 'crucial case' (Eckstein, 1975) for three reasons. First, in comparison with other groups of immigrants or minorities, Poles came in several immigration waves during the last 150 years: at the turn of the 19th to the 20th centuries, internal migrants moved from the former eastern regions of Prussia to the Ruhr area. And seasonal workers from the territory then occupied by Czarist Russia to these eastern agrarian regions. During World War Two, the German authorities forced labor convicts from Poland to work in Germany. Immediately after World War Two, many Germans emigrated from the territories which were to become Polish. In the 1970s and 1980s Polish asylum seekers arrived. The number of *Aussiedler* increased dramatically during the late 1980s, followed by the *Spätaussiedler* – late-coming ethnic Germans since 1993. Currently, cyclical migrants such as seasonal workers, cross-frontier commuters, contract workers and unregistered domestic helpers move back and forth between Poland and Germany. The category of cyclical migrants also includes some persons who eventually settle down, though most of them keep their main residence in Poland and commute. Thus, we have both circular migration and settled immigrants.

Second, the emigration from Poland to Germany has also included people of German descent who should be most prone to assimilation, right from the start of their stay in Germany. These ethnic Germans have enjoyed a constitutionally guaranteed right to settle in Germany because of their *German descent*, the ethnic Germans – *Aussiedler*.

Third, there is a broad range of legal categories in which these immigrants fall – ranging from seasonal workers and asylum seekers to permanent immigrants such as ethnic Germans – so that we can gauge the impact of legal status on integration. Among these categories are labor migrants, *Aussiedler*, refugees and asylum seekers, seasonal workers, and unregistered workers. In Germany, there is no other category of immigrants or minorities showing a similar wide range with respect to the legal status. Legal status is a crucial determinant of chances for long-term integration. Among the two million people from Poland – a rough estimate (Trzcielińska-Polus, 2000, p.191) – about 1.2 million *Aussiedler* form the largest group. Many of the *Aussiedler* naturalized in Germany also possess dual citizenship. Among the other categories, more than a quarter of a million have solely a Polish passport and are permanent residents in

Germany; and about 100,000 persons are recognized asylum seekers. Therefore, when taking country of origin as an indicator, immigrants from Poland constitute the second largest ethnic minority in Germany, immediately followed by people of Turkish origin. However, a caveat has to be added. If we look at the first generation and the 1.5-generation immigrants only, i.e. those who were born in Poland or experienced their formative socialization in Poland, the number is cut into half. Since 1980 about one million persons emigrated from Poland to Germany, most of them between 1987 and 1990 (Pallaske, 2000). Seen in this way, immigrants from Poland comprise the third-largest group, right next to those from former Yugoslavia.

The term *immigrants* denotes persons who have settled down in a country different from their country of origin for a significant period of their lives, usually more than 3 years. And *interstate migrant* designates those who intend to stay in another country for a significant period in their lifetime. Thus tourists, for example, do not belong to this category. There are two broad categories of immigrants from Poland: First, the term includes *immigrants of Polish descent*. Even a terminologically meticulous analyst such as Max Weber never exactly defined the term 'Poles' in writings such as his sharp-tongued and provocative inaugural lecture 'The Nation-State and Economic Policy' (1894). He alternately referred to Poles as citizens of the German Empire who used to be small farmers in the eastern provinces and to Polish seasonal workers hailing from the parts of the present Republic of Poland, then occupied by czarist Russia. Clearly, the term referred to very different legal and occupational categories. By contrast, the fanatic German forces at the turn to the 20th century had no problems with prejudicial definitions: They rummaged out the old stereotype 'Every Pole is a Catholic'. During the German-Polish tensions in the Ruhr District in 1907, the Polish-language paper *Wiarus Polski* retorted: 'The Polish people know the German Catholics quite well and conclude that every German is a hidden Lutheran' (Kleßmann, 1984, p. 500; own translation, TF). Second, the term 'immigrants from Poland' here also refers to a large category of people who have *some kind of German descent*, ethnic Germans – the *Aussiedler* and *Spätaussiedler* who mostly hail from Upper Silesia viz. Śląsk (the Polish term for Silesia).

3 The Models Applied

Applying the three basic analytical approaches of immigrant integration to the Polish case, we arrive at the following propositions (see table 13.1).

Table 13.1 Models for the analysis of immigrant integration: Assimilation - old and new, cultural pluralism and transstateness

Model of integration	Assimilation – 'old' model	Assimilation – 'new' model	Cultural pluralism	Border-crossing expansion of social spaces
Integration	amalgamation with the majority society	convergence of immigrant and majority groups	internal integration: colonies / minorities	transstate spaces: 'in' and 'between' states
Spheres of Integration				
Economic	socio-economic parity: socio-economic equality with the autochthonous population	- see the 'old' assimilation model -	niche and enclave economies: concentration of employment (self- or dependent) in selected sectors	cross-frontier flows of labor and entrepreneurs: transstate networks and collectives based on kinship and exchange
Political	national citizenship: uniform and homogenous national political culture	toleration of dual citizenship: diverse subcultures within a common framework (e.g. constitution)	multicultural citizenship: recognition of cultural diversity: polyethnic rights and possibly rights of self-government for minorities	recognition of dual citizenship: overlapping (dual) and nested (supra-state) citizenship; complementary to the national citizenship
Cultural	acculturation: adaptation to values and behavioral patterns of the majority core	mutual & asymmetric acculturation: more emphasis on the immigrants' influence on the majority culture(s)	cultural transplantation: transfer of culture from emigration to immigration countries	border-crossing syncretism: diffusion of culture and emergence of new types of plural identities

All three stylized perspectives on integration *cumulatively* promote a better comprehension of the most important aspects of the integrations of immigrants from Poland:

1. *Assimilation* models assume the eventual *amalgamation of the minority with the majority group* in the immigration country. This means, for example, participation of immigrants in professional and public life, such as membership in German trade unions, participation in political parties or soccer clubs. We would expect this to be true for the Poles in the Ruhr area – the so-called *Ruhrpolen* – who are nowadays in the fourth or fifth generation (Kleßmann, 1978), and – in terms of acculturation and social integration – of first- and second-generation ethnic Germans, the *(Spät-)Aussiedler*.

2. The concepts of *cultural pluralism* focus on the longevity of immigrant cultures, which were transplanted from the country of origin to the country of settlement. The main emphasis is on the *internal integration* within the *minority,* the formation of *colonies*. This means internal integration in the Polish community or communities – the so-called *Polonia* – for example, the Polish Catholic Mission or Polish cultural associations. These processes can be analyzed in more detail considering the refugees who emigrated from Poland in the 1970s and 1980s.

3. The newest approach, *border-crossing expansion of social spaces*, is based on the existence of *transstate spaces*. Transstate spaces are pluri-local ties of persons, networks, communities and non-state organizations – reaching beyond the borders of sovereign states. These spaces are characterized by a high density, frequency and stability of social and symbolic ties. This form of integration occurs *within the border-crossing, viz. transstate spaces between Germany and Poland and in the European Union (EU).* It relates to extremely diverse phenomena such as close kinship and friendship networks comprising Poland and Germany, posted workers in transnational enterprises, or network channeling of unregistered workers. In essence, integration in transstate spaces means that immigrants maintain social and symbolic ties to both country of origin as well as settlement.

All three models will now be discussed in greater detail.

3.1 Assimilation – From Amalgamation with the Majority Core to a Rapprochement of Ethnic Groups

The assimilation model has often been declared dead, but it still offers the most sophisticated description of immigrant integration. According to assimilation theory, the *amalgamation* of immigrants and their children with the core of the concerned majority group in all fields of private and public life will only be completed after the third generation. The assimilation model envisions three broad, successive stages of integration (Gordon, 1964). *Acculturation* or cultural assimilation means that immigrants and their descendents adopt the language, norms and ideals of the majority group. *Social integration* or structural assimilation holds that huge numbers of immigrants participate in the institutions of the immigration country, and finally even marry with members of the majority group. *Identification* or civic assimilation refers to the feeling of immigrants as an integral part of the majority group who, in the end, regard the immigrants as belonging to 'us'. This third form of assimilation implies the absence of value and power conflicts between immigrants and the majority group. Acculturation and social integration constitute the decisive stages. Once these steps have been taken, civic integration follows more or less automatically.

These three stylized stages – which do not necessarily show a linear pattern but may also proceed along a 'zig-zag' line (Gans, 1992) – lead from the experience of the first generation that is often connected with poverty and discrimination to a fast acculturation and a gradual socio-economic upward mobility, beginning with the second generation. Assimilation theory predicts that distinct cultural and language characteristics will have virtually disappeared in the third and fourth generations. In a first conceptualization of the Chicago School of Sociology, the term assimilation connoted the existence of a homogenous core culture. The pioneers of the assimilation model defined assimilation as a process of interpenetration and fusion of the minority group with the majority during which immigrants gradually acquire the majority's memories, feelings and attitudes. The idea of amalgamation here refers to the *socialization of the second generation* and, therefore, represents a crucial step towards societal trust and solidarity – the outcome of long and protracted processes (Park and Burgess, 1969, p. 510, p. 735). Thus, to expect assimilation on the part of the first generation would be a completely unrealistic idea. At best we could speak of temporary adaptation, i.e. a certain orientation towards the behavioral norms of the immigration country. Nevertheless, assimilation by no means indicates that all characteristics pointing to the ethnic, religious or national origin of immigrants will vanish into thin air. Religious peculiarities as, for example, the Mariolatry of some Polish immigrants and folkloristic elements do not, of course, present a problem to assimilation.

More recent interpretations have relieved assimilation theory from its earlier ideological underpinning of assimilationism. Assimilationism meant that there is a cultural core and a homogenous majority culture to which the immigrant should adjust. Instead, newer approaches start from the assumption that minorities of immigrants do not necessarily amalgamate with the dominant core. Rather, different cultures *converge* (Morawska, 1994) under the umbrella of a binding constitution and a common language. This 'thin' constitutional-cultural frame allows for a rather 'thick' ethnic and religious cultural life of immigrants. On the level of ethnic cultures, the convergence thesis assumes that minority and majority cultures influence the overall cultural set-ups in *asymmetric* ways, immigrant cultures exerting much less influence than receiving cultures. This revised assimilation model is not the same as the idea of segmented assimilation which means that new immigrants may adjust to various subcultures. Rather, the emphasis of the revised model is on the area of civic assimilation, on the integration of immigrants into a common political-legal framework and minimal cultural prerequisites such as a shared language. Thus, introducing the idea of convergence, the supposition of cultural homogeneity of all groups living in a sovereign state can be relaxed, without throwing the assimilation model as a whole overboard. So, the starting point is a more plural structure of cultures in immigration countries. In Germany, for example, a common framework consists of the Constitution (Basic Law) and a common language – German. This still leaves room for varied sub-cultures (Berger and Hradil, 1990, on changing life-styles in general).

Strictly speaking, the 'old' assimilation model makes the following predictions (see table 13.1). In the economic realm, the end result is parity with the majority group or a rapprochement of the immigrants to a supposed middle class. In the field of politics, amalgamation means a single, unique and indivisible civil loyalty, usually to the nation in the country of settlement. In the cultural realm, the process results in acculturation – the adoption of all essential values of the dominant group.

The 'new' convergence model of assimilation leads to significant modifications pertaining to the political and cultural spheres. In the political area, it aims at a public culture that is as homogeneous as possible and, nevertheless, allows for overlapping memberships such as dual citizenship in order to facilitate integration. An appropriate example in this context is the *Aussiedler* whose multiple nationality the German government has tolerated for many years – although dual citizenship is not allowed as a rule in Germany and in Poland. In between 1981 and 1990 the number of dual citizens increased to two million. Most of the rise was attributable to the tolerance of dual citizenship among the *Aussiedler* (Goes, 1997, p. 20). In the cultural area, the model predicts an approximation and mutual enrichment of the German and Polish cultures – with the caveat that the dominant culture of the immigration country, i.e. the German majority culture(s), is the most influential.

The 'old' and 'new' assimilation models seem to be most promising when applied to the following five categories of immigrants from Poland in Germany:

1. The first category is fourth and fifth generations descendents of the earlier internal migration of the Polish minority in the German Reich, the *Ruhrpolen*; about 80,000 to 100,000 of them are estimated to live in North Rhine-Westphalia. This category also includes descendents of Mazures from East Prussia.
2. The Nazis forced about 1.7 million Polish workers to labor in Germany during World War Two. A few stayed after World War Two. These so-called *displaced persons* refer to about 45,000 Poles who remained in Germany.
3. In the wake of the 1956 riots *refugees* fled to Germany, about 200,000. They were very conscious of their 'German-ness'.
4. In the course of the 1968 'March Emigration' several thousand *intellectual Jews* came to Germany.
5. *Aussiedler* are, in terms of figures, by far the largest group: Between 1980 and 1994 alone no less than 800,000 arrived in Germany. From 1950 to 1989, a total of 1,238,310 *Aussiedler* emigrated from Poland. From 1980 to 1989 the number increased to 632,000 immigrants – most of them came between 1987 and 1989: 438,985. After 1989 the figures rapidly decreased: 1989: 133,872; 1991: 40,129 and 1992: only 17,742.

The first and the fifth group are numerically the most important for contemporary integration processes. Certainly, the socio-economic integration process has been completed for the descendants of the *Ruhrpolen*. Also, socio-economic integration seems to have been relatively successful even for the fifth group, especially for those who arrived in the late 1980s and early 1990s during an expansionary economic period in Germany (Diehl, 2000). Yet regarding the cultural integration of this category, the sparse empirical evidence is not conclusive. Clearly, the relatively *low cultural distance* between 'Poles' and 'Germans' may explain why *Aussiedler* from the former Soviet Union are faced with much more difficulties in their process of integration into the German society than those from Poland (Mrowka, 2000, p. 231; Schmidt, 2000, p. 283). *Spätaussiedler* from the GUS states often belong to the Russo-Orthodox church instead of the Catholic or Protestant Christianity.

Undoubtedly, the assimilation process has been completed for the first category, the children of the *Ruhrpolen*. In many cases, only family names in telephone directories bear witness to Polish origins (Wóycicki, 2000, p. 243). If we regard mixed marriages between Germans and Poles as an indicator for one of the last phases of assimilation, we find few before the World War One. In the decades after (1918-1933), however, mixed marriages amounted to almost one third of the children of Poles. Here, we must take into consideration that the Germans who they married also belonged to the group of internal migrants (Kleßmann, 1984, pp. 499-500). However, a caveat should be added in terms of self-selection. In the early 1920s, two thirds of the *Ruhrpolen* moved to France and Belgium, or returned to Poland. Probably those remained who were most willing to assimilate.

However, the situation becomes much more complex when we look at the specific form of the acculturation of Polish *Aussiedler*, most of whom hail from Upper Silesia viz. Śląsk. Instead of acculturation, we often find *over-adaptation*. One of the reasons can be found in the particular legitimation of their immigration. *(Spät-)Aussielder* face a peculiar predicament. On the one hand, their German descent and traditions has enabled them to immigrate to Germany. On the other hand, this legitimation for immigration prevents them from claiming a 'Polish' past, which is also part of their history. Many, especially among the elderly *Aussiedler*, did not dare to live their Polish side openly in the public, for example, speak Polish in public spaces. And just think of the curious fact that many did not dare to install satellite dishes for fear of being accused of watching the channel 'TV Polonia'. They were the ones who greeted the advent of cable TV with great relief. This brief anecdote indicates that the *Aussiedler* publicly cannot lay claim to an alternative identity different from 'German-ness', which could prevent over-adaptation. Over-adaptation implies that immigrants have no chance to resort to their past, their traditions, in order to cope with the present and future in the country of migration. This is especially important for groups who face non-acceptance and discrimination by groups in the country of settlement. Indeed, *Aussiedler* from Central and Eastern Europe have not been easily accepted as 'Germans' in Germany (Bade, 1997).

Therefore, there is an important reason to go beyond the 'old' assimilation model. It does not clarify the role of immigrant culture for acculturation and the role of immigrant associations for social integration. And while the 'new' assimilation model conceptualizes state-citizen relations in terms of a 'thin' constitutional framework and a 'thick' immigrant culture, it does not provide a basis for analyzing the function of immigrant colonies. For example, there are the organizations of 'Polonia': 'Federation of Poles' (*Bund der Polen*) and the 'Union of Poles' called *zagoda*, meaning harmony or unity. Of course, the existence of such immigrant associations does not necessarily indicate non-integration. For example, the Greek immigrants' national schools, which have existed since the 1960s, have not resulted in a discrimination of their children in the educational system (Hopf, 1987). This is important with regard to Polish-language teaching in Germany, or the function of the Polish Catholic church and its pastoral activities in Germany.

3.2 Cultural Pluralism: Colonies and National Minorities

It is still an open question why immigrants of Polish descent in Germany have – notwithstanding their comparatively high numbers and longstanding history – hardly become visible in Germany's de facto multicultural mosaic. Therefore, it is useful to deal with a perspective that, in contrast to the assimilation model, puts more emphasis on the integration of newcomers and minorities within their own organizations, neighborhoods and groups.

Unlike the assimilation model, cultural pluralism does not form a consistent theory. Instead, it is a loose set of propositions which privileges the analysis of those cultural characteristics which allow distinguishing between immigrants and non-immigrants in the immigration country. On a theoretical level, only political theorists have gone at length to justify on normative grounds why certain minority groups should have group rights (Kymlicka, 1995). But there is no coherent set of positive, empirically-oriented theory detailing the many facets of cultural pluralism. Very much like assimilation theory, groups of immigrants from Europe and the USA at the turn of the 19th to the 20th centuries formed the empirical basis upon which far-reaching claims emerged (Glazer and Moynihan, 1963). Another commonality is that the first concepts of cultural pluralism also assumed a sequence of stages. Accordingly, immigrant dissimilation develops in four phases (Kallen, 1996, pp. 82 and 87): In a first phase immigrants strive to acculturate and to join the mainstream in all walks of life. However, usually they are exposed to heavy discrimination and, thus, in a second phase, revert to country of origin traditions. This process, third, leads to the opposite of assimilation – *dissimilation*. This does not necessarily imply segmentation in the sense of complete separation of the respective groups. The stylized fourth phase, then, is that of fully developed *pluralism* which means the coexistence of different cultures of nations in one country, or – in later versions – of ethnic or religious groups.

Cultural pluralism holds that immigrants eventually develop into *minorities*. This also means that immigrant minorities best integrate if each ethnic group has the opportunity to live its very own cultural traditions and practices. From this point of view there is no contradiction between overall societal integration and cultural diversity. In essence, cultural autonomy represents a more or less desirable form of integration into the immigration country. More recent versions of the model emphasize *cultural resistance* to majority cultures. Even when immigrants partially acculturate in the second or third generations, they usually preserve a significant number of social and cultural ties to persons, groups and organizations of the same ethnicity – particularly towards families and small communities such as neighborhoods but also towards larger language communities. For example, minority members use the language of the emigration country, viz. their parents' language, when communicating with actual or fictive kin (Fishman, 1966).

Cultural pluralism thus gives primacy to *internal integration in fairly homogenous immigrant colonies*. These socio-cultural agglomerations allow for the pooling of resources to help eventual integration in the country of settlement. Manifold examples exist, such as immigrants creating their own credit supply systems like 'rotating credit associations', or fulfilling social protection functions in organizing self-help insurance for illness and death (Breton, 1964). It is not totally clear, however, to what extent internal integration in ethnic, national or religious colonies represents a transitory phenomenon leading to eventual assimilation or to dissimilation. It could be that it depends on the degree of discrimination encountered by the newcomers and their children. The history of the *Ruhrpolen* prior to World War One could be interpreted as an example of partial dissimilation. Whereas up to the 1880s Poles from Upper Silesia, viz. Śląsk, Poznán and Mazuria, were integrated without any problems in local religious and social associations, this drastically changed during the mass immigration from the eastern regions of Prussia in the 1890s. Harassment and discrimination of Poles by Prussian authorities played a decisive part. The Prussian administration was afraid that the workers of Polish descent in the Ruhr area would support an independent Poland. Hence Poland's unresolved 'national question' and Prussia's policy of preventive discrimination formed the framework within which national tendencies in the associational life flourished (Kleßmann, 1984, pp. 494-8). In their heyday, more than 1,700 associations mushroomed in the booming coal and steel region, advocating an autonomous Polish state, and religious instruction for their children in Germany in the Polish mother language.

Nevertheless, if dissimilation is actually a correct description of these developments, it was limited to the late 19th and early 20th century. The *Ruhrpolen* who, by virtue of their religious, class and national affiliation were originally exposed to harsh repression during the German Empire, founded their own labor union in 1902, the Polish professional association ZZP (*Zjednoczienie Zawodowe Polskie*; Stefanski, 1995, p. 388). Yet this union was disbanded after World War One, and Polish workers joined the mainstream German trade unions. Nonetheless, this example suggests that internal integration may mobilize a minority's first generation much more than the direct incorporation of immigrants in the associations of the majority society. In this way, it may even be thought to contribute to the eventual amalgamation.

However, it would be misleading to extrapolate from the older Polish experience to integrations in the contemporary period. On the one hand, there are indeed similarities. For example, like one hundred years ago, organizations such as the Catholic Church function as parallel institutions. Many immigrants from Poland in Germany attend Polish-language services performed by Polish priests posted in German cities, serving under the jurisdiction of the Polish episcopate. On the other hand, times have significantly changed. The German government does not pursue politics and policies of assmilationism towards immigrants from Poland. Rather, ours is an age of a politics of recognition. This means that Polish associations in Germany are able to voice their interests and express cultural identities in a liberal democratic system. Nowadays, cultural pluralism is much more part of the German political culture compared to about a hundred years ago.

Nowadays, the *cultural pluralism* model should best fit three groups:

1. There are still German minorities in Poland, concentrating in the western region of contemporary Poland; reliable estimates speak of about 250,000 (Münz and Ohliger, 1997). Because of changing state borders between Poland and Germany, they are – in a way – the functional equivalent to the Polish minority in the eastern regions of the German Empire a hundred years ago (Urban, 2000).
2. *Political refugees* who have emigrated from Poland during the 'Gierek' era in the 1970s – about 120,000 persons.
3. The second group of refugees comprises people who sought asylum during the 1980s, the *Solidarność emigration*, some 250,000 immigrants. Categories 2 and 3 had a precarious legal status during the 1980s. They were only 'tolerated', and usually did not receive a work permit. They had to either draw social assistance or work illegally (Pallaske, 2000, pp. 135-6).

These two latter categories refer to first generation immigrants, so that the prediction of assimilation theory – the amalgamation with the majority society – could hold true. It is the somewhat increased level of tolerance of German society towards alternative cultural ways of living which today is higher than during the German Empire. And this openness could contribute to reduced discrimination and, thus encourage people of Polish descent to assimilate by convergence. The era of Bismarck's 'cultural struggle' against the Catholic Church and Polish language teaching, for example, seem to belong to the remote past. Nevertheless, discrimination of Polish immigrants in Germany is still strong. A representative survey suggests that in 1994 those youngsters who thought themselves superior to other nationalities felt so even more towards Poles than Turks (Pallaske, 2000, p. 137) – the prototypical cultural 'other' in German public discourses.

The cultural pluralism model contains the following expectations about the integration of Poles (compare Figure 1 above). In the economic realm we expect to find sectors and trades in which immigrant minorities are highly concentrated, even over-represented. Yet, this is clearly not the case – except in seasonal work and the building industries, both of which are examples of border-crossing activities and transstate spaces (see below). Also, compared with immigrants of Greek, Italian or Turkish origin who engage in niches such as restaurants or tailor's businesses for alterations, Poles do not form a parallel economy. Culturally and politically, we should find that a minority culture exists in the public realm. Again, this is questionable when looking at the claims of some Polish organizations that people of Polish descent constitute a minority.

Given the fact that Poles are a largely invisible or a sort of crypt minority, the central question then is: what are the organizational problems of the Polish minority in Germany? Spokespersons of *Polonia* organizations have repeatedly declared that Poles in Germany constitute a *national minority*. National minority denotes ethnic, cultural, language and religious minorities – according to the recommendation 1201 of the Council of Europe of 1993 (cf. UN Commission on Human Rights for the Prevention of Discrimination and the Protection of Minorities, 1979, quoted in Pan, 1999, p. 18). The characteristics are:

1. The number is *smaller* than the rest of the population of a certain state,
2. The group holds *non-dominant political and economic positions*,
3. The members – as *citizens* of the country of settlement – show ethnic, religious or language characteristics *which markedly differ* from the rest of the population,
4. The group possesses – even if not explicitly expressed – a sense of solidarity aimed at the *preservation* of their culture, tradition, religion and/ or language.

Here, criteria 3 and 4 are particularly relevant. The diverse discourses in international law and comparative law agree that a person's membership in a minority first of all depends on his or her will, i.e. the subjective factor, and that objective factors play a complementary role.

Criterion 3: The dominant opinion in international law holds that people do not belong to a minority unless they are citizens of the country (Janusz, 2000). Clearly, one could argue that most people from Poland do eventually naturalize in Germany – and the largest category, *Aussiedler*, are German citizens as soon as they enter Germany. However, this majority opinion is currently subject to criticism. Nowadays, some observers claim that groups of foreigners should be counted as minorities if they have been living in the country for a relatively long period of time (Franke and Hoffmann, 1992, p. 403). In this context an auxiliary criterion is also contested. In Germany, the status of officially recognized minority is bound to the existence of an ancestral place of settlement. This applies to the Sorbs who occupy the status of 'people' in the sense of nation, Danes who form a 'national minority', and North Frisians who are recognized as an 'ethnic group'. Sinti and Roma, however, are an obvious exception. But, according to the criterion of a 'coherent and fenced off territory', the category of people who came from Poland and settled in Germany do not constitute a minority. As distinguished from the Danes, Sorbs and North Frisians, the Poles in the present territory of the Federal Republic of Germany do not form a group that has been settling in a certain region for centuries. This is in sharp contrast to the German minority in Poland who – as we would have expected – concentrate in the former eastern regions of the German Empire (Kiwerska, 2000, p. 297).

Criterion 4: The question arises as to whether – following the central subjective criterion: 'a minority are all people who believe they belong to it' – immigrants and their descendants from Poland in Germany do form a uniform and relatively homogenous national minority. Until now, only one fact is quite certain: Within *Polonia* it is contested to which degree one could speak of a common intention that aims to preserve the ethnic, religious and language heritage. A closer analysis of *Polonia* associations is important, since political representation of non-governmental groups in Germany takes place through corporatist integration. In this context *corporatism* means that non-governmental institutions – such as the Christian churches, employers' associations or trade unions – attain a quasi-public status. This status gives them the opportunity to participate in central political institutions as bodies of public law. The respective public bodies include, for example, councils of public radio stations or the Federal Bureau of Labor (*Bundesanstalt für Arbeit*). Considering national or ethnic minorities, the recognition as people, national minority or ethnic group provides a similar privileged legal and public status. In sum, compared with other countries, the barrier for immigrants' and minorities' associations to join corporatist institutions is relatively high. Nonetheless, in case such an exclusive corporatist status can be achieved, extraordinary benefits are waiting.

Two examples indicate the problems faced by Polish associations:

1. In the early 1990s, the Federal Ministry of the Interior encouraged Polish associations to establish an umbrella organization analogous to the German minority in Poland. This would have given the German authorities a chance to bargain with only one partner in a corporatist fashion. Although some umbrella organizations, such as the Federal Association of Polish Councils (*Bundesverband Polnischer Rat in Deutschland e.V.*) have existed in Germany since 1997, several important Polish associations are not members of this top organization, for instance the Polish Congress in Germany (*Polnischer Kongreß in*

Deutschland e.V.), *Zgoda e.V.* and *Rodło e.V.* The Polish associations are not only split but also totally at odds with each other. This clearly restricts their efficiency as lobby institutions. Also, the number of *Polonia* associations declined from the mid-1980s into the 1990s (Stefanski, 1995, p. 394), and 80 per cent of the members are over 60 years old (Mrowka, 2000, pp. 220 and 232). Nowadays, there is not even a Polish-language press, which sharply differs from the situation of the *Ruhrpolen* around 1900 or that of today's Turkish immigrants.

2. *Polonia* associations differ widely in their stance towards the numerically largest group of people of Polish descent, the *(Spät-) Aussiedler*: some of the *Polonia* associations do not want to speak up for the interests of all *Aussiedler* from Poland but only for those who declare their support for the Polish cultural heritage (Mrowka, 2000, p. 226). This points to the fact that there does not exist the slightest consensus on what 'Polish' culture could mean in practice.

Against this background, the German government's hesitation to call the 'Poles' in Germany a minority caused fierce discontent. Indeed, the 'Treaty between the Federal Republic of Germany and the Republic of Poland on Good Neighborliness and Friendly Cooperation of 17 June 1991' does contain a striking *asymmetry*: On the one hand, the agreement speaks of a 'German minority in Poland'. On the other hand, the corresponding term is 'persons holding German citizenship who are of Polish descent or confess to Polish language, culture or tradition'. While this matter of mutual recognition has great symbolic importance, it is also true that the German government has affirmed in writing to grant the people of Polish descent in Germany the rights of a minority. In fact, this lives up to international standards (Deutscher Bundestag, 1995; Gras, 2000, p. 128; Hofmann, 1995, pp. 76-80, pp. 119-22). Nevertheless, substantial asymmetries persist, e.g. with regard to the right to vote: The German minority in Poland is exempted from the 5 percent clause. In addition to the established and recognized Sorb, Danish, North Frisian and Roma and Sinti minorities, only the Jewish group is currently considered as a potential minority in Germany. The situation was completely different during the Weimar Republic. The Weimar constitution had actually provided the status of a 'national minority' for the Polish minority. The respective article read: 'Legislation and administration must not impede those parts of the Empire's people who speak foreign languages. This concerns their free traditional development and, in particular, the usage of their mother tongue at schools and in procedures of internal administration and justice' (WRV, Art. 113; own translation, TF). This article would have given the Polish minority a chance to set up Polish schools and school classes, but it was never implemented. The reasons were the tense relationship between the German Empire and Poland, the disappearance of the Polish sub-culture in the Ruhr area and assimilation (Kleßmann, 1978, p. 177). Nevertheless, it seems that the early Weimar Republic experienced the peak of legal Polish activities in Germany. 1922 saw the founding of the already mentioned 'Federation of Poles in Germany' (*ZPwN/Zwiazek Polaków w Niemczech*). As the financially strongest minority association, it set up the umbrella organization for all minority groups in Germany in 1924, the 'League of National Minorities in Germany'. In addition to the Polish minority, Sorbs, Danes, Frisians and Lithuanians participated (Stefanski, 1995, p. 392). The Federation of Poles looked after the national interests of Poles in Germany and at the same time urged Poles to be loyal towards the German state (Kiwerska, 2000, p. 19). The situation completely changed when the National Socialists ignored minority rights and brutally pursued *Polonia* representatives – many of whom died in concentration camps.

Some researchers consider the organizational deficit of the German *Polonia* to be caused by its status – the lack of recognition as an ethnic-cultural minority (cited in Sakson, 2000). Then, however, the question comes up why the organizational density of other groups, which also do not possess the legal status of national or ethnic minority, exceeds that of the Polish minority. Take immigrant associations from the former 'guest-worker' countries like Spain (Schöneberg, 1993). In short, the legal recognition as minority cannot be the only reason for the relatively low degree of organization among people of Polish descent. We have to go beyond the official recognition of immigrant cultures by states to unearth the contribution of immigrant associations towards integration or segmentation.

One possible, though by no means sufficient, explanation for the relatively low organizational density may be that the great majority of recent immigrants from Poland are *Aussiedler* who were socialized in Poland during the Communist regime. Unlike the – proverbial – 'club culture' in Germany, informal meetings and circles of acquaintances characterized cultural life in Poland. It is remarkable, for example, that individual *Aussiedler* still act as informal organizers of sporadic cultural events and do not cooperate with *Polonia* associations (Schmidt, 2000, pp. 278 and 283). Moreover, courses in Polish language instruction teaching, offered in several German *Länder*, are only poorly accepted by parents and students (Stefanski, 1995, p. 399). The participation of *Aussiedler* in the *Polonia* is also low – the reasons range from their ambivalent identity (Wóycicki, 2000, p. 261) to the fact that some traditional *Polonia* organizations often expose an either-or mentality: German or Polish.

The relatively low organizational density might also point to a low degree of continuity between the 'old' Polonia and the relatively 'new' Polish language community in today's Germany (Wóycicki, 1999. p. 245). While Jews have also experienced a horrid break with the Holocaust, there is nevertheless a greater sense of historical continuity. Interestingly, Jewish organizations in Germany make great strides to integrate newcomers from the former Soviet Union. One possible explanation for this difference is probably the Jewish minority's global diaspora tradition. The difference becomes even more striking when we look at Jews and *Aussiedler* from the GUS.

To sum up, the cultural pluralism model throws light upon Polish organizational life and gives some reasons for the relatively low degree of organization among immigrants from Poland. It also helps to raise issues such as contentious minority politics. However, the model portrays a *static notion of culture* as heritage and as a transplant from the emigration countries. It does not consider the many changes immigrant cultures undergo as a consequence of integration. It is remarkable how much the assimilation model and the cultural pluralism perspective resemble each other in their static interpretation of cultural life: while the 'old' assimilation theories supposed a fairly homogeneous core culture, cultural pluralists have assumed a high degree of cultural homogeneity within immigrant colonies and minorities. In a way, they are simply mirror images of each other. Therefore, it is necessary to look at conceptual alternatives in order to interpret facts, which do not correspond to the eventual amalgamation in the immigration country or the unmodified transplantation of cultural traits.

3.3 Transborder Expansion of Social Spaces: Transstate Integration

As distinguished from the assimilation and cultural pluralism models, the transstate perspective looks beyond the *container space* of sovereign states towards the border-crossing networks of immigrants' social and symbolic ties. These networks are usually determined by both internal and transstate factors and do not normally reach a global or universal extent. Transstate spaces tend to be restricted to migration systems. In order to analyze integration that comprises the spaces in and between the emigration and immigration countries, one needs to consider the border-crossing sets of ties within small kinship groups, issue networks, border-crossing communities such as diasporas, and transstate organizations such as religious congregations and transnational companies. In the border-crossing perspective, the following integration results emerge (cf. table 13.1): In the economic area, for example, transborder migrants maintain a main household in the emigration country as well as a shadow household in the immigration country – as do Polish seasonal workers during a certain part of the year. In the realm of political integration multiple and nested citizenship are conceivable – without raising the specter of a nation weakened by its citizens' multiple loyalties. And in the cultural area syncretist and multi-dimensional identities are possible. For example, in a representative inquiry among Poles in Germany in the late 1990s, 71 per cent or the respondents expressed that they felt a longing for Poland. Nonetheless, 36.7 per cent stated to have found a new home in Germany (Jonda, 2000). In a nutshell, border-crossing ties may advance internal integration – examples include religious diasporas – the obvious reference is pastoral care for Polish Catholics by Polish clergy. The Catholic Church has continuously operated as a transstate organization that far exceeds the emergence of modern states. Historically, Catholic church activities have been highly supportive of the Polish national endeavors. According to the transstate perspective, the desirable and normatively prescriptive target is not (mutual) acculturation, as in the assimilation model, or cultural difference and the maintenance of a distinct cultural basis as a background to a context of choice, as in the cultural pluralism model. Rather, it draws attention to the analysis of immigrant integration in transstate spaces, populated by persons, networks, groups and organizations – with interstitial ties crossing borders.

In the economic realm, we find numerous examples for interstitial spaces. There are about 30,000 cross-frontier commuters, an even higher number of seasonal workers in agriculture and the restaurant business, and commuting workers in service industries as well as domestic helpers. Politically, the most contentious category was posted, viz. contract workers. Polish construction companies enjoy temporary and numerically limited freedom of services as a consequence of the *1991 Agreement on Work Contracts* between Germany and Poland. This bilateral agreement, which Germany also concluded with other countries in Central Eastern Europe and Turkey, allows for work contracts between German general contractors and Polish sub-contractors. Polish companies bring machines as well as workers, who are subject to the rotational principle. The workers have an extra-territorial status. While working in Germany, they are subject to Polish labor and social law. Posted workers from Central Eastern Europe are paid German wages, but are less expensive because only social wages by Polish standards apply. The quota of contract workers from Poland, however, was cut back significantly after unions in Germany accused Polish companies of 'wage dumping' and employers decried an alleged 'distortion of competition'. So, after a peak of about 60,000 annually in 1993, the German government reduced the contingents. Thus, the number of Polish workers declined to about 30,000 in the late 1990s – much to the regret of the Polish enterprises and Polish government. After 1993, incidentally, companies from within the EU – especially from Portugal – began to take advantage of the freedom of services. At the same time when the number of Polish workers declined, those of Portuguese workers multiplied manifold, up to 300,000 annually during the 1990s. This actually put downward pressure on wages and jobs in the German construction industry. Low-skilled workers but also small companies were hit especially hard. A German law, akin to regulations in France and Austria which raised wages and working conditions among posted workers, and the EU guideline on posted workers could only offer partial relief. Finally, the construction sector has increasingly become seamless, state borders within the EU matter little. In Germany, unions and employers in the construction industry thus think back nostalgically to bilateral agreements which still allowed for unrestricted control by nation-states of industrial sectors and labor markets.

Considering political integration, the model of the border-crossing expansion of social spaces suggests that immigrants quite often maintain ties reaching into several countries. Therefore, dual citizenship serves as an institutionalized expression of these border-crossing relations. Two forms of cross-border membership can be differentiated: overlapping and nested citizenship.

First, *overlapping* – dual or multiple – citizenship of immigrants from Poland is significant for the integration in Germany, as held by the 'new' assimilation model. After all, a majority of immigrants in surveys has repeatedly held that when being able to keep the citizenship of the country of origin, the willingness to naturalize in the immigration country is higher. Going further, dual ties and even multiple loyalties of citizens towards several *democratic* states do not constitute any risk to the civic integration. Multiple ties across borders – akin to those within borders – do not necessarily put into question the loyalty of citizens to the immigration states. In the German-Polish case, virtually all *(Spät-)Aussiedler* possess two passports - up to one million. That many *Aussiedler* do not publicly show their affinities to the Polish culture in public is certainly not caused by dual citizenship as such but by negative clichés connected with 'Poles'. It is interesting that both Germany and Poland have refused to officially recognize dual citizenship. However, de facto, citizens of Polish origin are probably the largest category of persons holding dual citizenship in Germany. Vice versa, the majority of citizens of German descent in Poland also carry two passports. But even to these rather restrictive countries the tolerance – not recognition – of dual citizenship seems to be a feasible solution to ensure the loyalties of de facto national minorities or immigrant groups.

Second, *nested citizenship* in the form of supra-state membership, such as European Union Citizenship since the Treaty of Maastricht (1991), means that citizens of EU member states are also citizens of the Union, the respective member state, and also local and regional entities. All of these are embedded within the broader EU citizenship. Accordingly, EU citizens may participate in communal elections in other member states, vote for the European Parliament, take recourse to ombudspersons and enjoy diplomatic protection in third countries. This form of citizenship, however, is only open for citizens of the member states and not for full members of (associated) third states, the so-called *extracommunitari*. It is related to the membership in federal states in so far as the formal membership in smaller political units as provinces is integrated in that of the EU proto-federation. Both federal states and the EU are multi-level governing systems. Nonetheless, there is a decisive difference: In federal states like the Federal Republic of Germany, there is a strong political center with the federal government and the corresponding authorities at the head. By contrast, the governing institutions of the EU – such as the EU commission, the Council of Ministers, the European Court of Justice and the European Parliament – are part of a much looser political multi-level system. Though Polish citizens are not EU-citizens yet, it is to be expected that Poland's forthcoming accession to the EU will promote a nested understanding of membership: Polish and EU-citizenship do not contradict but complement each other. Overlapping and nested forms of citizenship are thus closely interrelated: Member states accept the naturalization of citizens from other EU states without asking the applicant to give up the original citizenship.

When looking at the cultural realm of nested collective identities, issues become more thorny. Many Poles feel they belong both to Poland *and* Europe, or Poland *and* Germany. Self-descriptions that include multiple national belongings are not the exception but the rule (Jonda, 2000, p. 322). This is also true for the *Aussiedler* from Upper Silesia. They lived in traditionally mixed areas. In their history, people in Silesia – the so-called Ślązak – have been exposed to forced assimilation by both German and Polish authorities, 200 years of Prussian rule and 40 years of Communist government. Most *Aussiedler* define themselves as Silesians or Ślązak first and second, as Europeans – but only a minority also perceive of themselves as Germans or Poles (Wóycicki, 2000, p.252). This is a form of nested identity, with a high emphasis on regional and supra-state identities, while national feelings do not carry the same importance. This can be interpreted as a response to discrimination by the dominating German and Polish authorities respectively – for example, in access to jobs and to xenophobic violence.

The model of border-crossing expansion of social spaces helps to reinterpret the relatively low density of Polish associations in Germany. There is a puzzle: There are numerous border-crossing ties between Germany and Poland, for example, Polish-German city partnerships. However, this space does not fulfill a strong bridging function. The organizations of *Polonia* do not participate in these endeavors. Perhaps the geographic proximity of Poland makes it more difficult for a tight network of Polish-German networks to emerge. For instance, Polish immigrants do not need to organize to experience Polish culture. Instead, they simply take their car and drive to Poland. Many Poles in Germany travel to Poland several times a year (Jonda, 2000, pp. 323-4). Nonetheless, it would still be fruitful to further explore the question why the influence of the German *Polonia* traditionally has been less pronounced than the Polish diasporas in the Ukraine or in the USA (Posern-Zielinski, 2000, p. 45). Probably, the tensions between Poland and Germany have been too high during the 20th century to allow the blossoming of Polish organizations in Germany. Because of the contiguous German-Polish frontier, the transstate spaces may play a crucial role for the integration of Poles in Germany. In this respect, the German-Polish case shows similarities with the Mexican-American scenario. While the border region has been a subject of tremendous academic interest in the Mexican-US case (Scott et al., 1996), it is relatively understudied in the Polish-German context. This fact may be connected with the long and violent history of the border regions.

There is also a downside to transstate spaces in the Polish-German case, best shown in the tensions within the Catholic Church. In northern German cities, where we find high concentrations of Poles and a diasporic situation for Catholics, immigrants from Poland decelerate the massive loss of churchgoers and taxpayers in the Catholic Church. There is also a direct transstate connection because the Polish Catholic Church sends priestly shepherds to take care of its flock in Germany. These Polish priests are proud to still engage in a truly spiritual mission, while they and many of their believers perceive the German Catholic church as being too much influenced by the Second Vatican Council, allegedly emphasizing the social mission of Christendom. It is therefore not surprising that immigrants from Poland favor Polish-language Sunday service with Polish priests. Also, due to the growth of Polish believers, Polish Catholics try to get their own churches – sometimes, old church buildings threatened by destruction. However, the German church administration has refused to yield to such demands. This example indicates that religious identities as Catholics from various backgrounds may not be easily reconciled (Krampen, 2001).

The model *border-crossing expansion of social spaces* best applies to the following categories of immigrants from Poland:

1. *Seasonal workers* who engage in cyclical migration; *border-crossing commuters*; *posted workers* who are subject to a strict rotational principle; and Polish citizens who take advantage of *visa-free travel* to recurrently work for short periods of time in Germany. In the late 1990s, the first three groups comprised about 300,000 to 400,000 workers annually,
2. Dual citizens who hold ties and loyalties to groups in both countries. Among them we find *Aussiedler* but also former refugees,
3. Polish citizens who are *permanent residents* in Germany and maintain dense and continuous social and symbolic ties spanning German-Polish spaces.

All of these examples are but the latest and sixth period of German-Polish transstate integrations. It is obvious that the contemporary state of affairs after the end of the Cold War and the collapse of communist regimes all over Central and Eastern Europe is particularly conducive to transborder ties when compared to earlier times. The first phase was when the German Reich, the Russian and the Austro-Hungarian Empire had divided Poland up until the end of World War One: circular migration characterized the transstate ties; yet, there was no sovereign statehood on the Polish side, only strong strivings towards autonomy. The power asymmetry between Poland and the three dividing powers thus was enormous – while the Catholic Church took over some nationalist functions. The second period refers to an independent Poland in the inter-war period and the Weimar Republic. No dense transstate space existed in economic terms. But, politically and culturally, there were important foundations laid for the recognition of Poles as a national minority. The third phase was the most devastating for the development of transborder ties. National Socialists in Germany abolished all rights for minorities, and political opposition in general. The Nazis annihilated transstate spaces by the politics of territorial annexation. Right after the War, there was massive expulsion of Germans from the former eastern provinces, now the western provinces of Poland. In the fourth phase, during the Cold War, Poland and the German Democratic Republic (GDR) on the one hand and the Federal Republic of Germany (FRG) on the other hand, found themselves as parts of power blocs. The respective governments instrumentalized non-state actors, such as Polish associations and refugee organizations, for ideological purposes. After the reunification of Germany, the fifth period, the two governments have created a higher degree of civil and political rights for the German minority in Poland and the Poles in Germany by the German recognition of the Oder-Neisse line as the German-Polish border and by the 'Treaty on Good Neighborliness and Friendly Cooperation' – albeit in an asymmetrical fashion concerning the official minority status. Nowadays, in the sixth period, the accession of Poland to the EU is impending. Thus, the nested dimensions of membership of Poles in Germany and Germans in Poland will probably come to the fore. One caveat should be added. Even this cursory glance at the history of transstate spaces in and between Poland and Germany suggests that there has been no linear progression towards an ever-increasing density of non-state relations.

4 Conclusion: Towards a Multi-Perspective Analysis

All three models of integration – assimilation, cultural pluralism and border-crossing expansion of social spaces – capture essential parts of the experience of Polish immigrants in Germany. In the crucial Polish-German case, the assimilation model is most useful in portraying long-term processes of adaptation in the socio-economic sphere. The 'old' assimilation model is less useful in describing and explaining processes of integration in the political and cultural sphere under conditions of the politics of recognition. New conceptual extensions of the assimilation model help to describe two-way processes of accommodation between majorities and minorities and put greater emphasis on civic assimilation. The cultural pluralism perspective is most fruitful illuminating the 'internal' integration of immigrant minorities – issues of immigrant viz. minority community formation, organization building, and state-citizen relations. It is of much less help in understanding issues of cultural difference and persistence. Finally, the transstate model is well suited to unearthing the multiple ties immigrants maintain not only within but also across the borders of emigration and immigration states. This is particularly productive when analyzing modes of adaptation which seem – at first sight – to indicate non-integration. In addition, while the transborder perspective can claim no exclusive purchase on capturing syncretist cultural elements, it rejuvenates theory and empirical work on novel forms of cultural pluralism. While cultural pluralism may exist without transborder integration, there is certainly 'no transnationalism without multiculturalism'.

One may now critically object to the third and last model – transssstate integration – that its predictions, such as integration 'between emigration and immigration countries', refer to transient phenomena. Indeed, despite the caveats already mentioned, the history of the *Ruhrpolen* dating back to the late 19th century would support such a critique. However, to transpose these historical lessons to the contemporary period would be preemptory for two reasons. First, all three integration models shed useful light on the current processes of integration. None of the models seems to be superior to another when applied to the late 20th and early 21st century experience of Poles in Germany. This result seems to strongly support a multi-perspective analysis along the lines hinted at in Friedrich Nietzsche's introductory epigraph – without necessarily giving up the strong and at times competing assumptions in each of the three models used. And it is simply too early to predict the future of Polish integrations in Germany. Second, even if the predictions of the revised and 'new' assimilation model eventually carried the day, it would still be an open question how results such as amalgamation with the core or convergence of sub-cultures come about. A higher tolerance for cultural pluralism is an outstanding characteristic in contemporary liberal democracies, despite resurgent and high levels of xenophobia and populism. Ironically, it may well be that in the absence of forced assimilation, a vanishing assimilationist ideology and a crumbling cultural core, policies and trends favoring cultural pluralism and border-crossing exchange form the most effective mechanism for eventual cultural convergence.

References

Bade, K. J. (1997), *Migration Past, Migration Future: Germany and the United States*, Providence, Berghahn Books.

Bauman, Z. (1991), *Modernity and Ambivalence*, Cambridge, Polity Press.

Berger, P. A. and Hradil, S. (eds) (1990), *Lebenslagen, Lebensläufe, Lebensstile*, Special Issue, Soziale Welt, No. 7. Göttingen: Schwartz.

Breton, R. (1964), 'Institutional Completeness of Ethnic Communities and the Personal Relations of Immigrants', *American Journal of Sociology 70*: pp. 193-205.

Deutscher Bundestag, 13. Wahlperiode (1995), Antwort der Bundesregierung auf die Kleine Anfrage der Abgeordneten U. Jelpke und der weiteren Abgeordneten der PDS, Drucksache 13/628 vom 31.03.95.

DeWind, J., Hirschman, C. and Kasinitz, P. (eds) (1997), *Immigrant Adaptation and Native-Born Responses in the Making of Americans*, Special Issue, International Migration Review 31.

Diehl, E. (2000), *Aussiedler*, Bonn, Bundeszentrale für Politische Bildung.

Eckstein, H. (1975), 'Case Studies and Theory in Political Science', in *Handbook of Political Science*, edited by F. Greenstein and N. W. Polsby, Vol. 7, Reading, MA, Addison-Wesley, pp. 251-303.

Esser, H. (1980), *Aspekte der Wanderungssoziologie. Assimilation und Integration von Wanderern, ethnischen Gruppen und Minderheiten. Eine handlungsorientierte Analyse*, Darmstadt, Luchterhand.

Esser, H. and Friedrich, J. (1990), *Generation und Identität : theoretische und empirische Beiträge zur Migrationssoziologie*, Opladen, Westdeutscher Verlag.

Fishman, J. (1966), *Language Loyalty in the United States*, The Hague, Mouton Publishers.

Franke, D. and Hofmann, R. (1992), 'Nationale Minderheiten – ein Thema für das Grundgesetz?', *Europäische Grundrechte Zeitschrift* (EuGRZ) 19, 17, pp. 401-409.

Gans, H. J. (1992), 'Comment: Ethnic Invention and Acculturation: A Bumpy-Line Approach', *Journal of American Ethnic History* 12, pp. 45-52.

Glazer, N. (1997), *We are all multiculturalists now*, Cambridge, MA, Harvard University Press.

Glazer, N. and Moynihan, D. P. (1963), *Beyond the Melting Pot*. Cambridge, MA, MIT Press.

Goes, N. I. (1997), *Mehrstaatigkeit in Deutschland. Verfassungsrechtliche Kriterien, internationale und europäische Determinanten, Rechtsvergleichung*, Baden-Baden, Nomos.

Gordon, M. (1964), *Assimilation in American Life*, New York, Oxford University Press.

Grabe, W. (2000), 'Oberschlesische "Aussiedler"', in *Polen in Deutschland*, edited by A. Wolff-Powęska and E. Schulz, pp. 177-87.

Gras, A. (2000), 'Rechtslage der Polen in Deutschland', in *Polen in Deutschland*, edited by A. Wolff-Powęska and E. Schulz, pp. 123-45.

Hofmann, R. (1995), *Minderheitenschutz in Europa. Völker- und staatsrechtliche Lage im Überblick*, Berlin, Gebr. Mann Verlag.

Hopf, D. (1987), *Herkunft und Schulbesuch ausländischer Kinder: Eine Untersuchung am Beispiel griechischer Schüler*, Berlin, Max-Planck-Institut für Bildungsforschung.

Janusz, G. (2000): 'Nationale Minderheiten in Deutschland', in *Polen in Deutschland*, edited by A. Wolff-Powęska and E. Schulz, pp. 67-101.

Jonda, B. (2000), 'Besondere Bindungen an Polen', in *Polen in Deutschland*, edited by A. Wolff-Powęska and E. Schulz, pp. 319-28.

Kallen, H. (1996), [1915], 'Democracy versus the Melting-Pot: A Study of American Nationality', in *Theories of Ethnicity. A Classical Reader*, edited by in W. Sollors. Houndmills, Basingstoke, Macmillan, pp. 67-92

Kivisto, P. (2001), 'Theorizing Transnational Immigration: A Critical Review of Current Efforts', *Ethnic & Racial Studies* 24, 4, pp. 532-61.

Kiwerska, J. (2000), 'Einstellungen zum deutschen Staat', in *Polen in Deutschland*, edited by A. Wolff-Powęska and E. Schulz, pp. 288-308.

Kleßmann, C. (1978), *Polnische Bergarbeiter im Ruhrgebiet 1870-1945. Soziale Integration und Subkultur einer Minderheit der deutschen Industriegesellschaft*, Göttingen, Vandenhoeck & Ruprecht.

Kleßmann, C. (1984), 'Integration und Subkultur nationaler Minderheiten: das Beispiel der "Ruhrpolen" 1870-1949', in *Auswanderer – Wanderarbeiter – Gastarbeiter*, Vol. 2, edited by K. J. Bade, Ostfildern, Scripta Mercaturae Verlag, pp. 486-505.

Krampen, N. (2001), 'Minderheiten im kollektiven Gedächtnis. Vom Vergessen und Erinnern der historischen polnischen Minderheit in Deutschland', in *Die Migration von Polen nach Deutschland*, edited by C. Pallaske. Baden-Baden, Nomos, pp. 77-94.

Morawska, E. (1994), 'In Defense of the Assimilation Model', *Journal of American Ethnic History* 13, 2, pp. 76-87.

Mrowka, H. (2000), '"Polonia" - Organisationen und ihre deutschen Ansprechpartner', in *Polen in Deutschland*, edited by A. Wolff-Powęska and E. Schulz, pp. 213-35.

Münz, R. and Ohliger, R. (1997), *Deutsche Minderheiten in Ostmittel- und Osteuropa. Aussiedler in Deutschland. Eine Analyse ethnisch privilegierter Migration*, Demographie aktuell, no. 9, Berlin.

Nietzsche, F. (1999), [1877], *Jenseits von Gut und Böse. Zur Genealogie der Moral*, in *Sämtliche Werke*, vol. 5, edited by G. Colli and M. Montinari, New Edition, München, Deutscher Taschenbuch-Verlag.

Pallaske, C. (ed.) (2000), *Die Migration von Polen nach Deutschland. Zu Geschichte und Gegenwart eines europäischen Migrationssystems*, Baden-Baden, Nomos.

Pan, F. (1999), *Der Minderheitenschutz im Neuen Europa und seine historische Entwicklung*, Wien, Braumüller.

Park, R. E. (1950), [1928], 'Human Migration and the Marginal Man', in *Race and Culture. Essays in the Sociology of Contemporary Man*, Chicago, University of Chicago Press, pp. 345-56

Park, R. E. and Burgess, E. W. (1969), [1921], *Introduction to the Science of Sociology*, Reprint, Chicago, University of Chicago Press.

Portes, A. and Zhou, M. (1994), 'Should Immigrants Assimilate?', *The Public Interest* 116, pp. 18-33.

Posern-Zielinski, A. (2000), 'Zwischen Assimilation und Bewahrung der Identität', in *Polen in Deutschland*, edited by A. Wolff-Powęska and E. Schulz, pp. 41-66.

Sakson, A. (2000), 'Teilnahme am gesellschaftlichen Leben', in *Polen in Deutschland*, edited by A. Wolff-Powęska and E. Schulz, pp. 309-18.

Schmidt, J. (2000), '"Aussiedler" – zwischen Polen und Deutschen', in *Polen in Deutschland*, edited by A. Wolff-Powęska and E. Schulz, pp. 270-87.

Schöneberg, U. (1993), *Gestern Gastarbeiter, morgen Minderheit*, Frankfurt a.M., P. Lang.

Scott, J., Sweedler, A., Ganster, P. and Eberwein, W.-D. (eds) (1996), *Border Regions in Functional Transition*, Regio, Series of the IRS No. 9, Erkner, Institute for Regional Development and Structural Planning.

Stefanski, V. (1995), 'Die polnische Minderheit', in *Ethnische Minderheiten in der Bundesrepublik Deutschland*, edited by C. Schmalz-Jacobsen and G. Hansen, München, C.H. Beck, pp. 385-400.

Trzcielińska-Polus, A. (2000), 'Besondere Situation: Polen in Ostdeutschland', in *Polen in Deutschland*, edited by A. Wolff-Powęska and E. Schulz, pp. 188-212.

Urban, T. (2000), *Deutsche in Polen. Geschichte und Gegenwart einer Minderheit*, München, C.H. Beck.

Vermeulen, H. (ed.) (1997), *Immigrant Policy for a Multicultural Society*, Brussels, Migration Policy Group.

Waldron, J. (1995), 'Minority Cultures and the Cosmopolitan Alternative', *University of Michigan Journal of Law Reform*, 25, pp. 751-793.

Weber, M. (1988), 'Der Nationalstaat und die Volkswirtschaftspolitik' (1895), in *Gesammelte Politische Schriften*, 5th edition. Tübingen: J.C.B. Mohr (P. Siebeck), pp. 1-25.

Wolff-Powęska, A. and Schulz, E. (ed.) (2000), *Polen in Deutschland. Integration oder Separation?*, Düsseldorf, Droste.

Wóycicki, K. (2000), 'Polen, Deutsche, Europäer... Identitätsbewußtsein und Gruppenbildung am Beispiel Düsseldorf', in *Polen in Deutschland*, edited by A. Wolff-Powęska and E. Schulz, pp. 237-69.

Chapter 14

Postscript:
Cultural Difference and Collective
Identity in Processes of Integration

Rosemarie Sackmann

1 Introduction

The collection of papers contained in this volume address the theoretical and empirical connection between collective identity and integration. The different contributions prove to have some findings in common:

- It can be clearly determined that migrants are involved in processes of assimilation (compare Karakasoglu; Prümm, Sackmann and Schultz; Sunier; Sauter). This supports the proposition put forward by Peters (in this volume) that - given the conditions prevalent today - in the long term, processes of integration are likely to result in assimilation.
- There does not appear to be any inverse connection between ethnic collective identity and identification with the host societies (ibid).
- Host societies need to develop a public culture which reflects the fact of migration and the thus connected (further) pluralization of society (Bauböck; Engbersen; Apitzsch; Karakasoglu; Sunier).

By way of conclusion, here I should like to place the contributions of this volume into relation with the broader research landscape. This is to once again focus on the question of the significance of cultural difference and collective identity for processes of integration. Distinctly culturally different categories of migrants are usually seen as problematic cases with regard to integration processes. Over the years, Muslim migrants in particular have become the center of focus in the public eye and integration research. They are third-country-nationals and they belong to a religion which in Europe (mostly) is seen to be foreign and whose strong influence on the everyday lives of believers impacts in a particularly visible way.[1] This has made them into typical case studies of cultural difference.

But, why should cultural difference constitute a problem for integration in societies which are culturally pluralistic? A first answer to this question is the observation that cultural difference obstructs contact between population categories.[2] Cultural difference combines with social separation. This is heightened in cases where the religion delimits circles of contacts and, notably, circles of marriage. Culturally - and in particular religiously - different groups do not socialize. This alone, though, can hardly be seen as a particular problem for integration in modern plural societies. Another assumption involves factors that refer to the integration of society. Here we must distinguish between two different lines of argumentation. In the one, it is assumed that cultural segmentation implies an absence of identification with the host society. Migrants remain resident foreigners who feel no connection with the host country. In the second line of argumentation, the focus is shifted to the host society. When host societies refuse to accept culturally different migrants as full members of society, this can lead to a problem of integration for society as a whole.

2 Absence of Identification with the Host Country?

With reference to the different stages of integration processes developed by Gordon, assimilation research works on the assumption that identification with the host society occurs at the point in time when migrants have become completely culturally assimilated, especially with regard to their social relations (Gordon, 1964). Identification with the host society was perceived to represent the last stage in the process of assimilation. And assimilation was seen as an inverse process, in the course of which migrants were integrated within the host country to the same extent that they relinquished relations with their group of origin. Nowadays, this concept has become a subject of controversy (Hutnik, 1991; Berry, 1980).

---

[1] The perception of foreignness is heightened by the tendency to equate the religion with its most extreme forms in fundamentalist Islamic states. The terror attacks attributed to Muslims on 11th September 2001 has surely strengthened the public perception of Islam as a threat to western democracies. Muslims themselves report that the climate in their social environment has deteriorated as result of this. We still have to wait for results of research into the possible consequences on the integration of Muslim migrants in Western societies in the aftermath of the terror attacks.

[2] We shall not consider here whether migrants actually pursue the acculturation necessary for integration in the functional systems of society (like the labour market). At this point we simply assume that, as a rule, this is the case.

Theoretically the possibility is perceived that identification with the host society can indeed come about whilst maintaining identificatory relations to the group of origin. Empirical research reinforce this asumption (Berry et al., 1989; Sayek and Lasry, 1993).

The case studies of Muslim migrants in Europe presented in this volume also confirm that identification with the country of migration is possible whilst upholding relations of origin. Modood, for example, shows that migrants in England consider themselves as part of British society (Muslims *of* Britain). And young Turks in Frankfurt regard themselves as 'Turks of Frankfurt' (cf. Sauter in this volume). The contributions in this book also show how processes of localization come about. Sauter's investigation analyses how the sense of belonging to the group of origin and to the city-suburb, where the migrants live, are placed in relationship in processes of self localization. And the contribution by Prümm, Sackmann and Schultz shows the need to distinguish between belonging with regard to an ethnic-cultural group and belonging with regard to a location. The formulation 'Muslims of Britain', or 'Turks of Frankfurt' stand for a combination of feelings of belonging often common to migrant communities.[3] The distinction between different forms of belonging most probably facilitates identification with the host society. Research with regard to Turks in Germany has revealed a notable finding; namely that the interviewees feel a sense of belonging primarily to their German place of residence, despite thoroughly rejecting any identification for themselves with 'the Germans'. The preoccupation of research with identification in the group dimension would thus appear to underestimate the true extent of identification with the host country.[4]

Constructs of identity and the definition of membership connected with them are thus subjected to change. We observe transformations from national towards ethnic constructs of identity among immigrants (Sackmann, 2003). Whereas in the case of constructs of identity which are connected with nationality it is the group which determines membership, ethnic identity constructs come about via the personal identity of potential group members (cf. Alba, 1990). Here it is the individual who decides whether to be considered as member of the group – there are no criteria for

---

[3] In France Muslim organizations have changed their names. They call themselves now 'Muselmans de France' (Muslims of France) instead of 'Muselmans en France' (cf. Covreur, 1998).

[4] Many research findings confirm there is a high degree of identification among Turkish migrants with the German society they live in. A majority identifies strongly with the constitutional state and the system of democracy and many feel a strong sense of loyalty towards the host country (cf. von Willamowitz-Moellendorff, 2001; Sackmann et al., 2001).

membership (apart from descent) on the basis of which membership may otherwise be decided (Sackmann, 2003). The change from constructions of national identity to ethnic ones manifests itself not only in the second generation, but also in the first. It develops in different ways; there is more than one pathway for the transformation of collective identities.

Today's criticism of earlier concepts of assimilation is not restricted to the assumption of inverse relationships in the area of identification. Rather, it also challenges the (subsequently connected) assumption that complete cultural assimilation is a necessary prerequisite for assimilation to be successful. It challenges the assumption that complete cultural assimilation constitutes a prerequisite for processes of integration (Brubaker, 2001). It may also be questioned whether interactive assimilation is absolutely necessary for the social integration of migrants. This opens up the general possibility for conceivable variations in processes of assimilation and integration.

Empirical research findings reveal the existence of different paths towards integration. These paths vary according to the type and extent of assimilation involved. By revealing the possibility for partial integration, for instance, Brubaker implies the possibility of a process of assimilation which remains 'incomplete' (ibid.). This is just one possible step in the direction of grasping the multifaceted nature of assimilation and integration processes. Other authors refer to segmented assimilation as a specific integration strategy. They point out that integration processes involving migrants are not subject solely to the classical connection between assimilation and integration. For example, let us consider the path of social advancement. Research often treats the realization of goals involving upward-mobility as complete assimilation, including severance from the group of origin. There are other possibilities, though. One can imagine complete assimilation at the workplace, for instance, whilst in the private sphere intensive social contacts are upheld within the group of origin (Neckerman, Carter and Lee, 1999). Additionally, it is quite conceivable that contact to the group of origin may be preferred to assimilation in the country of immigration. This may be the case when migrants in the country of immigration find themselves allocated a lower social rank. Where in such situations migrants separate themselves from the host society, concentrating on preserving group-specific values and preferring social contacts within their own ethnic group, they are in effect rejecting the discriminating positioning on the part of main stream society. The upholding of group specific values may even facilitate integration, as Min Zhou points out with regard to US American society:

In the contemporary American context, certain general characteristics of immigrant families, such as the intact family and the respect for elders, may help children advance in any segment of the host society. If, however, these families live in social environments that are not conducive to academic achievement and upward mobility, then these characteristics may take on even greater importance. (...) In disadvantaged neighborhoods where difficult conditions and disruptive elements dominate, immigrant families may have to consciously preserve traditional values by means of ethnic solidarity to prevent the next generation from acculturating into the underprivileged segments of American society in which their community is located (Zhou, 1997, pp. 996f.).

The mobilization of group-intern, socio-cultural incentives for advancement connected with strict social control can improve chances for upward mobility.[5] In addition to these functional aspects, it must be considered that conflicts of loyalty, which are often connected with social advancement, may be eased due to being incorporated in the group (Neckerman, Carter and Lee, 1999; Portes and Hao, 2002).

The new approaches and research findings shift the focus onto group cultures as a repertoire of orientation that can be mobilized in different ways to serve processes of integration in the host society. This opens up a wide field for research. For instance, the role of cultural repertoire can be investigated in the shaping of an individual biography (cf. Apitzsch in this volume). Another example provided by Margaret Spohn (in this volume) shows that processes of cultural change not only take place by means of taking over the other culture. Rather, change can be manifested by means of a changed selection of cultural possibilities a group has at its disposal. This moves the question of assimilation with regard to migrants in the proximity of general theories of social or cultural change.

All in all, the research results presented in this volume lead away from the question as to whether cultural difference represents an obstacle to integration. Rather, they give rise to the question as to how the cultural

---

[5] Research on segmented assimilation has its origin in the USA. The existence of an 'underclass' defined by race (color) occupies an important position in this branch of research. Two elements are of particular significance: for colored migrants, labeled as such, there is the danger that they may be discriminated against due to labeling and subsequently excluded from chances for upward mobility. Persons discriminated or stigmatized in such a way often develop resentments against main stream society. For their part, they separate themselves from the people who discriminate against them. In turn, the subsequent growth of 'counter cultures' present obstacles in the path of upward mobility. This situation provides research within the USA with a frame. It would be interesting to investigate whether forms of segmented assimilation only occur in such problematic constellations.

orientation space migrants occupy in processes of integration will be effective and to what transformation processes they are connected with.

2 The Role of Immigration Societies

Up to this point we have approached the question as to whether cultural difference is to be regarded as an obstacle to integration from the side of the migrant. Let us now take a look from the perspective of the immigration society. In countries where, in the wake of migration, societies fail to accept the existence of culturally different population groups, their integration will subsequently be impaired, possibly also obstructed in the long term. Such a situation is problematic. As a rule, it leads to the marginalization of the migrant population. A situation which not only results in serious problems for the migrants, but also to economic and social costs for the country of immigration. In the context of modern democratic societies built upon principles of equity, the marginalization of large parts of the population poses a serious problem of integration. And marginalization is a difficult process to reverse. To avoid the subsequent costs of marginalization is better than to allow the situation to occur in the first place.

Is it then the country of immigration which is to blame when integration is held up because migrants are not capable (willingly or otherwise) of comprehensive assimilation? This question belongs to the domain of normative theory (see Bauböck in this volume). It is a widely held opinion that a society organized as a state should be able to decide itself whether persons are admitted as new members of the community, or not.[6] It is a widely held belief that society may expect cultural similarity, more or less, from its migrant populations. However, a distinction is drawn between admission to territory and to inclusion in the political community. Whereas the admission to territory is perceived from some normative positions to represent an issue to be freely decided by the countries involved, this is different with regard to membership of long-term resident migrants (cf. Barry and Carens, 1992; Booth, 1997).[7] Although a communitarian

---

[6] Normative theorist do not accept this opinion unequivocally (cf. Booth, 1997; Barry and Carens, 1992), although politicians as well as broad sectors of the public may well generally ascribe to it. Here we will not go into the different theoretical positions, since the following argumentation is supported by broad agreement in normative theory that there can be no legitimation for continuing to exclude permanently resident migrants in democratic societies.

[7] Libertarian and liberal positions reject any admission to territory criteria based on ethnic-cultural factors (cf. the contributions in Barry and Carens, 1992; Schwartz, 1995).

understanding of society perceives the culturally determined selection of potential immigrants to be legitimate, this standpoint cannot be applied in order to exclude already resident migrants from membership in the community (cf. Walzer, 1983). Otherwise, a modern democratic society would find itself in contradiction with its proclaimed principles of equity (cf. Bauböck, 2001; cf. Engbersen on the problem of the contradiction between dimensions of social integration in this volume).

The exclusion of culturally different migrants from membership - rejection of the recognition of belonging - is not without a political cost for the host countries. This ethnic-cultural wall against migrants supports general ethnic concepts of nationality. In its final consequence, the exclusion of ethnic groups leads to an emphasis on a particularist understanding of justice (cf. Apitzsch in this volume). The universalist principles of liberal societies, a corrective against the exclusive particularism, could be weakened in this way. This would entail the loss of important reference points of western democracies.

In more than one way, it is in the interest of immigration countries to build up a public culture in which culturally different migrants are also perceived to be members (cf. Bauböck in this volume). To be true, it can generally be assumed that eventually a state of widespread assimilation of migrants will come about (cf. Peters in this volume). Notwithstanding, the process of integration can be either of long, or of short duration, and for migrants as well as immigration societies, it can take place with more or less possibility of conflict.[8]

4 Integration Processes in Context

In many cases, new research endeavors emphasize the diversity of processes of integration. A number of factors can be relevant for integration processes - there is no one development path, but several. Thus, at the same time the focus moves to the relevance of different contexts and migrants as actors. Theories of transnational or transstate spaces are examples for this (cf. the contributions by Kastoryano and Faist in this volume). Structural conditions are seen to be crucial for the formation of special strategies for connecting relations of origin and of migration, but the social spaces which straddle borders are created by the migrants themselves by way of their

---

[8] It can, however, be assumed that at the micro level of direct contacts even then a considerable potential for discrimination and conflict will continue to exist when the public culture of the immigration societies becomes multiculturized. Cf. Blokland (2003) on conflicts at the neighborhood level.

social relationships (cf. Glick Schiller, Basch and Szanton, 1992). Institutional structures play an important role, be they already existent or be they of the type that first have to be built up by the migrants themselves. This is illustrated by the contribution by Riva Kastoryano, who shows how immigrants from Turkey utilize the EU platform for their positioning, with regard to both their country of origin as well as their country of migration. The EU provides them with an opportunity structure. Its usefulness and the way it is used are, however, dependent on whether and how the migrants deploy to build up representative lobbies at this level.

In the above mentioned examples on the role of group relations in processes of integration, the combination of situation factors with strategies of action is an important characteristic of the research approaches. This shifts the level at which academic generalizations are put forward. This perspective is not concerned with development of a general theory of assimilation or integration which is divorced from time and space. Rather, it postulates different courses or pathways for integration for which, by means of migrants' strategies of action, specific opportunity structures and the orientation repertoire at their disposal can be connected. By so doing, this procedure thus avoids the justifiably criticized tendency to reify ethnic groups so prevalent in previous research (cf. Anthias, 1998; Benson, 1996). The contributions collected in this volume and related research elsewhere demonstrate that the investigation of integration processes can provide insights into social processes which are of significance also outside the domain of research into migration.

References

Alba, Richard D. (1990): *Ethnic Identity. The Transformation of White America*, Yale University Press, New Haven.
Anthias, F. (1998): 'Evaluating "Diaspora": Beyond Ethnicity?' in: *Sociology*, Vol. 32(3), pp. 557-580.
Barry, B. and R. E. Goodin (eds), (1992), *Free Movement. Ethical Issues in the Transnational Migration of People and of Money*, Pennsylvania State University Press, University Park.
Bauböck, R. (2001): 'Integration von Einwanderern – Reflexionen zum Begriff und seinen Anwendungsmöglichkeiten', in: H. Waldrauch, *Die Integration von Einwanderern. Ein Index der rechtlichen Diskriminierung*, Campus, Frankfurt am Main, pp. 25-52.
Benson, Susan (1996): 'Asians Have Culture, West Indians Have Problems: Discourses of Race and Ethnicity in and out of Anthropology', in: T. Ranger, Y. Samad and O. Stuart (eds), *Culture, Identity and Politics. Ethnic Minorities in Britain*, Avebury, Aldershot, pp. 47-56.
Berry, J. W. (1980): 'Acculturation as Varieties of Adaptation', in: A. M. Padilla (ed.), *Acculturation. Theories, Models and Some Findings*, Westview, Boulder, pp. S. 9-26.

Berry, J. W., U. Kim, S. Power, M. Young and M. Bujaki (1989): 'Acculturation Attitudes in Plural Societies', in: *Applied Psychology: An International Review*, Vol. 38 (2), pp. 185-206.

Blokland, T. (2003), 'Ethnic Complexity: Routes to Discriminatory Repertoires in an Inner-city Neighbourhood, in: *Ethnic and Racial Studies*, Vol. 26(1), pp. 1-24.

Booth, W. J. (1997), 'Foreigners, Insiders, Outsiders and the Ethics of Membership', in: *Review of Politics*, Vol. 59, pp. 259-292.

Brubaker, R. (2001): 'The return of Assimilation? Changing Perspectives on Immigration and its Sequels in France, Germany, and the United States', in: *Ethnic and Racial Studies*, Vol. 24(4), pp. 531-548.

Couvreur, Gilles (1998): *Musulmans de France. Diversité, mutations et perspectives de l'islam francais*, Les Éditions de l'Atelier, Paris.

Glick Schiller, N., L. Basch and Ch. Blanc-Szanton (1992): *Towards a Transnational Perspective on Migration: Race, Class, Ethnicity and Nationalism Reconsidered*, New York Academy of Sciences, New York.

Gordon, Milton M. (1964): *Assimilation in American Life. The Role of Race, Religion, and National Origins*, Oxford University Press, New York.

Hutnik, N. (1991): *Ethnic Minority Identity. A Social Psychological Perspective*, Clarendon Press, Oxford.

Neckerman, K. M., P. Carter and J. Lee (1999): 'Segmented Assimilation and Minority Cultures of Mobility', in: *Ethnic and Racial Studies*, Vol. 22(6), pp. 945-965.

Portes, A. and L. Hao (2002), 'The Price of Uniformity: Language, Family and Personality', in: *Ethnic and Racial Studies*, Vol. 25(6), pp. 889-912.

Sackmann, R (2002): Formen kollektiver Identität und Selbstverortungen türkischer Migranten in Deutschland, in: Jutta Allmendinger (ed.), Entstaatlichung und soziale Sicherheit. Verhandlungen des 31. Kongresses der Deutschen Gesellschaft für Soziologie in Leipzig, 2 Bände und CD-Rom; Leske und Budrich, Opladen (in print).

Sackmann, R., B. Peters, T. Schultz und K. Prümm 2001: Zur kollektiven Identität türkischer Migranten in Deutschland. Forschungsbericht, InIIS, Bremen.

Sayek, L. und J.-C. Lasry (1993): 'Immigrants' Adaptation in Canada: Assimilation, Acculturation, and Orthogonal Cultural Identification', in: *Canadian Psychology*, Vol. 34, pp. 89-109

Schwartz, W. F. (ed.), (1995), *Justice in Immigration*, Cambridge University Press, Cambridge.

von Wilamowitz-Moellendorff, Ulrich (2001): 'Türken in Deutschland – Einstellungen zu Staat und Gesellschaft', *Konrad-Adenauer-Stiftung Arbeitspapier* Nr. 53/2001, Sankt Augustin.

Zhou, M. (1997), 'Segmented Assimilation: Issues, Controversies, and Recent Research on the New Second Generation', in: *International Migration Review*, Vol. 31 (4), pp. 975-1008.

Walzer, M (1983), *Spheres of Justice. A Defense of Pluralism and Equality*, Basic Books, New York.

Index